GUIDING
THE SOCIAL
AND EMOTIONAL
DEVELOPMENT
OF GIFTED YOUTH

GUIDING THE SOCIAL AND EMOTIONAL DEVELOPMENT OF GIFTED YOUTH

A Practical Guide for Educators and Counselors

James R. Delisle

Kent State University

Longman
New York & London

Longman, 95 Church Street, White Plains, N.Y. 10601

Associated companies:
Longman Group Ltd., London
Longman Cheshire Pty., Melbourne
Longman Paul Pty., Auckland
Copp Clark Pitman, Toronto

Senior editor: Naomi Silverman
Production editor: Till & Till, Inc.
Cover design: Susan Phillips
Production supervisor: Richard Bretan

Library of Congress Cataloging in Publication Data
Delisle, James R.
    Guiding the social and emotional development of gifted youth: a practical
guide for educators / James R. Delisle.
        p.   cm.
    Includes bibliographical references and index.
    ISBN 0-8013-0568-3: $17.95
    1. Gifted children—Education.   2. Affective education.
I. Title.
LC3993.2.D35   1992
371.95—dc20   90-22282
                                                              CIP

1 2 3 4 5 6 7 8 9 10-MA-9594939291

Contents

CHAPTER 8: Specific Concerns of Gifted Adolescents   131

CHAPTER 9: Special Topics and Special Populations   154

CHAPTER 10: From the Homefront: Parents as Helpers   188

Epigraph

I believe that our own experience instructs us that the secret to Education lies in respecting the pupil. It is not for you to choose what he shall know, what he shall do. It is chosen and foreordained, and he only holds the key to his own secret. By your tampering and thwarting and too much governing he may be hindered from his end and kept out of his own. Respect the child. Wait and see the new product of Nature. Nature loves analogies, but not repetitions. Respect the child. Be not too much his parent. Trespass not on his solitude.

But I hear the outcry which replies to this suggestion: —Would you verily throw up the reins of public and private discipline; would you leave the young child to the mad career of his own passions and whimsies, and call this anarchy a respect for the child's nature? I answer, —Respect the child, respect him to the end, but also respect yourself. Be the companion of his thought, the friend of his friendship, the lover of his virtue, —but no kinsman of his sin. Let him find you so true to yourself that you are the irreconcilable hater of his vice and the imperturbable slighter of his trifling.

RALPH WALDO EMERSON
"Education," in *The Works of Ralph Waldo Emerson, 1883*

Form Follows Function:
A Reader's Guide

In the course of my school life, from first grade through university tenure, I have read hundreds of textbooks. This book, though, is my first attempt at *writing* a text.

To some of you, my lack of experience with textbook writing will soon become obvious. As you read through these pages, you will note a tone and a style that is not "typically textlike." There are cartoons, stories about and drawings of children, allusions to rock music and Jewish proverbs, and a few feeble attempts at puns. There are also more than 200 reference citations, critical analyses of some major issues confronting the field of education for gifted students, and hundreds of practical suggestions concerning strategies and materials that could be used to guide the social and emotional development of gifted youth.

I intersperse these two elements of my book—the erudite and the poetic—purposely. For, as I said, I have read hundreds of textbooks, and in doing so, I have become bored hundreds of time. When I'm bored, I don't learn. But the books that have guided me toward knowledge are those whose authors remained cognizant of themselves as writers; those who have taken the care to explain *why* a topic is meaningful or *how* it impacts my daily life, or theirs. In other words, these are authors who put their hearts and souls, not only their minds, into their work. This rare blend of professional relevance and personal insight is the balance I hope to have attained in this my first text. You, of course, are the individual judges of my success.

A few words about the book's format. In typical textbook fashion, I begin each chapter with some of the goals or intents of that chapter. Then, I introduce a child, or a situation, that serves to highlight the focus of that chapter—such as underachieving behaviors, adolescent concerns, or understanding giftedness. The "meat" then follows, as my ideas integrate with those of my colleagues. Each chapter ends, then, with a series of still-unanswered issues (I call them "Continuing Quests and Questions"), and a short list of some exemplary resources that I hope you can find, and if so, that you find to be useful.

That's it, except for the bibliography and the cover, which are pretty typical adjuncts to any textbook.

Form follows function: I hope you are able to use this book to better understand and work with gifted students in your care (that's the "function"); and by appealing to your heart as well as your mind, I hope that your tour through these pages is memorable (. . . and that's the "form").

Preface

WHY THIS BOOK?

In preparing to write this book, I asked myself a fundamental question: "Is this book necessary?" To be sure, there are many texts already available dealing with the subjects of gifted children and their education; the same is true for affective education. However, locating a resource that combines these topics proved a fruitless search. At best, textbooks about education for gifted children devoted one chapter to a review of affective education (or related topics such as counseling strategies), while authors of affective education texts seemed to address their topics with little regard for what works best with whom; certainly, specific affective concerns of highly able children were not addressed at all.

This lack of printed information on a topic that, to me, was important and necessary forced me to choose between one of two conclusions:

1. A book on affective education for gifted children needed to be written.
2. A book on this topic was unnecessary, for if needed, it would have been written by now.

Obviously, by the presence of this book, I chose to believe the first conclusion.

Here's why: In the more than two years between my original conception of this book's content and its completion, I spoke with thousands of parents and educators across this country and others, mostly on the topics I address in this book. Also, I sat on the board of directors of the *National Association for Gifted Children*. These professional experiences made me acutely aware of the need to address the implications of gifts and talents on the social and emotional lives of the children we teach. For even though a majority of the persons I spoke to or sat with saw gifted youth as having specific academic and intellectual needs, too few of them would acknowledge the presence of distinct guidance issues that result from (or, at least, are a part of) high intelligence. Even some of my colleagues who *had* written articles and texts on education for gifted children seemed stuck in the stereotypic thinking that "if you're smart, you can work out your own problems."

This book, then, is written for educators who see the need for affective education of gifted students and wish to address this topic in a classroom context. Also, it is hoped that school counselors, private counselors, and parents will find some use for the material between these covers. Last, this book is intended especially for the "nonbelievers," the unconvinced, those who equate giftedness with easily attained success, interpersonal competence, and intrapersonal satisfaction. If, after reading this book, the nonbelievers remain unconvinced of the need for affective education of gifted students, I invite them to talk with gifted students themselves about the importance of the topics included in this book. Still unconvinced? Then I haven't done my job and I will buy this book back from you.

To me, success in life is measured more by the places you've been rather than the things you've amassed. If you explored a road that had heretofore been untraveled, you've no doubt left an impression on it, and it on you. In my own career as an educator, I have worked with handicapped children and gifted students; teenagers and third graders; children happy with themselves and children unhappy with themselves. Whoever the child, I learned from him or her and hope that this book provides proof that each of these "journeys" led me to appreciate the importance and the individuality of each child as a thinking and feeling human being.

ACKNOWLEDGMENTS

There are many people, and one place, that helped make this manuscript become a book.

Naomi Silverman, my editor at Longman, convinced me initially that a book on this topic needed to be written. I thank her for thinking that I had the insights and the stamina to complete this book. If ever there is established an "Editor's Hall of Fame," Naomi will be a charter member.

In addition, I would like to thank my undergraduate and graduate students at Kent State University, each of whom gave me an insight or two (or twenty) about the content and focus of this book. I hope they see themselves, and their words and ideas, reflected in these pages.

Next, my typists. In this era of whiz-bang technology, I still compose with a pencil and paper. Emily Brna and Janie Knight have added a twentieth century touch to my words, and I am always amazed by their speed, their accuracy—and most of all, their incisive comments on my work.

Then there's the place: North Myrtle Beach, South Carolina. Our summer home, far removed from the tree-lined streets of Kent, Ohio, it provides a refuge, a reassurance, and a perfect place to compose. The ocean, in all its majesty, allows my ideas to flow freely.

. . . But what is a place without people? Even the Atlantic Ocean would lose its appeal without important others with whom I could share it. It's here that Deb and Matt, my family, enter the scene. Without their support, both vocal and silent, not only would this book not have been written, but it wouldn't even have been worth the effort to consider writing it. Deb and Matt, you are my guides, my teachers, my soul.

It's ironic. As a teacher, I am supposed to instill in my students a love of learning, fresh insights, and boundless curiosity. But it is *they* who have taught *me* whatever I needed to know about this world, or my place in it. So . . . a collective "thank you" to you all; I hope you think I have learned my lessons well.

Especially, thanks to Roger, wherever you may be. I hope you are happy and healthy.

CHAPTER 1

In the Beginning . . .

The intent of this chapter is to

Acquaint you with some historically relevant data, and the
individuals who created it, regarding the social and emotional
development of gifted children

Provide an overview of some of the specific social and emotional
issues that can arise among gifted students and the adults who
teach and live with them

Serve as a foundation for future chapters as regards the overall
nature of affective education for gifted students

Those persons who think that education for gifted children is a new idea or a
"passing fad" either have short memories or a limited grasp of history. Western cultures have been fascinated with human diversity—physical, ethnic,
intellectual—for centuries, and today's emphasis on the education of gifted
children is but one link in this long, long chain.

Consider, for example, Jean Itard. In the late eighteenth century, Itard
discovered a young boy, about age 12, in the forests of central France. This lad
had no history—at least he could not relate it—as he was mute, and his
behaviors were crude, unrefined. He was a feral child, and Itard assumed that
he had survived alone in the forest by instinct and innate intelligence. Itard
took this boy into his home, named him Victor, and went on to try to prove
that Victor could become both learned and socialized. This "experiment"
lasted for several years, but as Victor grew toward adulthood, Itard became

discouraged by Victor's lack of growth. Victor did respond to his adoptive name, and he spoke some words that related directly to his basic needs—when he wanted milk, he asked for *lait*. But overall, Itard considered his experiment a failure, and Victor eventually was left in the care of his nurse-maid until he died.

An intriguing story, perhaps, but what does it have to do with gifted children and their education? From my vantage point—plenty. Jean Itard was more than an early social psychologist; he was a diarist. Itard kept track of Victor's daily exploits, his learning styles and patterns, and his intellectual growth. In his book, *The Wild Boy of Aveyron,* Itard chronicled one of the first and most ambitious attempts ever undertaken to probe into a young, developing mind (Itard, 1962). Sure, others came later—Jean Piaget, Lewis Terman, Benjamin Bloom—and each contributed in his own way to our over-all understanding of children's development. Yet Itard experimented with a single child, and his role became that of a caring father as much as an objective scientist. Itard's attempts with Victor may lack the statistical precision shown by other, later scientists; yet what he may have lacked in precision was more than made up for by the depth and duration of his vision.

To this day, Itard's work remains the sine qua non of studies that have the goal of exploring the development of individual talents; educators of gifted children would do well to read Itard's account of his time with Victor. (Visual learners might prefer François Truffaut's 1970 film version, *The Wild Child,* for it shows the importance of observation in the full understanding of the human animal.)

Upon Itard's Introduction to Victor
His eyes were unsteady, expressionless, wandering vaguely from one object to another without resting on anybody; they were so little experienced in other ways and so little trained by the sense of touch, that they never distinguished an object in relief from one in a picture. . . . He was destitute of memory, of judgment, of aptitude for imitation, and was so limited in his ideas, even those relative to his immediate needs, that he had never yet succeeded in opening a door or climbing upon a chair. (pp. 5–6)

An Early Lesson Learned
Once when we wanted to make him take a bath which was as yet only lukewarm, and . . . seeing that his governess was not convinced of the cool-ness of the water by the frequent tests that he made with the tips of his own fingers, he turned towards her quickly, seized her hand and plunged it into the bath. (p. 17)

In a Letter about Victor's Progress, Five Years Later
To be judged fairly, this young man must only be compared with himself. Put beside another adolescent of the same age he is only an ill-favored creature, an outcast of nature as he was of society. But if one limits oneself to the two

terms of comparison offered by the past and present states of young Victor, one is astonished at the immense space which separates them; and one can question whether Victor is not more unlike the *Wild Boy of Aveyron* arriving in Paris, than he is unlike other individuals of his same age and species. (Excerpted from *The Wild Boy of Aveyron* by Jean-Marc-Gaspard Itard, translated by George and Muriel Humphrey, 1962, p. 53.)

LATER RESEARCHERS IN GIFTED EDUCATION

To relate the work of every twentieth century educator or researcher whose emphasis was gifted children's development would take much time. Thus, for the sake of time (both yours and mine) and to avoid redundancy (such historical documentation can be found in other texts), the focus here will be limited to those individuals whose work has emphasized the social and emotional development of gifted children. However, to include mention of some individuals while excluding others is always a subjective choice. Therefore, the purpose here is not to include every researcher whose writing *at some time* used the word "emotional" in its title; rather, it is to highlight the work of selected persons whose career has focused on the nonintellective aspects of giftedness. In this way, you, the reader, will be provided with a historical analysis that, though thorough, is not necessarily comprehensive.

LEWIS M. TERMAN

It is hard to overstate the effect of Lewis M. Terman on the field of gifted education. To this day, no other person has influenced the theory and practice of educating and understanding gifted individuals as has this one man.

Lewis Terman's work with and interest in gifted children began in his native Indiana in the late nineteenth century. There, as an undergraduate student of psychology at Indiana University, Terman prepared two reports for a senior class seminar: one report on mental deficiency and the other on genius. It was in preparation of those papers that Terman became acquainted with the work of his contemporary, Alfred Binet, a French psychologist who had recently developed the first edition of an intelligence test, the Binet–Simon Scale (Binet & Simon, 1905).

Terman's interest in high intelligence continued through his doctoral program at Clark University, where his dissertation involved a comparison of precocious and "mentally backward" boys on a number of intellective factors. In Terman's words, "The experiment contributed little or nothing to science, but it contributed a lot to my future thinking" (Terman, 1954, p. 222).

Indeed it did! For several years later, while on the faculty of Stanford University, Terman revised the Binet test with which he became acquainted as an undergraduate, resulting in the 1916 version of the Stanford–Binet Intelligence Test—an individual test that, through several revisions, remains today as one of psychology's most respected assessment tools. Charged with enthusiasm and an ambition to "study (gifted) children at the earliest opportunity," Terman obtained a sizable grant from the Commonwealth Fund of New York City in 1921 to locate and study children whose Stanford–Binet IQs were 140 or higher (Terman, 1954, p. 222). Thus began the most famous longitudinal study of gifted children ever conducted, *Genetic Studies of Genius,* the benchmark even today against which other longitudinal studies are measured (Terman and Oden, 1947).

Although this intensive study of 1500+ children with high IQs is both interesting and provocative, the purpose here is not to detail each facet and finding of Terman's research. For the topic at hand, though, some of Terman's discoveries as regards the social and emotional adjustment of these youth are relevant.

"So far," Terman states, "no one has developed post-adolescent stupidity!" (Terman, 1954, p. 227). This quote (and this finding) did much to erase the idea that gifted children would "lose" their intelligence prematurely as a by-product of early precocity. The timeworn (but erroneous) theory that "early ripe" led to "early rot" was effectively dismissed.

On the whole, the Terman group of gifted children was remarkably successful (including the publication of 70 books, 1400 articles, and the receipt of over 150 patents). Still, there was considerable discrepancy within the group as regards productivity. Given that the intellectual threshold for the group was IQ 140, Terman attributed these discrepancies to several nonintellective factors:

1. Family influences were important, as 50 percent of the most productive prodigies had parents who were college graduates, whereas only 15 percent of the parents in the least productive group had college degrees. Also, the divorce rate was more than double for parents of children who were least accomplished.
2. The most productive individuals, as children, were rated more highly than the least productive children in the following traits: self-confidence, perseverance, leadership, popularity, sensitivity to approval/disapproval, and desire to excel. (Ratings were done by parents and teachers.)
3. As adults, the most productive subjects differed significantly from the least accomplished subjects on the following attributes, as measured by self-ratings: persistence in the accomplishment of ends; integration toward goals as contrasted with drifting; self-confidence; and freedom from inferiority feelings.
4. Terman subjects who, as students, were allowed to accelerate according to intellectual potential were more successful in school than were those students who remained in classes with their chronological

agemates. This latter group, Terman related, found little challenge in school and often developed poor work habits which, in some cases, ruined college careers.

Everything considered, Terman found the greatest differences among his highly able children (and later, adults) to be in areas of the drive to achieve and in all-around emotional and social adjustment. Success—both career successes and interpersonal triumphs—was associated more with stability than instability; with the absence, not the presence, of internal or environmental conflicts; "in short," said Terman, "with well balanced temperament and with freedom from excessive frustration" (Terman, 1954, p. 230).

LETA S. HOLLINGWORTH

Thousands of miles away, in New York City, Leta S. Hollingworth began her research with gifted children in the same year, 1916, that Terman's revised Binet test was published. Then, as an instructor of educational psychology at Teachers' College, Columbia University, Hollingworth observed an 8-year-old child test 187 on the Stanford–Binet IQ test. As her previous experiences involved the testing of "thousands of incompetent persons," Hollingworth's experience with this boy left an impression so profound that it directed the course of her future career. "I perceived the clear and flawless working of his mind against a contrasting background of thousands of dull and foolish minds. It was an unforgettable observation" (Hollingworth, 1942, p. xii).

From that point, Hollingworth began to search for other children with similarly high abilities. Her quest became more systematic in 1922, when she worked with the New York City School Board to identify highly able children for a "special class" in P.S. 165. Then, in 1937, Hollingworth had the opportunity to experiment with the minds and talents of rapid learners, as she became a teacher at Speyer School, P.S. 500; here, she worked extensively with 50 children whose IQs ranged from 130 to 200.

The enrichment units offered by Hollingworth at Speyer School provided an educational experience that challenged even the ablest children in her care. For instance, the students designed and produced a handbook, "The Evolution of Common Things," to be used by teachers for educating gifted children. Also, each child learned to speak and read French; library research by the students at Teachers' College Library was used in completing many of the 100 biographies the students produced each year; and study continued in the areas of nutrition, music, dramatics, and chess.

Throughout each unit and each classroom activity, Hollingworth remained cognizant of one characteristic shared by all her pupils: "The minds of these children are occupied primarily with exploration of the world in which they have recently arrived. . . . This is the golden age of the intellect" (Hollingworth, 1942, p. 292).

In retrospect, Hollingworth's students remember *her,* as well as recalling the many benefits of her instruction. In a study done by White and Renzulli (1987), 20 of Hollingworth's P.S. 500 students were asked to recall their years with her. Now in their sixties, these adults recall fondly, and with great clarity, both Leta Hollingworth and the lifelong impact of her special class: "I would say that Speyer School was the most influential aspect of all of my education. As I look back, I realize that by the time I was in high school, I had an attitude about learning that I did not get from a conventional school" (White and Renzulli, 1987, p. 94). Indeed, Hollingworth's contributions to education for gifted students would have been remarkable if she had done nothing more than initiate special programs within the New York City schools. However, she was as fine a writer as she was a teacher, as evidenced in both her two books (one published posthumously) and her frequent contributions to professional journals. In *Children Above 180 I.Q. Stanford–Binet: Origin and Development* (1942), Hollingworth recounts much of what she did with her students regarding, in her words, "their emotional education." She believed that gifted children were truly the original thinkers of their generation, and as such, they needed instruction in developing attitudes and drives that would instill in them positive habits of conduct and leadership. Further, Hollingworth believed that to be *precocious* was to be *vulnerable,* so both her writing and her instruction stressed the resolution of special problems that might develop with children who have "the intelligence of an adult and the emotions of a child" (Hollingworth, 1942, p. 282). It is in this area that the gifted education field remembers Leta Hollingworth best.

Specifically, the problems that Hollingworth highlighted include the following:

1. *Problems of play and friendship.* Gifted children have conceptual levels above that of many agemates. They may prefer complicated games, with set rules, rather than unstructured playtime. Such a preference for structure and complexity might not sit well with less able agemates for whom the importance of rules is not yet understood. Further, gifted children's vocabularies or interests might overlap minimally with that of their agemates, causing social discomfort for both the gifted children and their playmates.

2. *Problems associated with a lackluster school curriculum.* According to Hollingworth, children above 140 IQ waste half their time in ordinary elementary classrooms, while children above 170 IQ spend practically all their time in "various sorts of bizarre and wasteful activities" (Hollingworth, 1942, p. 299). These inappropriate educational opportunities keep gifted children from developing respect for the efforts involved in *true* learning, as they seldom need to exert much effort in

completing school tasks. As a result, work and study habits may not develop, which may be the reason some adults are led to comment, "If they're so smart, why can't they keep their assignments straight?" (. . . or other such comments).

3. *The problem of becoming negative toward authority figures.* Hollingworth relates several anecdotes of gifted children being chided by adults who do not themselves understand precocity. In one instance, a student is chided by a teacher when the boy argues that the Chinese, not the Germans, invented printing (he was right, of course). In another example, an 8-year-old is prohibited from using any books but those available in the library's juvenile section, although he needs more advanced resources if he is to complete his project: inventing a new way for engines to go into reverse gear.

   The problem inherent in the situations described above is that highly intelligent children seek to "make good" the mistakes or misconceptions of adults. But, as Hollingworth states, "Many a reformer has died at the hands of a mob which he was trying to improve" (1942, p. 299). This juxtaposition of adult ignorance and childhood knowledge can cause difficulties for highly intelligent children.

4. *The problem of using the intellect to take advantage of others.* Hollingworth wrote that most of her students were capable of a high degree of "benign chicanery"; that is, the children often used their intelligence to their advantage—to get their own ways with less able others or to dodge distasteful academic or social tasks.

   Noting that such chicanery was probably, in the end, both helpful and commonplace among adults, Hollingworth's concern was that the children be aware of *when* they took advantage of their talents. Further, she tried to instill in her students the reality that others, though not necessarily as intelligent as they, could still become their friends (or, at times, mentors), depending on the social context or academic conditions.

Overall, Hollingworth's contributions are many, and they relate directly to the affective development of gifted children. Perhaps her greatest legacy of all is that she is remembered as a kind, sensitive woman by the individuals who knew her so well, for so long: her students. Too, the merits of her work are such that three generations after her death, Hollingworth's insights are as fresh today as they were in the 1930s.

RUTH STRANG

Research on gifted children and their education continued at Teachers' College following Hollingworth's death, under the guidance of Ruth Strang.

Sharing similar beliefs with Hollingworth, Strang examined the social and emotional components of giftedness, giving particular attention to the influence of the home environment on the gifted child. In her publication, "Mental Hygiene of Gifted Children" (1951), Strang detailed several areas of concern to parents of gifted children, and to the youngsters themselves:

1. Parental pressure and exploitation, as adults overemphasize the child's intellectual development
2. Parental indifference and neglect toward their child's precocity
3. Financial limitations caused by poverty or the unwise expenditure of funds that limit the child's educational options
4. Perfectionism, as the gifted child is driven to success by parents' too high ambitions for him or her
5. Parental boasting and possessiveness, in which the child's success is transferred vicariously from child to parent

These concerns are not meant to serve as indictments for all parents of gifted children; rather, they are cautions given by Strang to offset problems that could result from inappropriate parent–child interactions. In fact, Strang was a strong parent advocate, emphasizing in her later writing the importance of the home in fostering the full development of gifted children.

> There is no substitute for your own firsthand understanding of your child. Only you can note, day in and day out, what he can and cannot do, under what conditions he learns best, what gives him the greatest satisfaction. You have to believe . . . in the evidence of your own eyes and ears. (Strang, 1960, p. 3)

The careful, sensitive writing of Ruth Strang strikes a harmonious balance between detailing the high points and the hurdles of growing up gifted. Her advice to parents and educators is to be sensible—to recognize the specialness of intellectual talents but to remember always that beneath the intellect lies a fragile child; a child with emotions and fears, goals and frustrations. Especially for the parents of bright, young children, Strang offers down-to-earth advice that acknowledges the nurturant roles played by parents. "Let him try his wings, give him opportunities to develop his interests, but refrain from showing him off. He has to be himself; he must not become a martyr to your own unfulfilled ambitions" (1960, p. 29).

Ruth Strang's work is a combination of empirical and anecdotal research of the highest quality. And, in addition to the theoretical insights her words provide, Ruth Strang adds a semblance of reality to every point she makes; indeed, it is easy to see the child within Ruth Strang's work.

VIRGIL S. WARD

The field of education for gifted children is filled with researchers and practitioners, some of whom are highlighted on these pages; however, it has had few philosophers. The individual who has served this role most effectively is Virgil S. Ward.

In his book, *Educating the Gifted: An Axiomatic Approach* (1961)—the title gives the reader fair warning of what is to come—Ward presents a theory of DEG: *differential education for gifted learners*. Based on his belief that gifted children will assume adult roles involving "leadership and reconstruction at the frontiers of culture, as distinct from mere participation in the status quo," Ward proposed numerous "propositions and corollaries" that involve all facets of a gifted child's education: academic, physical, moral, and emotional (p. ix). Concentrating especially on the catch-as-catch-can manner in which schools enhance students' emotional lives, Ward contends "It is perhaps truer in the area of character development than in any other significant undertaking by the school that the theoretical bases are not understood, the goals are not clarified and the methodology is not explicitly developed" (p. 194). To remedy this problem of aimless practice, Ward proposed that scientific methods be used in instruction. Thus, using the laws of learning that govern all content domains—exposure, repetition, understanding, conviction, and application—even goals as lofty and challenging as character development can be reached.

Basing much of his own work on that of a colleague, Leta Hollingworth (there she is again!), Ward also stressed the importance of recognizing that gifted children's intellects may outstrip their emotional maturity—so teaching materials and methods must be chosen with this in mind. Further, he emphasized the merits of using students' personal experiences as springboards from which to launch discussions of abstract principles—an idea exemplified by such extraordinary educators as Sylvia Ashton-Warner in her book, *Teacher* (1963), or the semifictional John Hastings in the 1989 film *Dead Poets Society.* Too, once educators have done the best jobs they are capable of doing, Ward admonished them to evaluate their actions relative to students' academic and emotional growth—something too seldom done even in today's programs for gifted children.

Tall orders, to be sure. Yet it seems fitting that Virgil Ward presented educators with tasks that demanded hard work (and thought) if they are to be accomplished. Given the caliber of the students with whom they work, educators of gifted youth must demand from themselves an intellectual rigor that matches or exceeds that of the students they teach.

One interesting (at least to me) note: Ward's book was reissued in 1980 under the more reader-friendly title *Differential Education for the Gifted.* When asked if he wished to alter the original content—now 20 years old and, of course, in need of an update—Ward acceded by including a glossary of terms and by writing a new introduction. In it he challenged readers to take him (and themselves) more seriously, for after 20 years, his propositions and corollaries were as relevant and underapplied as they had been in 1961 . . . case closed.

DONALD C. SMITH

If the game was "Gifted Education Jeopardy," the name of Donald C. Smith would be a $1000 response. Like author Margaret Mitchell, whose *Gone With the Wind* was her sole literary success, and James Dean, whose Hollywood legacy was founded on but a few films, Donald C. Smith produced work that was limited in scope yet powerful in impact.

The 1962 publication of his monograph, *Personal and Social Adjustment of Gifted Adolescents,* was among the first studies to compare gifted and less able teens on specific socioemotional variables. Though citing the work of Terman and Hollingworth, Smith cautioned that their studies, while important, could hardly be considered representative of the entire gifted population. Here's why:

> All of Hollingworth's subjects, except for four, were Jewish.
>
> Terman's finding that gifted youth were "superior" in their social and emotional adjustment was tainted because the children studied were selected from among groups of socially responsible, well-adjusted students.
>
> The exclusion rate of black and Latin children in *both* studies was almost 100 percent.
>
> The socioeconomic status of the families of the children studied was far above the national average.

So, in his study, Smith equated gifted and nongifted adolescents on social class, gender, nationality, and religion. His findings did much to refute the idea that gifted persons are immune from personal problems, as the gifted and nongifted teens differed in only two ways: Gifted students were more independent in their actions and were more dominant in social spheres than were the nongifted teens. Other developmental issues common to "typical" adolescents—concerns about appearance, acceptance, identity—were also part and parcel to growing up gifted.

The most important implication of Smith's research is this:

> Although Terman, Hollingworth and others provided a real service in demonstrating that the intellectually gifted are *not less* well-adjusted than other individuals . . . it is perhaps equally as important that professional spokes-

men do not place unqualified stress on their superiority in adjustment. (Smith, 1962, p. 56)

Compared with other studies, Smith's was small. His sample consisted of 84 teens from Syracuse, New York—no more the center of the universe than is Stanford—so he could be accused of incorporating biases into his own study too. What cannot be argued, though, is Smith's impact on future researchers, who now began to notice that social and cultural factors, if omitted, can distort the findings of any research.

E. PAUL TORRANCE

When the researcher is E. Paul Torrance, then the topic is creativity. For over 50 years, Torrance and his associates have investigated ways of defining, measuring, and improving creative thinking in children and adults. Indeed, the *Torrance Tests of Creative Thinking* (Torrance, 1966) have become the standard against which all other creativity scales are measured.

Much of Torrance's work involved the interaction of creativity and intelligence—two distinct yet related talents. In many of his studies (he has published more than 1000 articles and 100 books!), Torrance showed that creative thinking—"divergent thinking"—can be improved through instruction. This is important because creative talents, when combined with intellectual skills, can result in a well thought-out, innovative solution to a once-vexing problem.

However, all is not well for children who choose to display their creativity in academic settings. Torrance believed that many teachers relegate creativity to those activities that take place in art or music class—certainly not in social studies! Yet, as Torrance wrote, "It takes little imagination to recognize that the future of our civilization—our very survival—depends upon the quality of the creative imagination of our next generation" (1962, p. 6) That's right—1962; that "next generation" is today, and Torrance's words seem as poignant and vital as ever. If creative solutions are to emerge to our most urgent problems, then it is time to broaden our thinking of creativity beyond the limited bounds of an easel, some canvas, and a string quartet.

As well as serving as a link between generations, creative thinking, according to Torrance, is a vital component to a person's mental health and adjustment. In this regard, Torrance suggested several ways that adults can guide creative thinking in children.

1. *Provide highly creative children with a "refuge."* Society in general is savage toward young creative thinkers, so parents and teachers must provide a haven where it is "safe" to think creatively; where "far out" ideas or suggestions are appreciated and, in fact, applauded.

2. *Help creative children understand their divergence.* Creative children are often puzzled by their own behaviors and may feel as a "minority of one" in a classroom (. . . a world!) full of convergent, "straight-ahead" thinkers. The explanation from a caring adult that creativity is a universal trait—although it is often squelched or hidden—is a good start toward helping creative children understand and appreciate their talents.

3. *Recognize the personal and societal benefits to expressing creative abilities.* Creative children who do not speak their minds for fear of ridicule from others learn an unvoiced lesson: "Divergence is bad." But, when given the chance to express openly their personal ideas or thoughts, creative children gain a sense of psychological freedom that benefits both themselves and the society in which they live.

In 1975, in response to his belief that creative children are the best hope for a world filled with strife, fear, and misunderstanding, Torrance initiated a small-scale project in several high schools in Georgia. The goal of this project was to prevent "Future Shock" by having students consider possible solutions to some of our most gnawing problems—pollution, nuclear fear, poverty. Knowing that bright, creative children saw these problems each day in newspapers and on television, Torrance wished to empower students by letting them propose solutions to these problems in a cooperative, nonthreatening atmosphere. Encouraged by his early results, Torrance invited his colleagues around the world to initiate similar programs in their schools. Today, this Future Problem-Solving Program (Crabbe, 1979) involves hundreds of thousands of children, grades 1 through 12, from across the globe. This vast, junior think-tank may be the best remaining hope for solving problems whose solutions will require both creativity and compassion.

E. Paul Torrance has left a legacy unmatched in the fields of creative thinking and gifted education. Yet more than any of his many books, articles, or presentations, Torrance's most remarkable contribution transcends the printed or spoken word. He has left us with the knowledge that the development of creativity is vital, both personally and as a species; and he has left us with the awareness that we can all be a bit more creative, and a little more appreciated, than we already are.

JOANNE RAND WHITMORE

In a word association test, the term *gifted* usually prompts such initial responses as *smart, successful, achievement.* However, not all gifted persons fit into this mold; indeed, there is a large number of gifted children (and adults) whose performance falls far short of their potential. We label these persons *underachievers.*

Joanne Whitmore investigated the phenomenon of underachievement and, in her roles as both teacher and researcher, discovered that underachievement is often a learned behavior. In *Giftedness, Conflict and Underachievement* (1980), Whitmore explained that the onset of underachievement in gifted children often occurs in the primary grades and "that the process of correction is severely complicated if it is delayed until secondary emotional disturbances have arisen from the initial failure experiences" (pp. 233–234). Thus, Whitmore advocated early identification of gifted children who do not achieve as expected, followed by school programs to help reverse these behaviors.

Looking beyond a child's daily school routine, Whitmore stated, "Negative self-concepts are the central trait distinguishing underachievers from those who are achieving" (p. 178). She then described classroom strategies that can be used to reverse underachieving students' negative self-perceptions (more about these in Chapter 7)—the first step to rerouting the child's school performance toward achievement.

We attend to Whitmore's work for the same reason that we attend to Hollingworth's: Her conclusions are based on a combination of theory *and* practice. For several years, Whitmore was a teacher of severely underachieving students in Cupertino, California. There, she worked intensively with her pupils on bolstering both their personal and academic self-worths. Basing her classroom interventions, in part, on self-concept research, Whitmore "invited" achievement by using several key methods:

Using each student's strengths—often, reading mastery, advanced conceptual thinking, superior oral expression, and a keen interest in science—as avenues for future social or academic growth

Organizing the classroom around experiential centers—art corners, reading nooks, and listening and viewing centers

Providing a classroom climate more akin to "family" than "factory," where the central focus was the child not the curriculum

Discussing problems openly, in the form of "class meetings," so that each child's individual worth was enhanced through active and frequent discussion

The success of Whitmore's methods can be noted by the most exacting barometer there is: her students' eventual success. Each of her students was able to return to a regular class environment where academic success became the rule, rather than the exceptional. In an interview, Whitmore related a comment by a 10-year-old boy named Tommy, a former member of her class (Whitmore, 1981). Tommy told her that "when he thought about how he felt about himself last year, his eyes got kinda wet." Student growth—when noticed even by the student—is a sure bet that something went right.

Realists know what idealists never consider: That in individual ways, each of us is, at times, an underachiever. We run on seven cylinders instead of eight, or we put-off to a faraway tomorrow that which we know we should accomplish today. Life—with all its complexities and pleasures—gets in the way. (More power to life!) Yet for some persons, including some children, success always seems elusive, and work that is very good in others' eyes holds little satisfaction for them. It is on these persons (and those who live or work with them) that Joanne Whitmore's careful and sensitive writing will have the greatest impact.

CONCLUSION

In one short chapter and eight personal histories, more than 100 years of educational research has been covered. Is this chapter incomplete? Does it omit some important persons and historical developments? Guilty as charged, on both counts. Yet the intent was to provide an overview; a synthesis of the best ideas and authors related to the area of affective development of gifted students (from a somewhat biased source, your author).

There is a timeworn expression that those who choose to ignore history are doomed to repeat it. In the case of this chapter, my hope is that those of you aware of the history of our field will be challenged to use it and, ultimately, to add to our base of knowledge by incorporating your own ideas and research into this existing body of expertise.

. . . Paul Torrance wouldn't want it any other way.

CONTINUING QUESTS AND QUESTIONS

1. Where have all the diarist's gone? We seem to learn so much from anecdotal research, similar to Itard's *Wild Boy of Aveyron,* yet in the world of academic scholarship, such studies are often considered pseudoscientific. Your task is to locate books, films, or other accounts that are as instructive as they are entertaining. And if you *can* locate these sources, apply the knowledge gained into your daily interactions with students. Furthermore, why not begin your own chronicle of a particular student or class of students from whom you are learning? Your own "personal best" (and that of your students) may emerge from a thorough inspection of your thoughts and theories.

2. Terman's longitudinal studies of giftedness are cited in virtually every textbook on the subject of gifted education. However, I believe that most of these textbook authors have never read Terman's original work; instead, they have familiarized themselves with excerpted summaries or analyses. Assign yourself the task of reading one of the five volumes of Terman's *Genetic Studies of Genius* (available at most university libraries). Whether you are interested in the original sample and research design (Volume 1) or the "Termites" as adolescents (Volume 3) or at midlife (Volume 5), you will find raw data, rather than the digested versions presented in

textbooks. Then, draw your own conclusions on the role of social and emotional guidance in the lives of these highly able individuals studied by Terman almost a century ago.

3. The work of Leta Hollingworth and Ruth Strang represents milestones in our understanding of the guidance needs of gifted children and the adults who care for them. Yet, their work is generations old. Does that imply that the concerns expressed *then* are passé in today's world? And what about any new concerns that may have emerged regarding the social and emotional development of gifted students? Has our "information age" of computers or instant and global communication created any new causes of concern? Does nuclear armament and disarmament leave an impact on the lives of children that could not even be foreshadowed by the great minds of Hollingworth and Strang? Where are we headed, emotionally speaking, and how similar are our objectives for children today with those of 50 years ago? There is a timeworn theory that "the more things change, the more they stay the same." Does this idea apply to our society's ideas of children's emotional growth?

4. What will be the long-term impact (if any) of the "back to basics" and teacher and student accountability movements that pervaded education in the late twentieth century? If E. Paul Torrance and Joanne Whitmore are correct (and their research shows they are), then creative talents will emerge naturally in children under conditions of intellectual freedom, openness, and openmindedness—none of which can be measured by standardized tests. How can teachers, counselors, and administrators do what they must to satisfy a public hungry for increased accountability, while maintaining a climate conducive to fresh, original—and often—unmeasurable ideas?

OUT OF THE WAY/OUT OF THIS WORLD
RESOURCES

Teacher, by Sylvia Ashton-Warner (Simon and Schuster, New York, 1963).
　　Among the best examples of changing curriculum to meet the needs of children (rather than vice versa), *Teacher* chronicles the experiences of a woman who instructs Maori tribe children in New Zealand. Implications for differentiating curriculum based on specific needs, talents, and cultural backgrounds of students emerge throughout this classic work.

How Teachers Taught: Constancy and Change in American Classrooms, 1890–1980, by Larry Cuban (Longman Publishers, New York, 1984).
　　This textbook presents a historical overview of classroom practices throughout the decades and poses the question as to whether so-called trends are actually "old wines in new bottles." Some fine descriptions of schools and classrooms are provided.

Gifted Children: Their Nature and Nurture, by Leta S. Hollingworth (Macmillan Publishers, New York, 1926).
　　Take out the sexist language and some of the archaic sentence structure and what remains is a treatise on living and working with gifted children that is as contemporary as they come. Always a pioneer, Hollingworth shows that common sense and appropriate practice know no time bounds.

Emile, by Jean Jacques Rousseau (translated by Barbara Foxby) (E.P. Dutton, New York, 1911).

Every person has an inner consciousness, which he or she alone must discover, listen to, and follow. Education, then, is a personal and lifelong experience, and Rousseau's description of the education of Emile shows the necessity to tend to the social and emotional components of learning. Involvement with one's world is paramount to gaining a full understanding of one's place in humanity.

Genetic Studies of Genius, by Lewis M. Terman and/or others (Stanford University, Stanford University Press). Volume 1, *Mental and Physical Traits of a Thousand Gifted Children* (1925); Volume 2, *The Early Mental Traits of Three Hundred Geniuses* (1926), by C. C. Miles; Volume 3, *The Promise of Youth* (1930), with B. S. Burks and D. Jensen; Volume 4, *The Gifted Child Grows Up* (1947), with M. Oden; Volume 5, *The Gifted Group at Midlife; Thirty-five Years Follow-Up of the Superior Child* (1959), with M. Oden.

To try to understand the field of gifted education without exploring at least one of the above volumes is tantamount to beginning a 1000-mile journey on America's back roads without a map: You'll end up somewhere, and it may be an interesting trip, but you'll have no idea where you are or where you're heading.

CHAPTER 2

Understanding Giftedness

The intent of this chapter is to

Review various definitions of giftedness and make implications about their appropriateness for use in identifying gifted children

Summarize two views of the construct of intelligence and report on their applicability to identification of children for gifted programs

Present a view of giftedness that takes into account the emotional underpinnings of this construct

Leave you with a clearer understanding of the general lack of agreement found among researchers whose topics are intelligence and its measurement

There is a popular tale told about blind men and an elephant. Each man, able to touch only one part of the elephant—its tail, its trunk, its leathery torso—describes the beast in a unique, idiosyncratic way. Of course, each man thinks his description is the best and most accurate—unaware that the others who have touched the elephant have sampled a very different portion of the pachyderm. As a result, each man becomes smug with the self-assurance that he, and he alone, knows the true measure of the elephant's physique and that what the others have described is a very different beast indeed. It is only when another man, sighted in *one* eye, happens by that the blind men realize their errors in making faulty (or at least, premature) judgments.

How similar this parable is to our own ideas on defining giftedness. Throughout the generations, virtually dozens of definitions have evolved, prompting two authors (Sternberg and Davidson, 1986) to edit an entire book—18 chapters long—devoted to the 17 definitions of giftedness they found in the current literature. In some respects, those who have attempted to define this phenomenon have avoided the pitfalls of the blind men, for they have built their own conceptions of giftedness on the work of others who have come before them. But others, through either arrogance or ignorance (or both) have chosen to put forth definitions of giftedness that are as singular as would be the description of an elephant if one were able to touch only its toes.

In this chapter, various definitions of giftedness, and their appropriateness as related to affective development, will be addressed.

JUST A LITTLE MORE HISTORY: THE DEBATE
OVER WHAT GIFTEDNESS IS

To understand the rationale behind many current-day definitions of giftedness, we must return again to the work of Lewis Terman. Prior to his study of gifted children in the early 1900s, giftedness was a visible, yet rather poorly defined, phenomenon. We knew giftedness when we saw it—in the music composed, the formulas presented, the inventions patented. But without the presence of large-scale standardized testing, giftedness, and its definition, was very much determined by a specific society's interpretation of what behaviors and traits were exceptional. Thus, the Ottoman Turks identified males with physical strength and beauty, whereas the Victorians chose to concentrate on birthright and privileged rank as the precursors of high talent among the populace (Laycock, 1979).

Terman's use of a standardized measure to pinpoint intelligence—the IQ test—did much to equalize the opportunity for children of various rank and backgrounds to "show their stuff." To be sure, the IQ tests of then *and* now can bias against particular subgroups, yet it cannot be denied that Terman's selection and testing procedures were far more equitable than they had been up until his time. It has been only recently, and in retrospect, that we note some of Terman's less-than-perfect methodology.

Since the publication of the first volume of his *Genetic Studies of Genius,* many other researchers in education of gifted children have tried to discount the merits of Terman's work by deemphasizing the IQ score (Terman and Oden, 1947). Instead, these researchers replace it with various other measurement scales, personality traits, or "gifted behaviors." Thus, the stage was set for a scenario that continues even today on what giftedness is (and isn't); a scenario which, at times, evokes images of elephants and blind men.

ACT I, SCENE I: SOME PRINCIPAL PLAYERS—
PAUL WITTY AND JOSEPH RENZULLI

One of the earliest—and most extreme—reactions to Terman's use of IQ came from Paul Witty who, in 1940, wrote that giftedness describes any child "whose performance is consistently remarkable in any potentially valuable area" (p. 516). Certainly, this was a far cry from Terman's use of a 140+ IQ score to determine giftedness, and it was one that put structure around the conceptual biases of earlier times: that giftedness lies not so much in the traits you have as much as in the deeds you do. A generation later, Renzulli elaborated on Witty's idea in arriving at yet another conception of giftedness. In "What Makes Giftedness?" (1978), Renzulli dismissed the idea that IQ alone is the determinant. In and of itself, this was not a novel idea; the originality within Renzulli's work came when he highlighted two other traits, *creativity* and *task commitment,* as elements of giftedness. As noted in Figure 2.1, it is when these two traits merge with one's intelligence that giftedness is present. Two examples might help explain this point:

Eric, a fifth grader, has an IQ of 142 and finds much of school either easy or tedious. Aware of his high intelligence, Eric's teachers offer him independent study projects that tie into his interest in aeronautics. Though Eric shows initial interest in his teachers' suggestions, he must be pushed, prodded, and reminded to use his free time to work on the aeronautics project he has agreed to produce. Eventually, his interest wanes to the point where even Eric's teachers stop expecting much and agree to accept a scaled-down version of his initial project. Eric *could* do more, perhaps, but he's just not committed to his work.

Maria, also a bright fifth-grade student, approaches her teacher with two questions: "Why don't rockets just blow up when they're launched? What makes them rise, instead?" Helping Maria to locate resources that explain propulsion, her teachers devise, with Maria's input, a series of readings and experiments that will

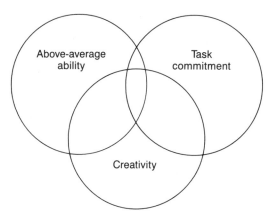

Figure 2.1. The three-ring conception of giftedness. (*Source:* J. S. Renzulli, *Revolving Door Identification Model.* Mansfield, CT: Creative Learning Press, 1981. Reprinted by permission.)

help her to answer her questions. Diligently, Maria works on her project during every free minute, and she eventually is satisfied that she has answered her questions—and more! Maria even shared her new knowledge by writing a short article for the school paper and giving a presentation in a sixth-grade science class.

Using Renzulli's conception of giftedness, Eric would not qualify—at least at this time—as a gifted child, for his behaviors give little indication of his intrinsic abilities. However, Maria epitomizes giftedness from Renzulli's vantage point, as she has taken her talents and produced something unique and purposeful. This utilitarian approach actually makes the term *gifted child* obsolete, replacing it with "a child with gifted behaviors." Thus, Eric might eventually "get his rings together" (intellect, creativity, and task commitment), but until he does, it would be incorrect to identify him as gifted—no matter how high his IQ. Conversely, Maria is the perfect candidate for a gifted program, as she is both creative and task committed—so, who *cares* what her IQ is?

Obviously, Renzulli's conception of giftedness has implications for the identification of and programming for gifted students—excuse me, "students with gifted behaviors." Further, this conception of giftedness has profound implications for children who, though intelligent, do not use their abilities in productive or visible ways. Both of these issues are discussed in a later section of this book, especially as they relate to affective development. For now, though, perhaps it is sufficient to state that Renzulli, like Witty, sees giftedness as a set of behaviors rather than a cluster of traits. This conception is a far, far cry from what Terman put forth, and one that differs greatly, as you shall now read, from the most popular definition of giftedness used in our country: the one put forth by our federal government.

ACT 1, SCENE II: ENTER THE FEDS

Each state in the United States has written its own definition of giftedness, and 34 of these states have used the United States Office of Education's (USOE) version as the basis of their own definition (Karnes and Koch, 1985). Originally adopted in 1977, and revised in 1981, the USOE's definition of gifted children is as follows:

> Children who give evidence of high performance capability in areas such as intellectual, creative, artistic, leadership, capacity, or specific academic fields, and who require services or activities not ordinarily provided by the school in order to fully develop such capabilities (Education and Consolidation Act, PL 97-35, Section 582, 1981)

Individual states are under no mandate to accept this federal interpretation of giftedness, so why would so many opt to do so? Because it is easily accessible?

(No; any good textbook in gifted education contains this *and other* definitions.) Because it fits individual state laws about educating gifted children? (Doubtful, as only one-half of the states require gifted programs to be provided.) Because most states want to emulate what happens in our nation's capital? (If you believe this, I've got a bridge I'd like to sell you. . . .)

No—the bottom line is that the definition provided by USOE *is good!* It is clearly written (specific areas of giftedness are listed), it allows for the identification of children with gifted behaviors and gifted traits (note the wording: "give evidence of high performance capability"), and it ties in the identification of gifted children with the necessity of programming for them ("and who require services or activities . . . to fully develop such capabilities"). In effect, the USOE definition provides two things too often lacking in federal documents: specificity and flexibility.

ACT II, SCENE 1: VARIATIONS ON A THEME: THE THEORIES OF ROBERT STERNBERG AND HOWARD GARDNER

Several of the big players in defining and understanding giftedness have come from the ranks of cognitive psychology. Robert Sternberg, of Yale University, and Howard Gardner, of Harvard, have put forth theories that consider giftedness within the wider context of their overall definitions of intelligence. Harvard and Yale, perennial rivals on the sports field and on the prestige meters, compete again within the conceptions of intelligence put forth by these two men. "As different as chalk and cheese," my mother would say: that's just how disparate the conceptions of giftedness are, as explained by Sternberg and Gardner.

Sternberg believes that intelligence has been shortchanged since the era of standardized testing began. In our quest for precision in measurement ("Is the child's IQ 126 or it is *really* 131?"), Sternberg contends that we have lost sight of what it is we are really trying to measure:

> There is a certain allure to exact-sounding numbers. An IQ score of 119, an SAT score of 580, a creativity score in the 74th percentile. . . . But the appearance of precision is no substitute for the fact of validity. Indeed a test may in fact be precise in its measurements, but not of whatever it is that distinguishes the gifted from everyone else. . . . The fact that a test score is (or appears to be) precise doesn't mean that it is any good. (Sternberg, 1982, pp. 160; 161)

Sternberg's conception of intelligence—his triarchic model (see Figure 2.1)—does take into account the verbal abilities that are generally measured by aptitude and achievement tests. These abilities, the first component of his model, Sternberg labels *crystallized abilities,* implying by this term that the abilities have had time to plant themselves firmly onto the mind of the person being assessed—pretty typical stuff.

However, he includes two other components to intelligence that are not so typical. These abilities have less to do with how well a person does in school and more with how well an individual manages day-to-day interactions with the real world. The second component of intelligence, social and practical intelligence, is often bypassed by most intelligence tests, but could be measured by one's response to a question such as this: "Fifteen percent of the people in a certain town have unlisted telephone numbers. You select 200 names at random from the local phone book. How many of these people can be expected to have unlisted telephone numbers" (Levine, 1987)? The answer, of course, is none, because if the telephone numbers are unlisted, they wouldn't be in the phone book at all. Trick question? Maybe. But Sternberg attests that picking up the nuances of situations such as this is an important part of successful manipulation of one's world.

The third component of the triarchic model is most aptly labeled "street smarts" (though Sternberg calls them *fluid abilities.*) These talents are illustrated in Sternberg's own example, which he provided to an interviewer for an article in *Discover Magazine.*

> I sit (my graduate students) down and explain the strategy of scientific publishing, how it's better to publish in a journal with a circulation of 40,000 than 4,000, and how to tailor a paper to a journal—things that many professors don't teach, in the belief that they're "sleazy." (McKean, 1985, p. 30)

This conception of intelligence, very different from the enduring notion that "intelligence is what gets measured on IQ tests," has all the markings of late twentieth century Western culture. It gives credence to the idea that real-world performance matters as much (perhaps more) than knowing the definitions of certain esoteric words; and it gives credit to the benefits of learning the ropes that lead to success in the marketplace.

Howard Gardner is just a Massachusetts Turnpike drive away from Sternberg, yet his ideas on intelligence are light years apart from those of his Connecticut colleague. Gardner's conception of intelligence is similar to the one developed by USOE, in that it categorizes talents into separate, yet related, compartments. Gardner lists at least seven distinct "intelligences," and in his popular book, *Frames of Mind* (1983), each of the following is explained in more detail:

1. *Linguistic intelligence:* Verbal facility, which is readily measured by current IQ and achievement tests and corresponds well with Sternberg's "crystallized abilities."

2. *Logical-mathematical intelligence:* More of the above, in this case, in the areas of symbolic reasoning.
3. *Musical intelligence:* Not only the ability to perform music, but the talent to perceive the delicate distinctions between a well-orchestrated piece and a mere collection of notes.
4. *Spatial intelligence:* Architects have this, so do expensive landscapers: it's the ability to arrange parts of the world in such ways as to inspire a sense of awe or beauty in others.
5. *Bodily kinesthetic intelligence:* You see this in the actions of Nadia Cominechi or Bo Jackson. Also, you see it in other athletic forms, such as lithe dancing, or mime, or the Broadway ensemble of *Cats.*
6. *Interpersonal intelligence:* If you know someone who can walk into a roomful of people and immediately pick up on "the vibes," or you watch a politician effectively turn an unruly crowd into a band of followers (or vice versa), then you have seen interpersonal intelligence in action.
7. *Intrapersonal intelligence:* Seldom valued openly in our society, this intelligence is the quietest; the most personal. Somewhat akin to Maslow's concept of self-actualization, intrapersonal intelligence is owned by persons whose self-knowledge is accurate and positive, and whose actions in daily living attest to their individualism and self-satisfaction.

That Sternberg and Gardner disagree so publicly about what constitutes intelligence is somewhat surprising, as one's ideas appear to both overlap and complement the other's work. Still, Sternberg believes that Gardner's work is based more on conjecture and wishful thinking than on research, while Gardner contends that Sternberg really still believes that intelligence is a one-dimensional concept that will eventually be able to be measured with great accuracy.

So, once again we have a clash of whose idea is *the* best. And although the final victor will probably not emerge for quite some time (if ever), the controversy does add new spark to the centuries-old dilemma of defining and measuring intelligence.

ACT II, SCENE II: ENTER THE CHILDREN AND MICHAEL PIECHOWSKI

Author and educator Neil Postman once said, "Children are the messages we send to a time we will not see." How true: both verbally and silently, teachers, parents, counselors, and clergy (not to mention store clerks and bowling alley attendants) give children messages literally thousands of times each day, through words and gestures, smiles and grimaces. Yet children are more than passive recipients of the world around them; they are also active participants— message senders—whose impressions of people, events, and ideas are both valid and valuable. This is true whether the subject is deciding on one's favorite color or discussing deeper issues, such as "what is giftedness?"

It seems appropriate for a book on the topic of affective development of gifted children to include some students' ideas about the topics under review, including the definition of the concept about which no two persons seem to agree: giftedness.

The earliest publication of gifted students' views on themselves was compiled by the American Association for Gifted Children in 1978, in a book titled *On Being Gifted*. In this book, 20 gifted teenagers wrote essays about the high points and hurdles involved with growing up gifted. True to form, these young people did not agree on a definition any more frequently than did psychologists or educators, but their impressions show an uncanny parallel to some ideas put forth earlier in this chapter:

> My definition of the phrase "gifted and talented" would mean someone who is naturally able to do certain things, such as a student who has the ability to do schoolwork without much difficulty or someone who can succeed even in small things which only require a particular skill. (p. 5)

> We know that scholars have tested, measured, researched, and described the characteristics of the gifted, but descriptions are a far cry from living in that sensitive skin. We think that in studying people like us, the researchers— scholars though they may be—lose track of some of the human aspects. (p. 8)

None of the 20 students mentioned test scores (á la Terman) in their descriptions of giftedness, and few gave descriptions that would approximate what Renzulli labels *gifted behaviors*. Instead, the students focused on differences they perceived–academic, emotional, attitudinal—between themselves and most of their classmates. Perhaps the most pervasive characteristic of giftedness cited by these young authors was intellectual curiosity—an intense desire to explore virtually any topic of interest. This "need to know" was cited again, a decade later, by another 19-year-old:

> I've met lots of people who get grades and aren't interested in the learning process . . . to me, they are not gifted. Gifted people question, and they love learning. They'll see a book and pick it up and love reading it, or they'll decide they want to learn to play the guitar and go out and do it. I guess I'm describing myself and the friends I have who I think are gifted. I'm constantly finding out that they're learning new things, making connections. (Delisle and Galbraith, 1987, p. 144)

Comparing these young persons' remarks with definitions of giftedness put forth in the professional literature may leave the reader—you—more confused than ever. Whether researchers seek the exact point that separates giftedness from average abilities or the task-specific behavior that qualifies one's efforts as outstanding, the students identified as gifted seem to note personality factors over all other traits. To be sure, there is a subtle connection between what the experts think and what the students believe to be true, yet this connection seems tenuous, at best. A forced fit may be better than no fit at all, yet there is still a disturbing gap between what researchers would have us believe and what identified gifted students tell us to be true.

Enter Michael Piechowski: a neurobiologist and psychologist (not too shabby!) whose work in understanding giftedness resulted in a theory that blends together cognitive and affective elements. According to Piechowski, gifted persons differ in degree, not kind, from others around them. That is, gifted individuals have *more* of a certain trait that is common to some degree in everyone; they do not possess different traits, just an overabundance of what might be expected. He labels this condition *overexcitability,* and explains what this means:

> It is often recognized that gifted and talented people are energetic, enthusiastic, intensely absorbed in their pursuits, endowed with vivid imagination, sensuality, moral sensitivity and emotional vulnerability. . . . These characteristics are found across different talents, in writers, composers, dancers, actors, scientists, inventors, civic and spiritual leaders. Often, they are as strong in adulthood as in childhood. . . . [They are] experiencing in a higher key. (Piechowski, 1986, p. 190)

These overexcitabilities can occur in various realms—intellectual, imaginational, emotional, psychomotor, and sensual. In effect, Piechowski has taken the idea of categories put forth by USOE, blended them with personality traits and observable behaviors, and created a conception of giftedness that should satisfy even the most ardent critic.

Of course, there are problems, the biggest of which is measurement. Is a school district willing to locate children who are overexcited intellectually? And just imagine the teacher-room comments when a junior high faculty is told that sensual overexcitability is a gift that *some* 13-year-olds possess more than do others. Hmmmm. . .

Still, Piechowski's work contains a feature that has been absent from the definition of giftedness since the days of Terman: research studies on gifted children that validate his ideas. As you recall, Sternberg's work considers what it takes to be successful in the marketplace, and Renzulli's three-ring conception is based entirely on the lifestyles and work patterns of eminent adults. The USOE definition, while good, is not based on research studies per se, and Gardner uses only case study data to validate his claims of multiple intelligences. So, we are left with Piechowski and his still-evolving analysis of a human condition that seems as evasive as it is important: the definition and enhancement of overexcitabilities—gifts and talents—in all their kaleidescopic dimensions.

CONCLUSIONS (TENTATIVE, ANYWAY)

If you're expecting to read a tidy conclusion combining the best elements of all the aforementioned definitions into yet-one-more conception of giftedness, you'll be disappointed. Would that it were that easy.

It is doubtful that any one definition of giftedness will be written—at least not in my lifetime—that satisfies the researchers, the educators, the huddled masses, and so on. Perhaps that is good; the way it should be. After all, the range of human diversity and exceptionality are so broad that any single conception of giftedness would likely be inadequate.

Maybe the time has come to put aside the notion that our field will progress further only after we have refined the concept of giftedness more uniformly than it is now. However, the teacher in me says that whatever the definition used, individual students will still need individualized educational options that take advantage of their *specific* gifts and talents. Therefore, let's allow the theorists to argue the relative benefits of one definition of giftedness over another; their disagreements will probably do no more harm than if they were trying to describe an elephant. However, in the meantime, let's continue to educate the young people who, by whatever definition or bias we care to intone, still have advanced abilities, talents, or insights.

CONTINUING QUESTS AND QUESTIONS

1. The IQ tests have become the assessment tools that educators love to hate. They are dismissed as worthless by opponents who agree that they measure only a few, specific aspects of intelligence. Proponents, however, contend that the tests themselves are blameless; instead, it is their misuse and misinterpretation by educators that have caused the brouhaha and heated debates. As we approach a new century, what place will IQ tests hold in the identification and school placement of gifted children? How much should teachers know about intelligence testing and interpretation of test results? And, if it is decided that IQ tests are inappropriate for identification of giftedness, what other psychometric measures should take their place?

2. Sternberg and Gardner present two new, but opposing, views of intelligence. Renzulli, Terman, Piechowski, and the U.S. government (among others) have put forth conceptions of giftedness. In each case, it appears that the individual researchers or agencies are trying to argue that their view is "best." Is it, then, a goal that the fields of psychology and education will eventually arrive at a universally ac-

cepted definition of intelligence and giftedness? What are the benefits and draw-backs to reaching such a consensus? In your own view, is it acceptable to have multiple definitions of the same construct—intelligence—or must unanimous acceptance of one view be our ultimate goal?

3. An intriguing component to both Gardner's view of intelligence and Piechowski's concept of giftedness is the emphasis on the social and emotional forms of intelligence. *Intrapersonal* intelligence (à la Gardner) and *emotional overexcitability* (from Piechowski) are seldom measured or appreciated by our society. These "gifts" are seldom seen as such and, in fact, might even be considered as detrimental to the attainment of eminence. ("You could really be successful if you could just be a little less emotional about things.") What part—if any—do these internal qualities play in the identification of and programming for gifted children? How would you convince policymakers that these affective aspects of intelligence are important enough to attend to in educational programs?

4. Consider the gifted education program with which you are most familiar. Looking at the children involved in this program, which of the conceptions of giftedness found in this chapter do they best fit? Now, consider children in your school who are *not* receiving gifted program services but who, in your view, are highly able. What factors do these children have in common—academically, emotionally, behaviorally? Last, consider your own ideas on intelligence and giftedness, and then decide which students in your school fit these conceptions. Compare the children you have selected with those currently in your school's gifted program. What is the degree of overlap, and what does this finding tell you about how well your concept of giftedness meshes with that of your school's views?

OUT OF THE WAY/OUT OF THIS WORLD RESOURCES

The Mismeasure of Man, by Stephen Jay Gould (Norton, New York, 1981).

This book is about the conception of intelligence as a single entity, the quantification of talent by using one number, and the use of these numbers to rank people from the continuum of superior to inferior. In short, this book is about the mismeasure of man (and woman).

The American High School Student, by John C. Flanagan (University of Pittsburg, Project TALENT Office, 1964).

This longitudinal study of over 400,000 high school students concerning their plans after high school graduation provides fascinating, and historically important, data and insights about gifted youth and their ambitions. The need for school counseling and parental support are strikingly similar to recommendations made even today.

Roeper Review: Special Issue on the IQ Controversy, edited by Linda K. Silverman (Volume 8, No. 3, February 1986).

This journal issue presents one of the more balanced series of articles on the pros and cons of IQ testing. The 12 articles presented are written by some of our field's most renowned researchers—Robert Sternberg, Alan Kaufman, Howard Gardner, and Michael Piechowski—as well as an interview with Elizabeth Hagan (coauthor of the *Stanford-Binet, Revision IV*) and a perspective on IQ testing written from a parent's point of view.

The Child Buyer, by John Hersey (Alfred A. Knopf, New York, 1960).

"Purchase of Boy Child, Town of Pequot, State Senate Standing Committee on Education, Welfare and Public Morality." So begins Hersey's extraordinary novel about Wissey Jones, a child buyer, who plans to purchase gifted children and convert them through drugs and surgery into brilliantly efficient thinking machines. A bestseller when first released, this novel presents a poignant description of everything we *don't* want gifted children to become, and it also contains an underlying theme of our cultural ambivalence toward children of high intellect.

CHAPTER 3

Specific Guidance Concerns of Gifted Students

The intent of this chapter is to

Provide basic information about the social and emotional needs of gifted youth by using a true and false quiz format

Familiarize you with individuals who have emphasized social and emotional guidance concerns in both practical and research settings

Emphasize the frequent "misalignment" that exists between gifted students' school placement and their academic and emotional needs

CRAIG

It was my first year teaching in a gifted program—first day, in fact, and Craig was the first student to walk through the door of my converted library/resource room.

"Hi," he said, "I'm Craig. I guess we'll be seeing a lot of each other." As I looked at him—10 years old, shirttail tucked-in here but tucked-out there, thick glasses, businesslike demeanor—I couldn't help but think that the stereotype was true: Gifted kids *are* like little adults, only sloppier.

Others arrived shortly thereafter. Fourteen children awash with questions, ideas, and concerns—and perhaps, an unstated fear: "What's this new teacher *really* like?"

The days turned into weeks, and . . . months. The students learned that I was no more an ogre than they were all angels. We each had individual quirks, interests, and talents. And that was okay.

Figure 3.1. Illustration by Maureen Canning Marshall. Reprinted by permission of the illustrator.

But Craig's qualities were very different from the others. He seldom completed his assigned projects, and he was "off task" as often as "on," which led his classroom teacher to wonder—out loud—whether Craig should remain in our gifted program. After all, other children not in the gifted program had higher grades and more task commitment than did Craig—weren't we rewarding his negative behaviors? Yet, to me, Craig offered a sensitivity that balanced our sometimes competitive environment (he lost at chess once, on purpose, because his opponent was "just learning," and Craig wanted to give him a chance to be good at something new). Also, in class discussions, Craig added shades of gray to our frequent black-and-white thinking. He always saw a new twist or new angle which brought initial confusion, but later led to legitimate conclusions; this surprised everyone but Craig.

But those unfinished projects! What *could* we do about Craig?

A QUIZ

Craig is not a typical gifted child. Or is he? *Typical* infers that general agreement exists on the topic or concept being defined, which certainly is not true in the case of the term *giftedness*. Yet, however we define them, gifted children historically have been seen in some stereotypic ways: physically (the "Coke-bottle glasses" type), intellectually (the bookworm who can define the word *football* but doesn't know how to throw one), psychologically (the absent-minded-professor type, as exemplified by the character in Figure 3.2), and socially (the gifted teen who would rather spend Friday night alone in front of a computer screen than on a date watching a movie screen).

Yes, unfortunately, the picture that is often painted of gifted children is not a pretty one; instead, it can be cruel, insulting, and bleak. Is it any wonder, then, that gifted children themselves, when told of their label, often deny it categorically? "Gifted?" they say, "Not me. I'm just a regular kid."

The following items constitute a quiz designed to test your *SQ:* *s*tereotype *q*uotient. [I thought that since we already test for *IQ*, eat ice cream at *DQ* (Dairy Queen), and catch up on the latest gentleman's fashions in *GQ*, this acronym would have a familiar ring.] It's a true/false quiz and, as such, many of you will want to respond "it depends" or "sometimes." These re-

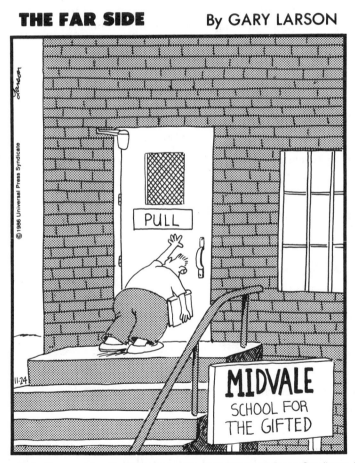

Figure 3.2. (*Source: The Far Side.* Copyright 1986 Universal Press Syndicate. Reprinted with permission.)

sponses are not allowed. (Sorry, but it's *my* quiz and *my* book.) But, don't be afraid of getting wrong answers either, as each of us at some time or another thinks in ways that are in need of reexamination. Just be honest.

Item 1: Children should be told when they are gifted.
True _____   False _____

Item 2: Once children have been identified as gifted, adults should expect higher grades or school achievement.
True _____   False _____

Item 3: Once identified, gifted children should be left on their own to pursue topics that interest them.
True _____   False _____

Item 4: Gifted children and gifted adolescents go through the same developmental stages as do their less able agemates.
True _____   False _____

Item 5: Gifted children can also have specific learning handicaps.
True _____   False _____

Item 6: If gifted children are rebellious or inattentive in school, it is their duty to conform to the situation.
True _____   False _____

Item 7: If school is "boring," gifted children will turn off to learning.
True _____   False _____

Item 8: Gifted children are apt to view their world from an adult vantage point.
True _____   False _____

Item 9: Gifted adolescents usually have very focused and refined career goals.
True _____   False _____

SCORING THE QUIZ

Item 1: Children should be told when they are gifted.

Correct Answer: True

Rationale: From the time gifted children are very young, they are able to detect differences between themselves and their agemates. They may note that, in speaking, they use words that other children don't understand, or they may prefer games with complex rules rather than the freewheeling melee of unstructured activities. In a now-classic study of gifted children's play patterns, O'Shea (1960) discovered that preschool-age children, when given the choice, self-selected playmates who were more like themselves in mental age over any other factor. Since this implicit knowledge that children can differ in unseen ways (for example, intellectually) is already noted in behaviors, gifted children benefit from being told explicitly, "This is how you are different, and this is what those differences mean."

Barbara Kerr, a psychologist and author, uses this analogy in her speeches to prove the benefits of enhanced self-knowledge:

Setting: A busy street corner.

Characters: Two people, one with a physical handicap, the other with no visible handicap.

Plot: Both characters prepare to cross the street.

As the traffic signal switches to "Walk," both characters begin to cross. The person with the disability takes longer than the other to achieve the goal, but both eventually reach the opposite curb. In terms of walking ability, the nondisabled person may be at the 97th percentile, whereas the person with the physical handicap may rank in the 35th percentile. These disparate levels do not imply that one individual is a *better person* than the other; rather, they denote that when the activity is walking, one of the characters excels while the other does not. Certainly, the physically handicapped person in this example would be more adept in some area than would the expert walker. A weakness in walking does not preclude talents in other areas.

Using this scenario, Kerr states that the nondisabled person would likely develop empathy for the curb-side partner—not resentment, or anger, but empathy: you understand the limits of the other and do not expect him or her to perform as well as you do.

The same is true, Kerr believes, when gifted children are informed about both the presence and the meaning of their specific talents. For example, a child in fifth grade who scores at the 98th percentile on a vocabulary test can, by dint of this test score, understand words (such as *dint*) and/or use them better than 98 percent of his or her classmates. Realizing this, verbally adept children can learn to appreciate that other fifth-grade students are not misunderstanding them *on purpose,* nor are they pretending to be ignorant of certain words— they simply may not have the verbal facility that some gifted children have.

When people understand that others are not being different to spite them; that ignorance or lesser ability in a certain area (for example, vocabulary) is not feigned; and that excellent performance is usually spread out among many people and many subjects, then their reactions are more likely to be emphathetic rather than critical. This is as true for first-class athletes as it is for first-class artists as it for first-class mathematicians. Each of us is better at some things than we are at others, which is the first step in recognizing that "better at . . ." is far, far removed from "better than . . ."; that just because an individual has a flair for words (is *better at* using words) that person is not intrinsically *better than* anyone else whose verbal facility is limited.

Gifted children who know about and understand the meaning of their specific talents will seldom become elitist—a common fear. Instead, they will see the limit and extent of their gifts in relation to their own particular strengths and those possessed by others.

> *Item 2:* Once children have been identified as gifted, adults should expect higher grades or school achievement.
>
> *Correct Answer:* False
>
> *Rationale:* Generally, it is incorrect to state that children are *identified* as gifted. *Identification,* in the dictionary sense, means that we put a name on something that heretofore has gone undiscovered. In the case of giftedness, children who earn this label are usually those who have done well on tests and in day-to-day academics; teachers and parents *already know* these children are bright and, therefore, their identification comes as no surprise. So, except in rare cases where a child with hidden talents is "discovered" by a specific test or an observant educator, *identification* is a misnomer. A more correct term would be *validation;* for, in fact, the process of locating gifted children generally results in a roster of students who come as no surprise to anyone. All we have done is validate our observations by putting some numerical parameters around the talents we knew to exist.

If this is, indeed, the typical scenario, then logic dictates that people should not expect higher performance from newly identified, that is, validated, gifted students. Thus, if a fourth-grade pupil commonly gets report card grades ranging from A to C, a variety of grades are likely to continue even if the gifted label is applied.

Expectations are often extremely high for gifted students. School, society, family, and self can contribute to the idea that peak performance should be the norm for students selected for gifted programs. If carried too far, these high expectations can lead to perfectionism, "the most overlooked and influential of those (personality) traits distinctly associated with individuals of superior intelligence" (Whitmore, 1980, p. 145). Although perfectionism can often breed excellence, it can also be destructive, leading gifted children to believe that the only efforts worth making are those that end in perfect achievement.

Therefore, except in that rare case where the label of *gifted* is applied to a student whose talents had been hidden or disguised by daily performance, it is wrong to think that the identification of giftedness will, on its own, improve the classroom performance of students.

Item 3: Once identified, gifted students should be left on their own to pursue topics that interest them.

Correct Answer: False

Rationale: There are two related misconceptions about gifted children and their education:

1. They are organized and well-versed in study skills and their application.
2. Gifted students learn independently; their teachers are superfluous.

Both of these widely held misconceptions can lead to big disappointments— for both gifted children and those who teach them. The first misconception assumes that able students can explore independent study projects on their own, thanks to an inherent sense of knowing what they want to learn and how to locate the resources that will get them there. In reality, there is no special gene possessed by gifted children alone that guarantees proficiency in learning how to learn. Like everyone else, gifted students require instruction about the difference between a dictionary and a thesaurus, and the relative merits of first-hand resources versus the encyclopedia. These skills may appear to be present in young gifted children, who can often rattle off fact after fact, like a computer with sneakers. The need for study skills instruction may only become obvious later, perhaps in middle school or junior high, when gifted students are no longer able to use mere memorization to recall both facts and assignments. Then, on closer examination, teachers often find that taking notes, locating resources, and managing time are foreign skills to their most able students. So, they (the teachers) backpedal, assisting these very same students who generally require curriculum extension, not remediation. The result? Everyone feels dumb—the teacher, for not recognizing earlier that study skills instruction was needed by able students, and the students, for not being smart enough to know what they don't know.

Also, students left to "fend for themselves" in exploring the various realms of content that strike their fancy or pique their interest lose out on one very important aspect of their education: interaction with a caring, competent teacher. The human-to-human contact between one who knows (that is, the teacher) and one who seeks knowledge (that is, the student) cannot be dismissed as trivial—a by-product of learning. Instead, the teacher needs to live up to the true purpose of an instructor, which is to educate (*educare,* the Latin root word for *education,* means "to bring forth" or "to lead to").

Should gifted students be allowed to do independent research? Certainly. Is the teacher's role to sit back and watch, as a spectator, while the student learns? Certainly not. The role of the teacher is to watch patiently (when appropriate), teach specifically (when needed), and show the student the importance of *d*ependence in *i*ndependent study.

Item 4: Gifted children and gifted adolescents go through the same developmental stages as do their less able agemates.

Correct Answer: True

Rationale: As is true so often in life, it's the timing that counts. Gifted children, like all others, have the needs to belong, to question, to rebel, and so on. Some emerge from these encounters unscathed and emotionally intact; others get through by sheer tenacity or the skilled guidance of adults or (sometimes) even other children. But the stages that are gone through and the milestones that are met are similar for children with below-average, average, and advanced IQs; what differs is the onset of particular developmental events.

For example, Nick Colangelo (1989) studied 125 gifted adolescents who were given the task of defining problems that were important to them. More than 50 percent of these students chose dilemmas that dealt with the topics of friendship and love relationships—a finding that shows the interconnectedness between gifted teenagers and all other teenagers. However, in addition to citing these rather typical spheres of conflict, the 125 adolescents also identified 36 different issues dealing with more adult themes such as public welfare (cheating, stealing, scandal) and life-and-death scenarios. Also, some of the problems cited dealt with more existential issues, as exemplified in these comments, as related by a tenth-grade boy:

> Some people have no direction in life. They just float through never trying anything that might challenge the first beliefs they encountered. They are lazy. They don't care. They assume a state of apathy. They try to out-nothing each other. They drift. They don't try to discover why they exist. (Colangelo, 1989, p. 11)

Gifted children and teens often ask questions or raise issues they are "not supposed to" bring up because they are "too young" to do so. What parent wants to discuss the pros and cons of voluntary school prayer with a 10-year-old who has watched the debate hatch daily in the local newspaper? What second-grade teacher looks forward to a classroom discussion of apartheid or Middle East politics led by a bright student during show and tell time? Eventually, these issues may become topics for roundtable discussions by students, but most likely the students will be college age and the class will be a course in philosophy. Still, it cannot be denied that some students will need to address these issues—*need* to—prior to the time preordained by our society as appropriate. And, most likely, if the brave teacher or parent does allow the discussion to ensue, the same students who were the most animated and vocal will, at the conclusion, *still* want recess, *still* want snacktime, or *still* complain (as most children do) that their parents treat them like little kids.

Dyssynchronous development: the very real situation that exists when gifted students have thoughts, ideas, and mental acuity that outpaces their handwriting skills or shoe sizes.

Item 5: Gifted children can also have specific learning handicaps.

Correct Answer: True

Rationale: How societally driven we are to pigeonhole ourselves and others into particular "camps": Republican/Democrat; conservative/liberal; athletic/wimpish; gifted/handicapped. The truth is, though, few of us exist exclusively in one domain, for as soon as we espouse one philosophy, belief, or course of action, we begin to see that believing wholeheartedly in our new-found truths is illogical. The other side, the opposite position, holds some merit and though we may disagree essentially with what exists there, we begin to notice that it, too, has its own sense of order.

How common, and how healthy. Some call it skepticism. Others call this ability to see all sides *intelligence.*

Luckily, within the past few years, the stereotype of gifted people as being flawless has begun to disintegrate as surely as does a sugar cube in hot, hot coffee. Due, for the most part, to the recognition of gifted persons who have overcome some handicaps, we have begun to notice that gifts and talents are often disguised or hidden by something beyond the control of its owner.

For example, Tom Cruise, whose early bouts with (and misunderstanding of) dyslexia led him to believe he was dumb and worthless.

Or Alexa Canady, our country's first black female neurosurgeon, who had to overcome the societal attitude that "your son you want to be the best he can be. Your daughter you want to be happy" (Lanker, 1989, p. 222).

Or Stevie Wonder, who in blindness sees pieces of our world and ourselves often not seen even by those with 20/20 vision.

Or the person with whom you work or live right now, whose abilities in a particular field or subject force us to note that a disability is not necessarily a handicap.

There have always been persons around us who have overcome a physical impairment or an environmental deprivation to excel in their chosen fields. We think of Helen Keller, Eleanor Roosevelt, or Abraham Lincoln. Still, these persons are the "stuff" of folklore—more historical than real—and our sense of affiliation with them is diminished, somewhat, by the tall pedestals on which we place them. They seem so removed from the world we know.

But we've seen Tom Cruise cavort (wholeheartedly!) with Kelly McGillis, and we know the sexual stereotype of which Dr. Canady speaks. "They" are "us" in a much closer way than the folk heroes of past generations have been, and due to their collective influence and honesty, we have the privilege of knowing that gifts and talents, though frequently laid dormant by personal imperfections or cultural biases, can also emerge and bloom.

So, can a gifted child also have a specific learning disability? Sure, and you probably know at least one such boy or girl. Can a gifted child be wheelchair-bound, be deaf, or have severe behavior problems? Of course. All these abilities/disabilities can coexist in a single individual, but to find the gift we may need to sift through some rough terrain to uncover it.

Item 6: If gifted children are rebellious or inattentive in school, it is their duty to conform to the situation.

Correct Answer: False

Rationale: A witty and wise college professor of mine, Dr. Grace Ellen Stiles, once told our "Methods of Teaching Social Studies" class, "If the teacher takes care to individualize the curriculum, then discipline will take care of itself." That sounded important—prophetic even—but at the tender age of 19, I had no idea what it meant. But I wrote it down anyway (like any good education student would do). Only recently have I been able to understand the depth of Dr. Stiles's insight, and its powerful potential to change for the better the school careers of gifted children. On examining her comments, I learned this: that blaming a child for his or her school failure is similar to criticizing the traffic cop trying to maintain order at a five-way intersection. Don't blame the individual in the middle of the problem for something that is flawed in design.

Gifted children who do not do well in school are not failing because they *enjoy* failure—who does? Instead, their weak performance may have its roots within Dr. Stiles's admonition, for when it comes to individualizing curriculum for gifted students, a good question to ask is, "Who's minding the store?"

A case in point is a recent inspection of mathematics textbooks by researcher James Flanders at the University of Chicago. He found "the average percent of new content in the three (most popular elementary) text series was less than 40 percent in grades 6 and 7, and only 30 percent in grade 8. Earlier grades were similar" (Driscoll, 1988, p. 3). For like reasons, the state of California in 1986 refused to adopt *any* of the elementary-level math textbooks submitted for statewide school adoption. The problem, dear reader, was not that the texts were so difficult that students were "turning off" because of frustration. Instead, they were "tuning out" because of a boredom that is the by-product of page after page after page of long division algorithms.

If a gifted student is rebellious, inattentive, or "underachieving" in a particular subject area, a problem does exist. The problem, however, may be *external* to the child—for example, within the textbook or the curriculum or the teacher—and until we determine the root of the problem, it would be both unwise and disrespectful to demand that the student do all the conforming. If later, after more thorough analysis, it is found that the student's role in poor achievement is a big one, then we are back to square one. Until this delineation is cleared up, though, it may be best to postpone both judgment and sentencing.

Item 7: If school is "boring," gifted children will turn off to learning.

Correct Answer: False

Rationale: Given the rationale for the previous response, it may seem contradictory to answer this item with false. However, the key word in Item 7 is *learning;* many gifted children turn off to *school,* but do they turn off to learning as well? Never. Listen as Ryan's mom details the distinction:

> When Ryan brought home a *C* in math last session, I asked him (nonchalantly, of course) what they had been studying. "Multiplication," he said. "Do you understand multiplication?" I asked. "Sure," he said, "it's easy."
> I proceeded to quiz him on his multiplication tables. No problem. "So, why the *C*?" I asked.
> "Guess I didn't do too well on the test," he surmised.
> "Any idea why that happened?" I probed further.
> "Well," he said, "the teacher told us we could do whatever we wanted when we were finished, and I was reading this *great* book on how to build your own robot, and it had all these really neat diagrams, and . . ."
> You should have seen his eyes light up. Who do you suppose actually learned more during that 20-minute math test? The students who carefully completed all the problems correctly, or Ryan, who went on to something more interesting, something unknown? They all had *A*s in math, and he had a *C*. This didn't bother Ryan at all though because he already *knows* that he understands multiplication.

If you recall Chapter 2, a 19-year-old's definition of giftedness spoke to the insatiable quest to know, to learn, and to explore, that was true of herself and other gifted students. It is an unfortunate reality that *school* and *learning* are not synonyms—or, at least, related—in the minds of some gifted children. Yet, this is sometimes true.

The goal of every educator should be to have children learn *because* of school, not *in spite* of it. Something more interesting, something unknown, which is Ryan's wish, will continue to happen in a mind as vibrant as his. How fortunate for him (and for us) if we become partners in his quest.

Item 8: Gifted students are apt to view their world from an adult vantage point.

Correct Answer: True

Rationale: The work of two of the finest researchers of education for gifted children, Annemarie Roeper and A. Harry Passow, provides the rationale for this response.

In an article on empathy and ethics, Annemarie Roeper related a common characteristic of gifted children:

> [They] are global thinkers, as they are apt to see the whole, the philosophy or the scientific framework, before they concern themselves with the details. . . . They are concept-oriented, and have an enormous desire to make sense of this world, to master it, and to make an impact on it. . . . They want to find out, they want to make discoveries, because of their inner need for intellectual and emotional order. (1989, pp. 9–10)

This heightened awareness of the interdependence among people, ideas, and environments gives gifted children the ability to concern themselves with right and wrong and to see the big picture on both a person-to-person basis and in relation to their world. As Roeper explains

> They get very emotionally involved and feel strongly for themselves and others. Even though they may be jealous of a sibling, they cannot stand it when they see their brother or sister punished . . . and they are often the ones who will, for example, befriend the child who is seen as strange. (1989, p. 7)

Such wonderful gifts—empathy, moral reasoning, a sense of justice! Yet when wrapped up in the body of a yound child, confusion sometimes reigns. For, at 7 years old, if you can see what should exist but doesn't, you want to know why it can't be fixed—right now! Politics be damned—if people are homeless, or hungry, or helpless, that needs to be made better.

"If only it were that easy," says the consoling adult. But the child may not *be* consoled, for things still aren't right; people still go hungry. An undefined sense of sadness, confusion, or rage might result, and a world that doesn't quite understand the gifted child looks on and rolls its eyes: "She's 10 going on 30," is its typical response.

A. Harry Passow, in sharing Roeper's views, suggests that educators concern themselves with the moral and ethical development of gifted children, and include such instruction within the curriculum provided to them. Research and school programs to guide the "development of caring, concerned, compassionate, committed individuals who develop and use their giftedness for society's benefit as well as for self-fulfillment" are needed, as are instructional programs in leadership development and creativity, among other topics (Passow, 1988, p. 13).

Both of these researchers, preeminent yet not singular in their thinking on these vital topics, know the benefits of reviewing with gifted children the many "big pictures" they encounter before adulthood—the time when they are *supposed to* be asking tough questions about their world. The dissatisfaction that gifted children may feel because their concerns cannot be addressed fully, or without regard for political and economic ramifications, will be diffused somewhat if caring adults at least take the time to acknowledge that the questions and concerns of these sensitive young people are valid.

Item 9: Gifted adolescents usually have very focused and refined career goals.

Correct Answer: False

Rationale: It's a question as old as humanity itself: "What do you want to be when you grow up?" A simple enough question (on the surface), the expected response is a career that involves doing things you enjoy and are good at, from brain surgery to business, from hotel management to homemaking. Yet for gifted students—those youth who seem to excel in so many areas—the question is not as simple as it sounds. One 15-year-old girl wrote about her aspirations in the following way:

> When I look for a career in my future, the clouds really thicken. There are so many things I'd like to do and be, and I'd like to try them all. . . . I'd like to be a physical therapist, a foreign correspondent, a psychiatrist, an anthropologist, a linguist, a folk singer, an espionage agent, and a social worker. (Hoyt and Hebeler, 1974, p. 285)

Marshall Sanborn, a researcher at the University of Wisconsin–Madison, ran the Research and Guidance Laboratory for Superior Students for more than 20 years. In that time, thousands of gifted adolescents were counseled and interviewed there, and career aspirations were a frequent topic of discussion. The frequency with which the laboratory personnel saw teens whose many interests and competencies made career choice a difficult problem led them to coin a new term: *multipotentiality.* This term, and its underlying impact on the lives of gifted adolescents, refers to the difficulty many able students have in selecting a career focus. Feeling somewhat like the spinner on the wheel of life (see Figure 3.3), gifted students often feel pulled in many different directions.

> I'd love to be an artist, but my mom says I should get a *real* job.

> When I told my dad I wanted to be a teacher, he said I was too smart for that—besides, there's no money in it. Oh yeah, he also added, "Boys aren't teachers."

Figure 3.3. Multipotential: an embarrassment of riches. (*Source: The Gifted Kids Survival Guide II* by James Delisle and Judy Galbraith, illustrated by Harry Pulver, Jr. Reprinted by permission of Free Spirit Publishing, Inc. Copyright © 1987. All rights reserved.)

> My guidance counselor says with *my* brains I could be anything I want to, which is great to know, but it doesn't help me focus on what I want to spend my life doing.

These quotations, though fictitious, are a reality for many gifted adolescents. Feeling somewhat like Benjamin in the movie *The Graduate* (when Dustin Hoffman's character, Benjamin, a young college graduate, is told to get into "plastics"; it turns out that he has his own ideas), gifted teens often feel a sense of pressure regarding career selection. (More on career guidance issues in Chapter 8.)

Do all gifted teens remain confused or unfocused about their life's profession? Of course not. Some young people know from the first day of first grade what they want to become, and they go ahead and do it. But for those who do feel purposeless, or committed to everything (at least for a week), career guidance is an essential, though often neglected, aspect of their education.

How'd You Do?

Or as the kids ask, "What d'ya get?" If you did very well (7 to 9 correct), you are either very astute about the affective development of gifted students, or you are a good test taker. Perhaps both. (If you have some extra time, you might consider writing your own book on this topic.)

If your score was 6 or below, consider this nine-item quiz as a pretest which, by intent, was designed so that your score could improve after some more reading, some more thinking.

Whatever your score, I'm glad you're here. For unless you are required to read this book by a college professor-type who thinks it will be *good* for you, then you are here out of choice, not mandate. (Even if you find yourself in the former category, I hope your reading time provides an insight or two.)

BACK TO CRAIG

Craig remained in our gifted program for two years, despite occasional out-cries from his classroom teachers. As he matured, he learned the importance of playing the game by at least *some* of the rules. His favorite line became, "Sometimes in life you have to be ready to compromise." So, he took a bit more care in completing his homework (though he saw most of it as a mere exercise), and in order to keep more on-task, he wrote out both daily and weekly work goals. He became more organized and more aware of his teachers' goals for him. School became a bit more pleasant for us all.

What Craig taught me and his other advocates is that student success and growth cannot be measured solely through completed projects or straight *A* grades. If Craig had been dropped from our gifted program in deference to a child more oriented to school-based achievements, we all would have lost. An artificial comfort would have been created that the greatest good was being served.

There are many Craigs in our schools today—sensitive children whose skills and talents transcend the measurable. Each one *needs* an advocate—perhaps you—to assure they receive an education commensurate with his or her abilities.

CONTINUING QUESTS AND QUESTIONS

1. If there is one point of agreement among highly able students, it is their universal dislike of the label *gifted*. Generally, the benefits of being identified as gifted are appreciated (for example, the special classes and advanced courses), yet the term itself, *gifted,* is both *un*appreciated and misunderstood. Why is this so? What situa-

tions in your own students' lives have caused them to view the term *gifted* as a liability? Should our field of study seek alternative terms to label students with high abilities, and if so, what terms can you suggest? Last, what suggestions do you have for making students feel more comfortable with the talents they possess, regardless of the label attached to these special gifts?

2. Many school programs for gifted students function with two distinct definitions of giftedness. The first definition—the ideal one—refers to children with high potential, while the second conception—the operational definition—is the one actually used in the selection process. This operational definition allows for a selection of only those children whose high potential is coupled with high achievement. Rarely would a student with a high IQ and low grades in daily classroom work be chosen for participation in the program for gifted children. How should the field of education for gifted children address this conflict between ideal and operational? In a world of limited school funding, which children should receive priority in special programs: gifted children with high achievement or students whose high aptitude is not matched by superior performance?

3. Many ideas espoused by education specialists of gifted children—teaching high cognitive thinking skills, problem-solving strategies, and independent study skills— have been "picked up" by our colleagues within regular education programs. You could say that education personnel of gifted children are doing their jobs so well that they might be putting themselves out of a job. If this is so, where should the "next generation" of education specialists of gifted children target their services? Which groups of underserved gifted children should receive our immediate attention? In other words, in 10 years from now, what will we consider to be our field's greatest new accomplishments in this decade?

4. What alternatives do exist, and what alternatives *should* exist, for gifted students who do not fit into the usual school's routine? If a creative child refuses to complete rote drill worksheets that emphasize what she already knows, what are our alternatives as educators? If a vocationally talented student is failing high school English, should this disqualify him from taking courses that advance his talent? How much does the student need to compromise when "school doesn't fit," and how much should the structure change to accommodate the child?

OUT OF THE WAY/OUT OF THIS WORLD RESOURCES

On Being Gifted, by the American Association for Gifted Children (Walker and Company, New York, 1978).
      This book, written by 20 gifted teenagers, reveals the high points and hurdles of growing up gifted. Although some sections of the book are beginning to "show their age," the majority of comments are still valid and can be used as fine discussion starters with students who question the merits of possessing strong talents.

New Voices in Counseling the Gifted, edited by Nicholas Colangelo and Ronald Zaffron (Kendall-Hunt Publishers, Dubuque, IA, 1976).
      Now out of print (yet available in many libraries), this book's "new voices" may

not be so new anymore, yet the expressions of need made by the authors regarding social and emotional growth of gifted students are still valid and important. Especially useful are the chapters on career development and identification of gifted students from minority groups.

There Are Those, by Nathan and Janet Levy (NL Associates, Hightstown, NJ, 1982).

An abstract picture book, *There Are Those* extols the benefits of individual differences. People who see things from a unique vantage point or those whose talents are expressed in creative ways will see themselves very much in evidence throughout this short book's words and drawings. In a quiet, subtle way, the author allows the reader to experience the joy of unique attributes.

Crow Boy, by Taro Yashima (Viking Press, New York, 1955).

This picture book (for children 7 and older) presents a sensitive tale of a young boy whose special gift is ridiculed by classmates, causing Crow Boy sadness and embarrasssment. Only when the other schoolchildren see how Crow Boy's special talent adds richness to their own lives do they come to accept and appreciate his differentness. A very special story to share with students and colleagues.

CHAPTER 4

The Gifted Child at School

Part 1: Self-Concept, School Achievement, and Invitational Education

The intent of this chapter is to

Familiarize you with the concept of *invitational education* and provide examples of "inviting" and "disinviting" school environments

Provide evidence of the natural link that exists between self-concept and school achievement and give examples of how these two interweave in classroom activities

Show how curriculum design, grading, and evaluation procedures, the school's physical environment, and disciplinary methods can invite achievement in all students, including those who are gifted

Give evidence that the educator's own self-concept contributes to or takes away from the inviting environment existing in schools

Remove yourself, for two paragraphs, from the place you are now to a site where you once vacationed. Lakefront, oceanside, near a pool or puddle, all you need for the mental picture to follow is a remembrance of water. Now . . . got it?

Next, pick up a pebble, or a seashell, and drop it gently into the water. Notice what it does. For one thing, it causes ripples, as wave after wave spreads out from the spot where the pebble was dropped. Even when gently dropping the object into the water, you change the image of anything reflected in it. Tall trees now waver, the sunshine is seen as uneven patches, not steady rays. All this caused by one small stone or shell.

These changes are temporary, of course. But imagine how often other objects—twigs, raindrops, toes—broke the surface of the water before you arrived and after you left your waterfront. So many changes, each one small, yet taken together they could create a large wave.

You probably see an analogy on the horizon. And there is one—a good one—and it is embodied in the form of Mrs. Sanders, a first-grade teacher I observed while supervising student teachers. Mrs. Sanders's class had 28 students, 3 of whom did not speak English and several more whose backgrounds, interests, and abilities made cluster grouping difficult. There are many qualities about Mrs. Sanders worth mentioning—her varied teaching strategies, her effective use of praise—but most special, most "rippling," was what she did at the end of each day.

As the children were preparing to go home—"walkers" on the right, "riders" on the left—Mrs. Sanders made a point to take each child and either squeeze a shoulder, rub a head, or make a funny face to force a smile from a reluctant frowner. Each gesture was accompanied by a verbal statement such as, "Good answer in math today, Mary" or "Nice sneakers, Jeff!" Each child, each day. A different gesture, a different expression.

I asked her why—"Why go to such trouble each day?" Her answer was

Figure 4.1. Illustration by Maureen Canning Marshall. Reprinted by permission of the illustrator.

simple, straightforward, and indicative of a teacher for whom 110 percent is merely typical performance.

She said this: "I have no idea what happens when the students leave school. Some ride on the bus and get ridiculed; others go home to an empty house; still more rush around from ballet to soccer to who-knows-what. I have no idea, and I have very little control. But," she added, "I *do* have control over how each student will remember his or her last moment of the day with me, and that memory will be a fond one."

Mrs. Sanders did admit that on some days, with some children, it was tough coming up with a positive statement. My favorite example of her ability to see improvement where others would likely see strife? "Good day for you, Eric, you didn't bite me so hard."

"But they're worth it," she said. "I dig until I find something good."

See the ripples?

SELF-CONCEPT AND SCHOOL ACHIEVEMENT: A NATURAL LINK

As explained in Chapter 3 (and, it is hoped, throughout this book), gifted children are, first and foremost, children. Their needs, wishes, and feelings are more like those of other children than they are different. This being so, the comments that follow may lead you to wonder, "But isn't self-concept development good for *all* children?" The answer is yes.

Still, this section is important in the affective development of gifted children, too, for the following reasons:

1. Gifted children, often more aware of reactions of others toward them, may begin to develop a self-concept at a very early age (Silverman, 1986).
2. Since many gifted students tie their success in school to their worth as a person, early attention to self-concept enhancement is essential (Whitmore, 1980).
3. The belief that perfection is an attainable and expected goal limits some gifted children from giving themselves credit—and therein, personal worth—for many of their lesser achievements (Adderholdt-Elliott, 1987).

If you read educational or psychological literature, it is tough to find a writer who does not link self-concept with school achievement. This is as true in articles in the *Journal of Educational Psychology* as it is in *Family Circle*. No writer (at least none of whom I am aware) states publicly, "Who cares if you think you're worthless, you can still learn, can't you?" Everyone, from everyday people to eminent scholars, seems to agree that attitude affects performance.

> Human behavior is always a product of how people see themselves and the situations in which they are involved. Although this fact seems obvious, the failure of people everywhere to comprehend it is responsible for much of human misunderstanding, maladjustment, conflict, and loneliness. Our perceptions of ourselves and the world are so real to us that we seldom pause to doubt them. (Combs, Avila, and Purkey, 1978, p. 15)

If there is any disagreement about self-concept and school achievement, it comes in the form of a chicken–egg conundrum: Which occurs first? Does a solid sense of self encourage a person to want to learn more, or does successful learning make an individual gain a more positive sense of self? An important question, perhaps, and an intriguing one, but I'm afraid my own callous response is, "Who *cares* which comes first?"

We know already that the two—self-concept and school achievement—occur as a pair, so the question of which precedes which is as meaningless as trying to remember which half of a happily married couple first said "I love you" to the other. For if the marriage is working, the point is moot. It's the same when trying to determine the roots of self-concept or achievement. Even if we *can* specify the exact point at which one or the other began, what good does it do? We're not living back then, we're living now, and this places a much greater need to focus on the present and the future. To be sure, educators cannot dismiss the impact of past experiences on one's present actions, as both common sense and research make us aware of the connection between "what once was" and "what now is" (Seligman, 1975; Chamberlin, 1981). Moreover, just as surely as we cannot ignore the past, we cannot erase it. We, as educators, have only *today* (usually, between 9:00 AM and 3:00 PM) to make changes, to influence lives. It's oh-so-easy (and oh-so-wrong) to think, "What good can *I* do, just look at her homelife?" or "His parents have *never* been supportive of him, so what can you expect?"

Expect? Expect much, dear reader, for you have only today, and a finite number of tomorrows, to affect the self-concepts and achievements of the students in your care.

A FEW MORE WHY-FORS

Franklin Delano Roosevelt once said, "The ablest man I ever met is the man you think you are." Not bad, especially since it came from a man whose dyslexia was so severe that he could not even read his own speeches. Still, he persevered, and the entire world was his ultimate beneficiary.

It's a daunting task, being an educator, bearing the responsibility for shaping both academics and attitudes. Accountability, as defined in today's schools, often measures the easy stuff: the math facts memorized, the commas placed correctly, the historical events sequenced. But the true measure of an educator's teaching performance is not so readily determined. No computer-scanned bubble sheet measures how our students feel about learning, or their biases toward self and others. These indexes, the true value of learning and education, elude detection and measurement, sometimes for years. And even if we *could* measure attitudes and biases—there are self-concept scales available to do just that—we might pick up general trends, but not specific thoughts (Coopersmith, 1967; Sears, 1963). For instance, answering "I like to take challenges" on a scoresheet is one thing, but signing up for an honors chemistry course, where receiving a B is likely, is quite something else.

So, the brave educators wishing to enhance both students' self-concepts and their achievements must be content with not knowing the immediate or long-term impacts of their actions. Yes, some changes will be noticeable; others will be stubbornly absent (at least in the short term). But as Mrs. Sanders knows quite well, ripples expand as they leave the central core.

. . . AND A FEW HOW-TO'S

A teacher I know very well—she happens to be my wife—worked for several years as a resource teacher of gifted students in a rural Ohio school district. She worked in four different buildings, seeing about 30 first through sixth graders daily. (4 schools × 30 students = 120 students per week.) A difficult task, even for an expert juggler, like Deb.

Meeting with each group of students only once per week created some gaps in continuity. Projects that were expected to be completed in the interim sometimes got "forgotten." Resource books, outlines, and notecards stayed buried under math texts and more pressing homework assignments. Most important, though, Deb found that even young lives can go topsy-turvy from one week to the next: Pets can die or run away, best friends can move, new babies can arrive, school awards can be won. A lot can occur between one Monday and the next that could affect the attitude and performance of students.

. . . Enter "New and Goods."

New and Goods is singular, not plural. It defines a time period—15 minutes or so—that began each resource room class that Deb taught. During New and Goods, students met in a group to review the week just passed. Each child (and the teacher too) was given the chance to share something new and good that had occurred since their previous meeting. Talking was encouraged, though not required, but most children took advantage and spoke of something real, something personal, something only theirs. Occasionally, as the groups became more intimate and trusting, a child would ask to share a "new and sad" or a "new and bad." This was allowed. The purpose of New and

Goods was to communicate; the content of what got shared was an individual choice.

Occasionally, as the year moved on and the pace became more hectic, class schedules became less predictable. Still, New and Goods began each resource room meeting—the children demanded it. Having been given the chance to express themselves freely, and without criticism (a key point), they were not about to forego this special time. Projects could wait. First, they shared news about one another.

New and Goods is just one example of the type of activity that serves the dual purpose of promoting both self-concept and achievement. It requires no materials, no budget, no preplanning; in other words, it is a teacher's dream. What it *does* require is a belief that listening to what children say is important to them and a willingness to take the time to do so within the crowded confines of a classroom schedule.

Now, let's broaden the picture. If New and Goods makes sense to you, then you will probably buy into the idea of *invitational education.* As defined by its authors, Purkey and Novak, invitational education is a "self-concept approach to the educative process and professional functioning" (1984, p. 2). It relies on four basic principles:

1. People are able, valuable, and responsible and should be treated accordingly.
2. Teaching should be a cooperative venture.
3. People possess untapped potential.
4. This potential can become realized in an environment that respects individual differences and preferences.

Based on statistical and anecdotal evidence regarding teacher effectiveness, Purkey and Novak maintain that students' perceptions of themselves are often derived from teachers' perceptions *of them* (Brophy, 1979; Good, 1981). Thus, if teachers convince students that they are capable, the students are more likely to act in ways that prove their competence. Conversely, if teachers tell students—verbally or through nonspoken cues—that they are "as dumb as they come," then it is likely that the students will behave in ways that confirm this impression.

An important contention underlying Purkey and Novak's theory is that most teachers are in the business of building character, not tearing it down. Thus, it is the rare educator who sets out for school on Monday morning thinking, "I wonder whose ego I can crush today." Such teachers *do* exist— every profession has its buffoons and its meanies—but it is unusual to find an educator who, *on purpose,* practices self-concept destruction. Instead, the teachers, counselors, administrators, and other school personnel who do destroy others' love of or desire to learn often do so unconsciously or, as Purkey and Novak phrase it, "unintentionally." These unintentional disinviters would argue vigorously that their aims are to *improve* student performance and attitude. What goes awry is this: The "messages" they send that are intended to instill pride in or a love of learning are interpreted by individual students as negative and critical. Perhaps an example of an unintentional disinvitation will help clarify this point:

> My grades were adequate, but I hated the pressure and the high level of competition [in my accelerated classes]. For example, in my math class, the seating was rearranged after every test, with the highest average in the right front, the lowest in the left rear. (Cox, Daniel, and Boston, 1985)

Most likely, the teacher responsible for this public declaration of who-got-what intended to reward the highest achieving students (those in the first row) while prodding the low achievers to do better. I'm afraid, though, that the effect on this student—now a 37-year-old award-winning geologist—was one of humiliation and fear. No doubt, many of us would have similar reactions if we were told to sit at our school's next inservice workshop according to our college grade point average.

Messages sent, messages received: Sometimes the lines of communication get crossed, and when they do, the end result is often no communication at all.

INVITATIONAL EDUCATION: A FEW EXAMPLES

Donald MacKinnon, a scholar in the field of creativity, once wrote, "The same fire that melts the butter, hardens the egg" (1978, p. 171). He was reviewing the elements of creative environments and discovered that few creative people agree on the ideal setting that prompts original thought. Some people love loud music, open spaces, and a beer by their elbow. Others demand quiet, herbal tea, and a closet with a light. The same is true for message sending and receiving: Their impacts are as individual as fingerprints or snowflakes.

Table 4.1 gives examples of how a singular message may have multiple meanings and interpretations. As illustrated by the variety of contexts in which messages are sent and received—social, academic, and other settings—it is easy to see the pervasive nature of the thousands of invitations that we give and get within even a single day. Nonverbal clues—the raised eyebrow, the broad grin, the pat on the back—are as common as are spoken statements. Often, they are just as open to interpretation, as expressed by a 12-year-old runaway who learned the hard way that what adults show and what they feel are often quite different:

> I am . . . one who doesn't "blend to fit with the blur" and am a target for critical assumption by many adults. Therefore, I have little faith in opening

TABLE 4.1. MESSAGES SENT, MESSAGES RECEIVED: DIFFERENCES OF OPINION

Message Sent	Message Received: Positive	Message Received: Negative
Social Messages		
"My, what a beautiful hair-cut!"	Gee, I guess I look pretty good.	Gads! Imagine what I must've looked like yesterday!
"I'd have invited you to my party, but you live so far away. I didn't want you to feel obligated to come."	How considerate—I was spared having to turn down an invitation.	That's only an excuse. If they really wanted me there I would've been invited anyway.
"Interesting meal: I *never* would have thought of glazing the chicken with orange juice."	I got their tastebuds talking—how exciting!	Everyone hates it—so much for recipe experiments.
Academic Messages		
"There was only one *A* on yesterday's test—can anyone guess who got it!"	I'll feel so proud if it's me; I really studied hard!	I'll *die* if it's me! How embarrassing to be picked out as "Mr. Smarty Pants" in front of your friends.
"What's your opinion, Sally? We can always count on you for the wildest ideas."	The teacher really appreciates my creative ideas.	My teacher thinks I'm weird; she even *expects* it when I give my opinion.
"Whoever finishes this assignment first will be my special helper for the day."	I'd *love* to help out—I'll work as fast as I can!	So, I'm only "special" when I'm fast? Forget it, I'm not into speed! Besides, I'll never finish ahead of everyone else.
Other Messages		
"Of course I trust you, but I never lend my car to anyone—really, it's not just you."	I can't argue with him if that's his policy for everyone. He'd say no to anyone who wanted to borrow his car.	He *doesn't* trust me.
"It's OK to be alone, some-times."	My parents understand that "alone time" is important to me.	If I'm not always on some sports team, my parents will think I'm weird.
"I'll bet that you'll be even more successful in life than your sister."	Gee, my family really wants me to do well.	I'll *never* catch up to her, so why try at all. I *hate* getting compared!

up, knowing too often behind a smiling face and persuasive talk, reveals a back stabber. I'll admit some people will do or say things unintentionally, and will admit they were wrong in their judgment, and express they do make mistakes. It's easier to forgive those who even have an understanding for their own weaknesses than those who enjoy hurting others. . . . Oh well, what do I know. I am just a kid. Happy New Year anyways to all of you who care, but just remember I am just one runaway [sic] among thousands of others whose stories go untold. (Allen, 1989, p. 8A)

Gifted children are especially apt at picking up the multiple meanings of these blatant and subtle messages. However, this precocity in perception is not always accompanied by a similarly advanced ability in *interpreting* these messages. Thus, the result can be a misreading of invitations sent by teachers or parents so that the gifted child notes the negative over the positive. For example, a child who is told that report card grades of *A*s and *B*s are signs of good work may *hear* the message as a warning to do better, rather than as an acknowledgment of strong efforts. These negative misinterpretations are most apt to occur in gifted children who are perfectionists or those whose self-concept is weak. In fact, if individuals believe something about themselves, they are likely to accept as true only those statements that validate their established beliefs or attitudes (Bandura, 1977). Thus, a child who thinks "I am stupid" will accept readily those messages—intentional or not—that go along with this belief. Likewise, a child with a strong self-concept will be more likely to interpret messages in a more positive way.

The importance of invitations, and their correct interpretation, has been proved through reams of research and years of human interaction. As adults, we often recall the times in our own childhood when we were either invited or disinvited, and these memories, if powerful enough, can affect our behavior even decades later. A teacher in Gary, Indiana, related the following incident to me:

> When I was in third grade, I raised my hand to answer a question, and the teacher called on me. I gave the wrong answer. To this day, I remember how she reacted. She said, "Oh, Catherine, you're just like an old hen. You cackle and cackle but never produce an egg." I'll remember how hurt I felt then—and now—for the rest of my life.

So now what? If you've read this far, you probably realize the importance of invitational education. But saying "I believe" and following through with appropriate actions are two very different things. What follows, then, are some clues for constructing an inviting environment—for yourself and for those you teach.

PSYCHOLOGICAL SMALL CHANGE AND THE FLORIDA FUND

In our home, November 1 is a very big day. Neither holiday nor birthday, this day after Halloween is the date we count up our "Florida fund."

If your household is like mine, you too have a Florida fund. Usually, it is a mayonnaise jar or a coffee can tucked away in a closet and filled with coins. This container gets frequent, albeit minute, deposits throughout the year, and on November 1 we take this small change to our local bank for redemption (monetary, not spiritual). Each year the teller returns with the good news: "$150.63" or "$221.02."

"Amazing," we say, "and to think it all began with a little small change."

Teachers can (and do) provide small change to their students each day— *psychological* small change. Their quiet encouragement equals a dime; the unexpected smile earns two bits; and an extra 5 minutes of recess on springtime's first warm day is worth at least a Kennedy half-dollar. Day in, day out, teacher actions and comments build up each student's psychological reserve. If deposits exceed withdrawals, students are left with a bank of resources that reap rich dividends in terms of self-concept and the desire to achieve.

There are at least five areas in which educators can provide psychological small change to gifted pupils:

1. Within the curriculum
2. In grading procedures and student evaluation
3. Within the classroom environment
4. In establishing disciplinary procedures
5. Through self-satisfying behaviors

WITHIN THE CURRICULUM

Provide Posttests as Pretests

It is more common than rare that gifted students know portions of the regular curriculum before instruction begins. If teachers allow able students to take the textbook-provided posttest at the *beginning* of a particular unit of study, then curriculum can be adapted to meet the *current* level of student functioning. This not only prevents many "I'm bored" comments, but it also gives students credit for their past accomplishments and present competence.

Ask Mrs. Foster

Topics for independent study projects can range from agronomy to Zambia, and students can show what they learn in many and varied formats, as explained by a 10-year-old girl:

> Before, I never used to like book reports, but ever since I did them with Mrs. Foster I've liked them. What she would do is have us either do a news report on it for the class or make costumes and act out our favorite part. (Delisle, 1984, p. 59)

Variety is the spice of successful teaching *and* learning; add a pinch or two to enliven the classroom tempo.

Coordinate Student Schedules

Many gifted programs operate in a "pull-out" format, where students leave the regular class for a period of time each day or week. Whether you are the "sending" teacher (in the regular classroom) or the "receiving" teacher (in the resource room), be aware of the scheduling dilemmas that are part and parcel of pull-out programs. Try to coordinate tests, special events, and the introduction of important topics so that students don't get caught in a bind as they try to serve two (or more) masters in their different classrooms.

Provide "Instead of" Not "In Addition to" Enrichment

Often, gifted students are told that they can work on special projects or in learning centers only *after* they have finished their assigned work. This is all well and good, except for those times when the assigned work is little more than a task requiring rote drill of an already mastered concept. "Instead of" versus "in addition to" enrichment is best noted in comparing these two teachers:

> *The "In Addition to" Teacher:* "Linda, once you've written your spelling words 10 times each and completed these three pages of math seatwork, you may work on your independent project."
>
> *The "Instead of" Teacher:* "Linda, since you scored 95 percent on both your math and spelling pretests, why don't you use your time to work on your science project."

This curriculum streamlining (the "instead of" enrichment) allows teachers to buy time within the school day for students whose past efforts have proved their competence in basic skill areas.

Termed *curriculum compacting* by Renzulli, Reis, and Smith (1981) and *telescoping* by Tannenbaum (1983), this provision benefits students whose knowledge base of particular curriculum areas precludes the need for extensive instruction.

Provide Incentives

Many teachers are frustrated by the seemingly haphazard attempt made by gifted students in completing simple tasks. For example, when a top math student makes 10 computation mistakes on a review worksheet, the student is often chided for making "careless errors." The student balks at redoing the assignment, with complaints of "I already *know* this stuff." The teacher agrees and says, "I *know* you can do the work—just be more careful." Thus begins a cycle of frustration for everyone concerned.

However, think how much of an incentive it would be for students if they were told, "There are 50 math problems on this page. Anyone who completes the first 25 examples with no more than two errors does not have to finish the remaining problems." This comment invites achievement in a way that rewards students who take the time to think about what they are doing, and it offers a "quality discount program" that prods attention to the task at hand. (Also, and not so incidentally, it cuts down on the teacher's grading time while ensuring that students have mastered basic concepts.)

GRADING PROCEDURES AND STUDENT EVALUATION

Get the Red Out

The ubiquitous red pen that is used to grade students' projects and papers is perceived as an instrument of torture by many children, especially those who are either perfectionists or extremely averse to criticism. Able children make the connection early: "The more red marks, the worse my grade." Solutions? Use any color but red to grade students' papers, or use red ink *only* to point out pupils' accomplishments or correct answers.

Encourage Students to Grade Their Papers

Every text has a teacher's edition; every workbook an answer guide. Hand these over to those students who finish their tasks early and allow them to grade their own work. Not only does this allow students a chance to determine the extent of their knowledge, but it also cuts down on *your* grading time—so everyone wins. Also, and most important, allowing students to grade their own assignments implies that you trust them to be honest about their errors. And, ironically, when most students are given the chance to cheat, they won't; there's no need to be dishonest when the person in charge respects your right to make errors.

Set Reachable Goals

Many gifted children select topics of study that are bigger than they are. "I want to study dinosaurs," they say, or "I'd like to learn about chemistry." Great topics, but each is hardly manageable in a lifetime, let alone a six-week independent study assignment. The first step, often, is setting one's limits in terms of the depth and breadth of the project focus. One strategy, curriculum "webbing" (a colleague calls them "spider plans"), is illustrated in Figure 4.2. By constructing such webs, students get to see the many facets of a topic that,

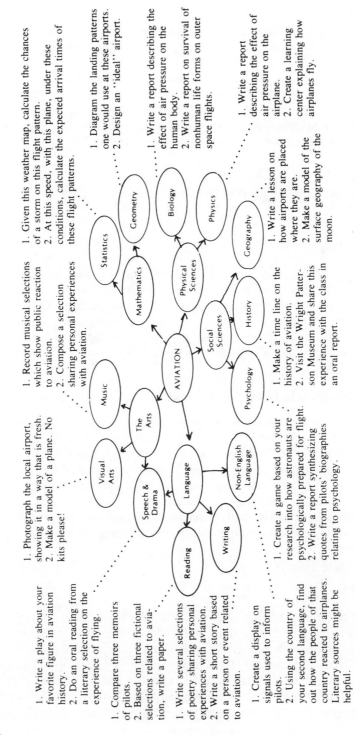

Figure 4.2. Webbing diagram for an interdisciplinary unit on aviation. (*Source:* G. F. Vars, *Interdisciplinary Teaching in the Middle Grades*. Columbus, OH: National Middle School Association, 1987, p. 15.)

at first, may have appeared one dimensional. Then, they may pinpoint their specific areas of interest within the broader scope of their initial topic idea and work on a scaled-down version of the original theme. Remember: Limiting one's scope is not the same as lowering one's standards, and most of us would prefer to succeed on a small scale than to fail in a grand fashion. Besides, if the spider plans are well thought out, the student can return to them if the new, trimmed-down project is just a tad too lean. (Translation: It's easier to build on a firm foundation than on patches of scattered thoughts.)

Determine Evaluation Criteria

Someone brilliant (Ashleigh, I think) wrote, "If you don't know where you're going, you'll probably end up someplace else." This is as true on interstates as it is in classrooms, and a road map to get you to your desired destination is valuable in both the glove compartment and the teacher's desk drawer. In this regard, students need to consider their entire project—including how they'll show the teacher or others that they've learned something—from day 1. The following outline is one type of curriculum road map:

Seeing It Through: A Guide for Independent Study

1. *Subject area, broadly defined:* (For example, dinosaurs, chemistry.)

2. *Subject area, narrowly defined:* (Select one or more topics from your spider plan and write a sentence or two about what you'd like to learn.)

3. *Resources you could use:* (Write enough information so you know where to locate your sources.)

   A. *Printed resources:* _____

   B. *Human resources:* _____

   C. *Audiovisual resources:* _____

4. *First steps:* (List the first five things you will do to begin your project. As you complete this list, add more items.)

   A. _____

   B. _____

   C. _____

   D. _____

   E. _____

5. *Possible problems, possible solutions:* (Write at least three things that could go wrong with your project and think of some ways to overcome these problems.)

A. *Possible Problems*   B. *Suggested solutions*

   1. _____   1. _____

   2. _____   2. _____

   3. _____   3. _____

6. *Sharing your work:* (What form will your project take: a report? a movie? a demonstration? Explain here what type of project you will do and to whom you want to show your results.)

7. *A timeline:* (Write the dates you expect to complete your project.)

8. *Project approval:*

_____   _____
Student   Teacher

It is designed to encourage students to consider a project's scope, its starting points, possible pitfalls and "escape routes," and evaluation criteria from the onset of the project. Of course, some parts of the plan may change as the student learns more about the topic (didn't you ever diverge from your scheduled itinerary?), but it is always easier to switch from a *known* direction than it is to set out blindly and hope for the best. Not all students may need this formal a plan to study a topic, but for those who do, a curriculum road map can save time and energy for both the students and the teachers.

Further, Treffinger (1975) presents a plan for independent study that takes into consideration the various levels of independence that students may show. His self-directed learning model contains three stages, each one progressing toward greater student independence. For example, a student at level 1 may choose an independent project from a variety of teacher-selected options, while a student at level 3 controls the topic choice and resources used. Likewise, evaluation at level 1 is done primarily by the teacher, while the student at level 3 is expected to determine the evaluation criteria and how well he or she met these criteria. Self-directed learning is a realistic approach to working with students whose abilities to work independently vary.

Praise and Critique Separately

Remember your last job performance evaluation? All "excellents" or "goods" I bet—except for maybe that *one* item about turning in paperwork on time or arriving at school before the students get there. One item (okay maybe two) on an otherwise flawless record. So, what do you remember? Generally, human nature prevails, and we recall the negative. The tendency to recall the bad over the good is termed the *Ziegarnik effect.*

Students, too, have this reaction. Thus, when we tell them, "Your essay was good, *but* you could improve your grammar" or "I like your picture, *but* elephants aren't *really* blue," our pupils may feel as if they just got kicked in the "but"—for what they remember is what *should have* been done rather than what *was* accomplished. When praise is coupled with criticism, it is usually the latter that is retained; so even though both types of comments might be appropriate and important, it helps to mention the points at two separate times. "I like your picture . . . period."

THE CLASSROOM ENVIRONMENT

What's Important to Them?

The typical school bulletin board is awash with students' accomplishments. Peppered with "A+," "100%," and "excellent job!" this wall of honor extols the virtues of perfection and flawless performance.

If given the choice, though, students might opt to post other examples of their work—nongraded papers, perhaps, or even difficult assignments on which they received grades lower than *A*—instead of a perfect paper that may have required little extra effort on their part.

Allowing students to display what is important *to them* shows your awareness that hard work and strong efforts come in many forms and grades.

Establish a Planning Council

Generally, a classroom's decor is designed by the teacher. Prints, posters, bulletin boards, and desk arrangements are all in place as the school year begins, and if changes are made throughout the year, it is due to the teacher's initiative.

Enter the Planning Council (PC). Chaired by the teacher (or a designee), the PC comprises students who are members of the class in question. It is *their* job to recommend changes in the classroom environment and to implement these suggestions, either by themselves or by "subcontracting" the job to an interested group of students. Of course, the teacher may request that an "environmental impact study" be done prior to any major changes. For example, will putting the desks in clusters instead of rows create unnecessary talking or congested traffic patterns? However, by establishing a PC the teacher is telling the students in a very real way that *this* classroom is *their* classroom. (As the year progresses, PC membership may change to involve as many students as possible.) Successfully implemented, the PC turns the classroom atmosphere from one of *factory* to one of *family*.

Taking the Classroom Temperature

Moods affect performance, no question about it. But moods are sometimes subtle and secretive, and it is easy to suppress anger behind a calm demeanor or to shadow disappointment behind the veil of a smile. Often, the very students who need the most caressing are the ones most adept at disguising their moods.

George Betts and Maureen Neihart (1985), a researcher and a counselor of gifted students, suggest that educators take the class temperature daily. By constructing cardboard thermometers that are placed on each student's (and the teacher's) desk, each student can monitor and record his or her mood throughout the day. For example, a student may have this type of day:

> 9:00 AM Feeling good after a bus ride seated next to my best friend—78° (very comfortable).
>
> 10:50 AM Picked last (again) for the recess kickball team—32° (cold and uncomfortable).
>
> 12:30 PM *Everyone* lost free time just because a few kids were fooling around at lunch, no fair!—95° (very hot and uncomfortable).
>
> 1:20 PM The teacher discusses the students' feelings about the lunchroom problem—82° (feeling a little better).
>
> 2:45 PM A good end to the day, a *B* on a test and a spur-of-the-moment popcorn treat—78° (comfortable again).

A simpler (but similar) suggestion is the use of a color wheel—the kind found in many board games—to detect moods. Red indicates anger, blue means sadness, green shows joy, and so on.

These nonverbal indicators of moods allow students to monitor their changing emotions throughout each day and help them pinpoint the events that get them angry or calm them down. Also, if teachers use a similar device, it lets students know that we, too, are affected by different moods as the school day unfolds. Imagine—a teacher, and human, too!

Design Classrooms that Respect Preferences

Just as people differ about the environment most conducive to creative production, they also vary in their styles and preferences for completing academic tasks. Some students love group projects, where each person participates actively in a cooperative learning venture. Others prefer solitude: A study carrel in a corner, where the outside world remains just that—outside. Some students learn most efficiently by reading, lecture, or drill, while still others prefer educational games, films, or class discussions.

The literature is filled with studies extolling the benefits of using multiple learning modes for gifted children (Dunn and Dunn, 1975; Stewart, 1981; Starko and Schack, 1989). There is, however, no consensus on which teaching style or setting works best. One thing *is* certain though: A classroom designed to allow for both private and group learning through a variety of techniques invites learning more than does a setting in which lecture alone is used to convey lessons. So vary the "menu." It will enhance and enliven any learning environment.

DISCIPLINARY PROCEDURES

Avoid Group Punishments

Your students are "chatty" in general, and your requests for quiet go unheeded—at least by some. Unable to determine exactly which children are responsible for the noise, you give one final warning: "If it's not quiet by the time I count to three, you will all lose your recess."

One . . . Two . . . Three.

It isn't quiet, so you smugly (or sternly) follow through with your plan. "OK, that's it; I'll see you all at 10:15."

There, you've done it. Ruined recess for everyone, yourself included.

Gifted students hate this form of punishment, as even young ones see the inequity inherent in punishing en masse. It is easy to see why the nontalkers get upset—after all, it wasn't their fault. Yet ironically, gifted students who are "guilty as charged" realize how unfair it is to punish others who are innocent. Some may even appear at your desk, repentant and pleading, asking you to lift the punishment from those who are blameless.

Avoid these situations at all costs, for it is hard to argue with the logic of a student whose only guilt is by association or whose sense of justice demands to know why "innocent until proven guilty" applies in the courthouse but not in your classroom.

Reward Incremental Improvements

Many gifted youngsters are stingy when it comes to giving themselves credit for a job well done. If there's a flaw, they'll find it; if there's a higher grade to be gotten, they'll wish they attained it. Too few of them notice incremental improvements in performance and, therefore, downplay their efforts until perfection is reached.

Educators can help students enjoy the fruits of their labors by pointing out to them their small successes. Comments such as "Ann, your cursive handwriting is really improving—I noticed it on the poster you designed yesterday" or "Compare these two assignments, Joey—notice how much more complete this second one is" go a long way toward sharing your satisfaction with day-to-day growth or progress.

Catch 'em Being Good

It is easy for educators to ignore or take for granted situations that neither bother us nor demand our attention. It is quite difficult, though, to tolerate a child who is misbehaving, disturbing others, or causing a general ruckus. In fact, we react strongly and swiftly to point out and curb these actions.

As R. L. Thorndike might say, "How soon they forget."

Thorndike's "law of effect" (we all learned about it in educational psychology 101) rests on the idea that people (and rats) are likely to repeat those behaviors for which they are rewarded. Thus, if we want to see a particular behavior *repeated* in someone's repertoire, we reinforce it; and if we want to *extinguish* a particular behavior, we douse it with feigned ignorance—we make believe it isn't there.

However, behaviorists usually work in labs, not schools, where it is easier to ignore rats in a cage than it is children in a classroom. And this behavioristic theory collapses in schools as soon as it confronts a child who sees negative attention (such as when a teacher chastises a child's behavior) as preferable to no attention at all.

Still, the impact of emphasizing the positive to children can't be argued. Imagine their surprise when a group of first graders hear: "I really appreciate the way you are sharing your crayons. It makes my job more pleasant when you behave so well." "Who is this?" they'll think. "The teacher from planet Nice-Nice?"

Yet they'll listen and incorporate this statement into their ever-growing (hopefully) reserve of self-concept comments that prove their value, their ability, or their responsibility. Pick on the positive, and see how much more pleasant a place school can become.

Discipline in Private

Okay, so *nobody's* perfect. Every student at some time will misbehave. Every student—even the most able and conscientious—will need a talking to. When this time comes, discipline in private. Though more time consuming, it is a more personal and meaningful way to point out the connection between the child's *action* and your *reaction*. For example:

(Said in front of class): "That is inappropriate language, Sue. Let's talk about it after class."

(Said in private): "Mike mentioned to me how bad he felt when you called him 'stupid' because he's not in the top reading group. Were you trying to make him feel bad?"

(Said in private): "I could have stopped my lesson and punished you in front of everyone, but I'd rather talk with you privately about your behavior."

Each of these statements conveys respect to the student, and each one begs the student to forge the connection between actions and consequences. Especially effective with intelligent children (who can see the correlation between their action and your response) and students who seldom get punished (and think it's the end of the world when they do), private disciplining can help students "save face" in front of their classmates. Also, it teaches an important lesson that an off-the-cuff public reprimand ("Behave yourself, Margaret; I expect better behavior from a smart girl like you") can never achieve.

SELF-SATISFYING BEHAVIORS

Establish a "Feel Good Folder"

Even eternal optimists have their "down days." Whether caused by bio-rhythms, bad Karma, or bad news, each of us has occasional second thoughts about the education profession we chose. "There have to be easier jobs," we think, "and more lucrative to boot." Still, we persevere; we get through; we find that second wind. And we go on.

To make the journey easier, keep track of the invitations *you* have received as an educator. Gather together some of the little rewards of our profession—the happy face drawn by a first grader and given to you as a present; the former sixth grader, now in college, who wrote to you once "just to say thanks"; the note from two parents who appreciated the "shoulder to cry on" you provided when they needed it most—and place them into a file: your "feel good folder." Then, on days that are rougher than you would like, open the folder and reread the messages that meant so much. You'll be surprised at how special those notes still are.

Leave School at School

Anyone who thinks that education is a 9:00 AM to 3:00 PM job or an occupation chosen by those who appreciate summer too much to work need to have their eyes opened and their mouths closed. In *any* human services career, teaching included, your job follows you home (where you get telephone calls from parents), to the mall (where you see your students), and on vacation ("Hey, isn't that Mrs. Jackson over there in the bikini?").

This situation isn't necessarily stressful, but if you find yourself talking about your job to people who aren't involved in education—spouses, neighbors, grandchildren—you might need to learn how to leave school at school.

Easier said than done, there are some tricks you can try:

Grade papers or plan tomorrow's lessons *before* you leave the school building and, sometime, leave your school empty-handed.

Plan an exercise routine—even 30 minutes three times a week—and stick to it. This could be as "serious" as racquetball or as leisurely as a walk around the neighborhood. Just do it.

Splurge occasionally: Have a massage. It's so invigorating and therapetic that the $40.00 you spend on it should count as a medical tax deduction.

Make a "school conversation schedule," whereby you agree to talk shop with colleagues or family for *only* 30 minutes a night. After that, all talk of school is *verboten*. (Even better: Attach a 25 cents penalty for every infraction of this rule. With luck, and a little effort, the pot will be empty and you will be happier.)

You're Not the Teacher Next Door

How frequently we downplay our efforts and accomplishments by comparing them with those of our colleagues! In our attempts to become "superteacher," we look around us and see what others have done that we have not. Even as the ink is still drying on the parent newsletter we're sending home on a monthly basis, we belittle its importance because "so-and-so down the hall thought of it first."

Educators' worst enemies are often themselves. To break this cycle of accomplishment–disappointment–accomplishment–disappointment, educators need to learn a lesson they so often teach to their students: Compare your efforts *today* with your efforts of *yesterday* or last week or last year, and, especially, not with the person down the hall. Remember: You're not the teacher next door, and that's okay.

You Don't Have Total Control

The vital lesson, realizing that you don't have control over your students' lives, is the one taught so well by Mrs. Sanders. An excellent teacher, a caring individual, she realizes, also, the limits of her powers. She knows too well that the lives of her students are not always easy or pretty. She acknowledges that some pupils enjoy homes of privilege, while others are never free from want—physical, environmental, or emotional.

Still, she goes on. Because she *can* help and she *does* help every day between 9:00 and 3:00 in a magical placed called "a classroom."

So do you.

CONCLUSION

The psychological small change given to students on a minute-by-minute, day-to-day basis is one of the most efficient ways to enhance both achievement and self-concept in the classroom. Students who feel good about themselves as human beings, not just scholars, grow to become (in the words of William James) "effective geniuses": young people in touch with both their hearts and their minds; adults as willing and able to *care* deeply as to *think* deeply.

CONTINUING QUESTS AND QUESTIONS

1. Many "innovative" techniques espoused by discipline experts—assertive discipline, tough love, corporal punishment—provide hard-core consequences for misdeeds done by students. The underlying mentality of these methods is that students are *going* to misbehave; therefore, they should know what will happen before they do the misdeed. What will be the long-term impact of such responses to students' misbehaviors? As they mature into the educators and policymakers of tomorrow, will they recall these measures and wish to use them on their own children? Or will they demand that more positive approaches to discipline be implemented? Also, what is the long-term impact of punitive discipline policies on students' self-concepts? How will *our* discipline strategies with students today translate into *their* discipline strategies with their own children tomorrow?

2. Examine your school's policies and procedures for promoting student self-concept and achievement. Are student successes lauded in *all* areas—athletic, academic, and creative? Are students rewarded for their *attempts,* no only their *accomplishments?* Do teachers, counselors, and administrators deal with each other respectfully, even if they disagree with one another about specific issues or concerns? Do a self-study of the climate that exists in your classrooms, your corridors, your cafeteria, and your teachers' lounge. Is *your* school a place you would choose for your own children (or grandchildren) to attend, and if not, what can you do to improve the inviting climate of your school?

3. Our nation has become so enmeshed in trying to count education's successes by improved test performance and literacy rates that it has neglected one very valuable measure: attitude toward learning. After high school or college graduation, there will be few formal occasions for which today's students will have to "hit the books." Beyond formal education, all people (yourself included) will have to decide individually what, how, and whether you will learn. This being so, what aid can we give to our students now to assure their desire to become lifelong learners? How can our schools measure this seemingly unmeasurable concept, and how can we convince a number-hungry public that *wanting* to learn is at least as important as knowledge itself?

4. Our nation's drop-out rate is both an international embarrassment and a personal tragedy for the student who quits. In generations past, drop-outs had legitimate reasons to leave school—operating the family business perhaps or getting a job to secure the family's financial solvency. While this is still true today to a limited extent, the majority of today's drop-outs do so not to go to something *better* than school, but to avoid the most banal and unfulfilling setting they know: a classroom. What can we learn from these drop-outs? What can *they* tell us about improving schools so that academic and emotional success is achieved? When will we gain the courage to ask those who leave school, "What did we ever do to lead you to take so drastic an action?"

OUT OF THE WAY/OUT OF THIS WORLD RESOURCES

One Hundred Ways to Enhance Self-Concept in the Classroom, by Jack Canfield and Harold C. Wells (Prentice-Hall, Englewood Cliffs, NJ, 1976).

When you finish this book you will ask yourself, "Why didn't *I* write that?" because most educators could write this book in a matter of weeks (and considering this book has gone through more than 20 print runs, you'll *really* wish you had written it). Essentially, the authors provide exactly what they say: 100 specific activities that will enhance your students' senses of self-worth, while also building group cohesion between students and educators.

Reaching Out: Interpersonal Effectiveness and Self-Actualization (4th edition), by David W. Johnson (Prentice-Hall, Englewood Cliffs, NJ, 1990).

This book is very much a primer on establishing positive and cooperative relationships. Intended for use by adults, it could also be a good resource for secondary students involved in psychology classes or courses that stress interpersonal relationships.

Self-Concept and School Achievement, by William W. Purkey (Prentice-Hall, Englewood Cliffs, NJ, 1970).

Other books have been written on the topics addressed in Purkey's book, and more recent research studies are available than are the ones cited in this volume. Still, this is the classic book on the topics of self-concept and school achievement, and the author's writing style is so informal and "fluid" that you will hardly know you are reading a textbook.

EDGE Learning Program, by Don Zadra and Bob Moawad (Creative Education Publishers, Mankato, MN, 1986).

This series of books, each about 50 pages long, deals with a specific aspect of growing up that can cause young people some grief. Such titles as "Mistakes Are Great," "Dare To Be Different," "How To Beat the Jitters," and "The Secrets of Goal Setting" indicate the social and emotional focus of these books. Great for use by students age 10 and above, these resources provide practical advice in a reader-friendly manner.

CHAPTER 5

The Gifted Child at School
Part II: Specific Adjustment Concerns of Gifted Students

The intent of this chapter is to

Introduce you to some specific adjustment concerns of gifted children in the areas of understanding giftedness, getting along with friends, and getting along in school

Bridge the research and practice gap regarding the emotional education of gifted youth

Focus your attention on the need for gifted children to get specific guidance regarding career development

Present evidence showing the need gifted children often have to understand life's more complex and existential issues

AMY

While teaching in a rural school in Connecticut, I met Amy. She was 8 years old then, and she fit into many situations. Amy was in love with a mysterious stranger who challenged her to see things in ways she had never seen them before. Amy was in love . . . with science.

As Gifted Program Coordinator for grades K through 8, I wore many hats. Twice a week—usually Tuesdays and Thursdays—I met with the junior high science club. We dissected and bisected; explored and experimented; postulated and predicted: In short, we were building our understanding that the *true* scientist, the one who really makes changes, always has more questions than answers.

Of course, Amy was not in our class. "Too young," I thought, "she'll never fit in. She needs to be with her peers." But due to the persistence of Amy's fine

Figure 5.1. Illustration by Maureen Canning Marshall. Reprinted by permission of the illustrator.

third-grade teacher, I was convinced to give Amy a trial run. It was a month before winter break, so if things didn't work out we could easily go back to our "big kids only" science club.

However, things *did* work out. Amy arrived fully prepared with her dissecting kit, her safety goggles, a pencil, and her stuffed cat, Pockey. Never afraid to ask "Why?" and never intimidated by the size of classmates whose thumbs were the size of her entire hand, Amy contributed a newness, a freshness, a sense of wonder.

Then, the holidays: two weeks of free time from studies and school. When classes resumed and science club reconvened, Amy seemed different—aloof. Even Pockey (her cat) got relegated to a seat on the floor, not alongside Amy at the lab table.

The psychologist in me said, "Something's wrong . . . something happened over vacation." I talked with Amy's teacher, but she didn't notice any change, nor did anyone else. Finally, I did what I should have done at first: I spoke with Amy. And there *was* a problem—a big one. "Before," Amy said, "when I came to science club, all I was missing was spelling. Now, we have a different schedule and I'm missing snacktime with my friends."

Amy taught me two important lessons. The first is that generalizations and assumptions are dangerous weapons in the mind of a would-be psychologist like me; I was too ready to attribute a change of attitude to something being wrong with the child. Second, Amy taught me that *peer group* is a relative term. For although she fit in very well academically with eighth graders embarking on puberty, Amy still was small enough, young enough, childlike enough to need the company of agemates: *other* friends, who saw Twinkies and milk as the day's most important activity. Amy, like all 8-year-olds, sometimes enjoyed the company of other 8-year-olds.

Amy is a child, Amy is a scientist, and Amy is a prime example of the reason to consider gifted children from vantage points that are based on individual needs and individual differences.

AN UNDISCOVERED GEM

In the previous chapter, we reviewed the importance of self-concept and invitational education as applied to gifted children. Although the strategies suggested are equally applicable for all students, whatever their ability levels, some specific adjustment concerns are uniquely applicable to the gifted population. These concerns are based on social and emotional guidance issues that are part and parcel of the lives of persons with high talent.

As Amy's story suggests, some of these issues revolve around peer interactions. Others relate to expectations, conformity, and career guidance. The underlying issue—the foundation on which all the others are based—is understanding giftedness and conceptualizing how and why intellectual differences can have such a big impact on day-to-day living.

As you might expect, researchers and other educators throughout the decades have highlighted these areas of social and emotional development in gifted students and have suggested classroom interventions and strategies to address these concerns. One of the most complete reviews of these issues was forwarded by James Mehorter who, in 1964, completed his doctoral dissertation on the topic of counseling gifted adolescents. Using the technique of *bibliotherapy,* which is "the use of reading material to help solve emotional problems and to promote mental health," Mehorter suggested excerpts from classical and current literature that address issues of social or emotional concern (Spredemann-Dreyer, 1989, p. xiii). Then, through an independent study curriculum that he developed called "Self and Society," gifted adolescents were invited to correspond with Mehorter regarding their own reactions to the literature he suggested. A long-distance dialogue resulted, as Mehorter and his "students" maintained communication through letters. The result was something rarely seen in higher education: a dissertation worth reading, and one that actually made a difference in the lives of school-age students.

Unfortunately, Mehorter's hard work went the way of most doctoral studies—it started to collect dust on his advisors' shelves. (His academic advisor was Virgil S. Ward, by the way—the "philosopher" of gifted education whom we met in Chapter 1.) It is still there, perhaps, far, far back on a tall, tall bookcase. Never published in article or book form, "Self and Society" remains today as one example of a good idea that was ignored (Mehorter, 1964). Lacking a publisher, it was denied its place in the spectrum of classroom materials that could have a very positive impact on the moral and personal development of gifted students.

James Mehorter died, a victim of suicide, shortly after completing his PhD. With him went his stunning insights into the lives and minds of gifted students. Perhaps now, more than a quarter of a century after his landmark work, it can have its well-deserved day in the limelight.

SPECIFIC ADJUSTMENT CONCERNS OF GIFTED STUDENTS: AN EXPLORATION

The concerns of gifted students that Mehorter wrote about cover all aspects of human growth and development and can follow gifted children from their early years through adulthood:

1. Problems associated with realizing the nature and significance of intellectual differences
2. Problems associated with intellectual frustration in normative (that is, "day-to-day") and life situations
3. Problems associated with the infrequency of wholesome interpersonal relationships
4. Problems associated with conformity
5. Problems associated with discovering, preparing for, and locating a satisfying vocation
6. Problems associated with developing a satisfying philosophy of life

Although stated here as *problems,* it should not be assumed that every gifted child, adolescent, and adult will be plagued by deep-seated stresses or anxieties. The areas addressed by Mehorter cover *potential* sources of intrapersonal and interpersonal conflict and serve merely to outline the various life situations that may cause discomfort among highly able persons. However, through preventive counseling strategies and open discussion with gifted students of the issues that they may confront as they mature, social and emotional growth should continue on a generally smooth course.

Issue 1: Problems Associated with Realizing the Nature and Significance of Intellectual Differences

Now let's be blunt: we are not 'normal' and we know it; it can be fun sometimes but not funny always. We tend to be much more sensitive than other people. Multiple meanings, innuendos, and self-consciousness plague us. Intensive self-analysis, self-criticism, and the inability to recognize that we do have limits make us despondent. In fact, most times our self-searching leaves us more discombobbled than we were at the outset. (American Association for Gifted Children, 1978, p. 9)

There is no one definition that encompasses adequately all the traits and behaviors incorporated under the term *gifted*. Likewise, there is no consensus regarding the most appropriate way to inform children of the presence of their specific gifts or talents. If we *do* tell them that they are gifted, won't they get egos as inflated as the Goodyear blimp? And if we *don't* tell them about their abilities, don't we run the risk of having highly able children "sitting back and sliding by," never fully using their talents? Given this ambivalence regarding which strategy is best, adults often defer to the middle ground: They'll talk about giftedness if the child brings it up; otherwise, why rock the intellectual boat? Unfortunately, this silence results, for many gifted students, in a spotty understanding of the nature and significance of their intellectual differences.

When left to fend for themselves in deciding what giftedness both means and implies, the gifted child's fall-back position often results in interpretations that are either naive or overblown. For example, Torrance (1962) found that gifted youngsters often view themselves as minorities of one: the sole person in the world (or, at least, the sixth grade) who prefers chess to checkers, philosophic discussions over spelling bees, or compromise instead of dogma. Further, this minority-of-one status makes it difficult for gifted kids to view any differences they do possess as giftedness: "Gifted? Who, me? C'mon!" A 12-year-old child made the following analysis: When I picture someone being gifted, I think of someone like John McEnroe or Beethoven, not someone in seventh grade (Delisle, 1984, p. 5).

Webb, Meckstroth, and Tolan (1982) advise that parents and educators need to help children better understand giftedness for two reasons. First, an explanation of the term will help children focus less on the label and more on its accompanying behaviors, such as "quick learning ability" or "a sensitivity to the problems of others." Second, an open review of giftedness helps prevent the child from equating the terms *better learner* and *better person*. It is important to point out repeatedly that other children have special talents that are different . . . but no less valuable. It is this repeated reminder of interdependency with others that will help prevent vanity (Webb, Meckstroth, and Tolan, 1982, p. 58).

Understanding giftedness through discussions and straight talk is an essential step in recognizing and accepting one's own personal strengths and weaknesses. The goal of such discussions is not to arrive at a consensus that defines giftedness to everyone's satisfaction, nor it is to try to nudge children into believing that there is one best way to interpret their talents. Rather, the goal is to listen to the children's perceptions and discuss possible misinterpretations that may have grown from years of avoidance of such issues.

When dealing with perceptions there should be no judgments involved;

no right or wrong answers. Instead, the end result of the discussion should be a medley of impressions and ideas that cause students to probe further and deeper into the nature and significance of individual differences—their own and those of others.

Issue 2: Problems Associated with Intellectual Frustration in Normative and Life Situations

> The story you are about to read is true; the names have been changed to protect the not-so-innocent. Brian and Todd, both 6 years old, were having a first-grade shouting and pushing match. Neither boy was at a loss for words when describing each other to me and the teacher in charge of recess duty that day. Todd began, "Brian's a pig. I hate him and he's stupid." Brian responded, "Well, that's nothing; Todd's a Neanderthal." Todd stood, mouth agape, looked at me, and shrugged his shoulders. He didn't know whether he had been insulted or not. The fight was called off on account of miscommunication. There was no victor and no victim, just confusion for Todd and frustration for Brian, whose 25-cent insult, "Neanderthal," didn't hit its target. "That's Brian," his teacher responded when I told her this story, "using vocabulary that no one understands but he and his teachers."

How common it is for gifted children to be misunderstood when they are trying merely to be themselves! Whether, as in Brian's case, it is due to an advanced understanding of and facility with words or perhaps to a heightened ability to see gray areas where everyone else sees just blacks and whites, the frustration these children feel is very real. No one—at least not a child—uses such big words as *obfuscate* to do exactly that; most of us speak out for the express purpose of communication—of being understood by others. If, in attempting to make a statement or venture a guess, our message is lost in the verbiage, we have several options: we can restate our message, only louder; we can rephrase our message if we know the source of others' confusion; or we can say "never mind," thereby losing our chance to be an active discussant.

In reviewing the frustration commonly felt by gifted youth in normative and life situations, Mehorter (1964) stressed that *verbal interactions* are just one source of this potential frustration. Other sources of misunderstanding can occur during *recreation,* when gifted children demand to play a game by the rules instead of just "for fun"; in *academic situations,* when classmates (or the teachers) can see only one right answer on a multiple choice test but the gifted child can rationalize why *every* answer is acceptable; and in *social interactions,* where the astute child or teenager refuses to accept group norms of dress, behavior, or attitude just because "everyone else does it/wears it/ thinks it." The result can be a sense of hollow isolation, as the able child wonders why no one else appreciates what seems so logical to him or her. One gifted adolescent put it this way:

There's the jock-prep stereotype and there's the heavy metal stereotype. I hang around with the heavy metal stereotypes. I hang around with the heavy metals because I smoke—that's probably the only reason I hang around with them. But even the heavy metals, who are so supposedly anti-snob, anti-prep, are just as snobbish as the preps are. There's a lot of hypocrisy. (Lockwood, 1989, p. 6)

The ability to see events or situations from a mature perspective that agemates do not yet possess is a source of confusion for many gifted children. If misunderstood, these differences in insight might take on the connotation of "weird." If a child is alone among classmates in being able to see nuances, shades of gray, or long-term ramifications, he or she may perceive this difference as "bad" and, therefore, ignore or deny the existence of these differences. However, the gifted child who refuses to accept that these perceptions do exist does so artificially, for the ability to see a problem or event from a variety of angles cannot be erased by wishing it were so.

Talking with gifted children about the drawbacks, benefits, and sheer reality of these variations in their perceptive abilities is one way to ensure that they understand that a difference is not necessarily negative and that their insights can actually be a valuable resource in their lives.

Issue 3: Problems Associated with the Infrequency of Wholesome Interpersonal Relationships

. . . Shades of Wonder Bread! A "wholesome" interpersonal relationship implies simpler times, when Ozzie and Harriet ruled the roost and parents' main concern for their children was that they avoid swear words and talking-out in class. Today, decades after Mehorter's delineation of this problem related to friendship, his words seem anachronistic. Or do they?

In a recent study of high-IQ elementary children's self-perceptions regarding friendship, 37 percent conceptualized themselves as differing from their peers (Janos, Fung, and Robinson, 1985). Although half of this group noted these differences as *positive* (for example, "I feel more mature"; "I can read better"), the other half of the sample were either *ambivalent* toward these perceived differences (for example, "I really can't explain how I'm different") or *negative* (for example, "I feel out of place in my class"). When results of the Piers-Harris self-concept scale were analyzed, the researchers found that "thinking of oneself as different proves to be associated with . . . diminished self-esteem" (Janos, Fung, and Robinson, 1985, p. 80).

Earlier, Tannebaum (1962) asked 615 high school students to rate eight imaginary teenagers described as brilliant or average, studious or non-studious, and athletic or nonathletic on 54 traits. The results showed that brilliant, studious nonathletes ranked significantly lower than all other types of students. The most socially acceptable student was the brilliant athlete who was nonstudious. This study showed that giftedness, in and of itself, is acceptable. It is only when it gets tied in with other variables that social nonacceptance appears.

In trying to understand these studies (and others like them which show similar results), it is worth considering the possibility that when gifted children view their differences as negative, it may be due to a misconceptualizing of the term *peer group*. For when a gifted child is perceived, by self or others, as not "fitting in" to an existing social structure, that child is often assumed to be the cause of the problem. In fact, however, the gifted child may be trying to fit into a situation that offers little personal satisfaction, so his or her attempts at socialization may appear half-hearted. Indeed, they may really *be* half-hearted and for a very good reason.

Peerness, a term defined and described by T. Ernest Newland (1976), helps explain why some gifted students might not fit in with their classmates.

> The gifted child's peers must be identified in terms of at least reasonable comparability in potential and skill in performing whatever task is to be undertaken, in comparability of interests relevant to that task, and in emotional accommodation. (Newland, 1976, pp. 100–101)

Thus, when gifted children are placed in academic or social settings that do not mesh with either their interests or abilities, the real problem exists within the *structure,* not within the child.

Consider this case: A gifted 7-year-old who is comfortable with advanced curriculum may find that his *intellectual* peers are in the fourth grade down the hall, not the second grade in which he sits. This same child may share many social interests, such as recess kickball or fantasy play, with his second-grade classmates. Thus, his *social* peers may well include children his own age. Emotionally, this same child may have keen insights into the inequities of life ("If I wasn't misbehaving, why should *I* be punished along with everyone else?"), so that his *emotional* peers are few and far between, at least in the primary grades. If these variations in development exist (and indeed they do), then adults should not expect that *all* gifted children will interact with *all* classmates at mutually satisfactory levels.

Peerness is little more than a term describing the realization that people get along with others for various reasons and in various contexts. In adults, peerness is common practice, as those people we associate with at work may be very different from those with whom we socialize outside of work. Elementary and high school are the only places in life where we are pigeonholed so precisely by our chronological age. If you, dear reader, are now 29 years old (for the third time perhaps?), do you *only* invite *other* 29-year-olds to your party? No, of course not. And if you take a graduate course at a nearby college, do you feel out of place because the age range of students within that class is so broad? Doubtful, because you know that other adults can learn alongside you, whatever the year of their birth. The same forces are at play in childhood: peerness exists, whether you are 14 or 40. Thus, when a gifted child says (or thinks), "I must be weird; I don't get along with my peers," he or she may be too self-critical, because the "peer group" with whom that child doesn't get along may not be a real peer group at all.

John Gowan, who recognized this disparity between gifted children and some of their classmates, wrote that "if you're one kid in a hundred you have to know one hundred other kids to find one like yourself, and half the time that someone is (of the opposite sex), so you're sunk" (1972, p. 14). But true peers need not be so distant. If adults are willing to accept as fact the concept of peerness and are able to structure academic and social settings that allow for the grouping of students based on interests, not just age, then the idea of multiple peer groups will be better understood. The common practice of grouping schoolchildren solely on the basis of age is a decision based on administrative ease rather than educational logic, and one that disregards what we know about the different developmental rates of children (Ward, 1980).

Issue 4: Problems Associated with Conformity

As children mature and become more socially conscious, they also become more aware of what behaviors are considered normal or regular by the majority. Often, in efforts to become (or remain as) a part of the mainstream, gifted children either acquiesce to group expectations or disguise their real interests or abilities in order to be thought of as typical. Conformity—adapting to the spoken or unspoken rules of group consensus—is seen as a means to an end: acceptance.

Hollingworth (1942) interviewed many gifted children who struggled with the issue of conformity. She found that many socially accepted gifted youngsters could not distinguish between times when they should go along with the crowd and other times when they should maintain their individuality. As a partial remedy, she advocated that children adopt a strategy proposed by no less a person than St. Paul: "For ye suffer fools gladly, seeing ye yourselves are wise" (Corinthians II, 11.19).

When people suffer fools gladly, they are playing life by the unwritten but well-understood rules of group consensus. As adults we play this game each time we waste two hours and $5.00 on a movie we knew we would hate but that our friends talked us into seeing. Or, if we eat lunch in the teachers' or employees' lounge merely to "make an appearance," we also suffer fools gladly. Going along with the crowd—not resentfully, nor sneeringly, but gladly—is a part of everyday life and has been so since the days of St. Paul. If it was good for him, and it works for us, then gifted children, too, should know it is okay.

There are times, of course, when conformity is not in a child's best interests or when "the crowd" is either silly or arbitrary in its judgments of what is acceptable. The ability to discern which events and situations require individualism and which are so menial as to be of little concern is a skill developed through both trial and error and the use of common sense. Most often, children report that going along with the crowd is appropriate if their loss of individualism is low, temporary, or meaningless:

> Sometimes I do go along just to fit in with the crowd. For instance, when my friends are playing something I'm really not interested in and I want to play with them, I play it. (10-year-old girl, California)
> I do things to go along with the crowd—like asking questions I know the answers to, just so they will treat me like one of them. [11-year-old boy, Illinois (Delisle, 1984, p. 51)]

In these instances, the students' self-worth remains intact although they reneged on personal wishes or abilities in order to gain approval from agemates. The intrusion on these children's sense of independence was small enough to be forfeited voluntarily for the quest of the greater goal of social acceptance.

However, gifted youngsters are equally united in stating that group acceptance is secondary in importance to maintaining integrity in a particular set of beliefs or values:

> Most of the time I stand up for the things I think are right. Sometimes my friends get mad at me because I don't do what they want, but I don't care because I know what I believe and nothing can change that. (11-year-old boy, California)
> If I know I'm right, you'll be sure to know. If I don't do what other people want and they get mad, I feel that's just their tough luck. [13-year-old girl, Connecticut (Delisle, 1984, p. 54)]

Neither inherently good nor bad, conformity is a life-skill strategy that is within the repertoire of most persons. The "goodness" or "badness" of conformity is decided by the degree of personal freedom that is lost by going along with the crowd. Depending on the particular situation, the greatest good for the child could be served either by giving in to the ideas of others ("who knows, the crowd might be right!"—10-year-old boy, New York) or by standing firm on an existing set of standards, beliefs, or values.

Issue 5: Problems Associated with Discovering, Preparing for, and Locating a Satisfying Vocation

For gifted children embarking on a successful school career, the cliches they hear abound:

"You're so bright you can become whatever you want to become."

"With your brains, you'll be able to write your own ticket."

"The world is your oyster." (Whatever *that* means!)

All meant as compliments, these statements serve to put the gifted child on notice: "You will be successful; your life will make a difference." So often, in the eyes of adults, gifted children share a privilege reserved for very few others: the option of selecting from among virtually any line of work as their future career.

Yet this multiplicity of talents holds problems as well as promise. For example, if a gifted student shows high interest in law, medicine, education, and archeology, how does she pursue *all* these interests in one short lifetime? For the talented artist, who also excels academically, how does he respond to others who suggest getting a "real" job in lieu of pursuing a fine arts career? For the highly able student who lives in an environment short on role models who are employed in any profession at all, where does she get the impetus to excel?

These and other problems exist for gifted children and adolescents, and it is my opinion (for what *that's* worth) that career education and guidance for gifted students is the most neglected area of their development. It is assumed (incorrectly) that when left to their own defenses and problem-solving strategies, gifted students will select both a high-profile career and a training program beyond high school that educates them for that career.

. . . Would that it were that easy:

> Nothing is so simple for me that I can do a perfect job without effort, but nothing is so hard that I cannot do it. This is why I find it so difficult to decide my place in the future. (Hoyt and Hebeler, 1974, p. 12)

This ambivalence about the future and one's place in it is shared by many gifted youths. Sanborn, Palvino, and Wunderlin (1971) discovered patterns of multiple interests and aptitudes among superior students in Wisconsin schools. Likewise, Khatena (1982) notes the complications that can arise when trying to select one career from among many viable options. Further, Perrone, Karshner, and Male (1979) cite the clash that may arise when an internal need to select a meaningful career conflicts with the external desire to find a high-paying job that may offer few emotional benefits.

Overall, the research is very clear: Although the sole generalization that can safely be made about gifted individuals is that they differ from each other in more ways than they resemble each other, it cannot be refuted that many capable youngsters have *multipotential*—the ability to excel at virtually any area of interest (Sanborn, 1979). Recognizing multipotential as a mixed blessing—something that can be as confusing as it is invigorating—is a start toward understanding the complexity involved in the gifted student's choice of a vocation.

Issue 6: Problems Associated with Developing a Satisfying Philosophy of Life

Several years ago, the US Army had an advertising campaign whose slogan was "The Army: It's not just a job, it's an adventure." This catch phrase, modified just a bit, could well serve as the gifted student's credo: "Life: It's not just a job, it's an investment."

Ah, life! What is its meaning, what is its basis, what is its goal? Heady issues, to be sure, made all the more difficult by the fact that no one answer suffices and no one philosophy prevails. Alice Walker, author of *The Color Purple,* prefers life to death "because it is less boring, and because life has fresh peaches in it."

But still, life is no more limited to fresh peaches than it is always the proverbial bowl of cherries. Life laughs, life hurts, life just *is.* "So how do I fit into the scheme of things?" gifted students ask. "What is my purpose in existing?"

These issues, as timeworn as human thought itself, plague each new generation with a fresh vengeance. Like a storm at sea that gathers steam, unleashing its fury on the shore, only to return to the ocean to reemerge later and stronger, the issues surrounding Mehorter's last facet of social and emotional development continue to meet today's youth as when, at an earlier time, they confronted each of us. Steve Allen had the following to say about life:

> I believe in mystery, not in any dark-shadows-and-incense way, but as a matter of fact. The world seems to me to be absolutely based on mystery. The three most important philosophical questions—those concerning God, Time, and Space—remain questions, which is to say no answer to them has ever been proposed that convinces all interested parties . . . [For example], time: either it began one morning, say, at 9:27—which is obviously ridiculous—or it never began, which appears equally ridiculous.
>
> As for space, either one can go to the end of it—which is absurd—or it has no end, which is equally absurd.
>
> . . . No matter how assured we may be about certain aspects of our belief, there are always painful inconsistencies, exceptions, and contradictions. This is as true in religion as it is in politics, and is self-evident to all except fanatics and the naive. (Berman, 1986, pp. 8–9)

So where do we go from here? How do we, as adults, convince our students that their questions are legitimate and worthwhile, even though "the" answer and "the" philosophy are as elusive to us as they are to them? And how can we respond to young people—sometimes *too* young—who see the inequities inherent when, for example, Dan Rather laments poverty in

America on CBS, a network that pays him millions of dollars a year to report nightly on a part of our world?

Developing a satisfying philosophy of life is a journey, not a destination. From year to year, day to day, minute to minute, children change. A quandary one week is an answered question the next; a ready solution to one problem no longer applies the next time a similar situation is faced. Helping gifted young people tolerate the ambiguity that is part and parcel of a well-lived life and encouraging their continued questioning of what was, what is, and what may be are sure signs that we are growing old gracefully. One is never too young to be intolerant of the status quo, nor too old to be unsure of even age-old beliefs.

CONCLUSION

Jim Mehorter paid a great service to the field of education for gifted children by detailing the specific adjustment concerns that might be faced by able persons in their lifelong development. His work paralleled that of his predecessors—Strang, Hollingworth—and it complemented the work of his contemporaries, such as Virgil Ward and Anne Marie Roeper. The legacy he left was one of hope; the suggestions he made were ones of integrity. He challenged gifted students to be themselves in academic and social situations and to learn to ignore the chorus to "blend in with the blur" in order to fit in with a world used to accepting the average.

Amy (remember her?) would like that. She would see the need to fit into a variety of peer groups, and she would not be averse to discussing scientific topics that are supposed to be "above her." She would not conform to make others content, a decision that, if carried throughout her life, will help her to choose a career and a lifestyle that best fits the philosophical framework that she espouses. But Amy can't accomplish all of this alone; life is not a solo mission, but a shared one. So, to set her on a path that we only hope she will continue to follow, we rearranged our junior high science club to accommodate Amy's snacktime. Then, we again enjoyed a pleasant journey with a stranger named science. Even Pockey liked it, as he reassumed his perch alongside Amy's elbows.

Sure, it was a small step, but as a Chinese proverb so truthfully states, a journey of 1000 miles begins with a single step.

Happy traveling, Amy!

CONTINUING QUESTS AND QUESTIONS

1. Frequently, gifted children state that classmates ridicule them because of their high abilities. "They think we're all stuck up nerds" is a common complaint. Parents of gifted children sometimes share this ambivalence about explaining their child's abilities to others, for they don't want to be seen as "bragging" or "being pushy" about their child's advanced development. How can educators help gifted children and their parents to accept these talents, while not feeling embarrassed about them in the presence of others? What, if anything, should nongifted students be told about children with special learning needs, including gifted children? What pitfalls should gifted children and their parents avoid in discussing high abilities with other people?

2. In rereading the six adjustment concerns presented by James Mehorter, it becomes clear that gifted program teachers often face these very same concerns as do the children they teach. For example, they might be considered by other teachers to "have it easy" because they teach the brightest students, and they may have to endure such teacher lounge comments as "If you teach gifted students, I guess *you're* gifted too. Are you?" How can teachers of gifted children respond to such comments, and how can they share with their students these concerns common to gifted children and their teachers?

3. How does social skills instruction for gifted students differ from that given to other students—or does it? Are there programs or strategies that can exist in our schools that help students to face peer pressure effectively, to resist conformity when it means relinquishing personal values, and to accept each other as individuals with varying talents in various areas? How willing are school administrators and boards of education to prioritize these areas so as to make such instruction a part of school curriculum?

4. The media portrays various views of gifted students. In old TV shows such as "College Bowl" and newer ones such as "Jeopardy," gifted students often come across as encyclopedias with legs. In movies such as *Lucas* or *Revenge of the Nerds,* social awkwardness is seen as a part of a gifted student's personality. What media sources can you find that help portray gifted children as the individuals they truly are, with strengths, weaknesses, quirks, and needs similar in variety to those possessed by any other student? Share these sources with various audiences to show that stereotypes place both the "typer" and the "typee" at a distinct disadvantage when it comes to understanding human diversity.

OUT OF THE WAY/OUT OF THIS WORLD RESOURCES

Self and Society: An Independent Study Course for Gifted High School Students, by James Mehorter (University Microfilms, Ann Arbor, MI, Order #64-10909, 1964).
    This one is hard to find, yet a successful search will be worth all the effort expended. Especially useful for secondary school educators, the self-study curriculum offered by Mehorter offers an in-depth and intense analysis of persons whose lives as gifted individuals were marked with both triumph and anguish.

Understanding Success and Failure, by Lois Roets (Leadership Publishing, New Sharon, IA, 1985).
    A brief and useful guide that provides structured lessons for use in grades 3

through 8 to help children better understand and accept their strengths and limitations. Thoughts of perfectionism will be banished as children learn about the many "failures" confronted by Walt Disney, Babe Ruth, Louisa Mae Alcott, and others. Also, some well-designed lessons on viewing all successes and failures as temporary can lead children to both pursue new goals and get beyond past failures.

Managing the Social and Emotional Needs of the Gifted, by Connie Schmitz and Judy Galbraith (Free Spirit Publishing, Minneapolis, MN, 1985).

A practical teacher guide that serves to introduce the reader to ways of reviewing sensitive topics with gifted students. Classroom discussions will be unavoidable (so be forewarned) as you address topics such as *being assertive instead of aggressive; coping with teasing; setting realistic expectations;* and *understanding giftedness.*

The Value Tale Series, various authors (Value Communication, La Jolla, CA, 1980 and on).

This 11-volume series deals with biographies of famous persons, but what makes these books unique is the emphasis on the childhood years of Charles Dickens, Jackie Robinson, Cochise, and Eleanor Roosevelt. Each book centers on a particular theme, for example, *The Value of Determination: The Story of Helen Keller,* or *The Value of Humor: The Story of Will Rogers.* For use with students age 7 through 12, the *Value Tale Series* does a fine job of developing each character as a *real* person, not just a celebrity.

CHAPTER 6

The Gifted Child at School

Part III: Strategies, Activities, Materials, and Conditions to Promote Self-Control and Achievement

The intent of the chapter is to

Show you that activities designed to enhance the social and emotional lives of gifted students can also be useful with other students

Demystify the methods of gifted program selection for you, so that you in turn can discuss this topic with students

Provide methods for students to take an active role in planning their own education, both in school and outside of it

Review methods and materials that can help gifted students in their social relationships with both intellectual peers and other students

Discuss sexism as it relates to both gifted girls and gifted boys

Provide ideas and activities that link together the cognitive and affective needs of gifted students

KEVIN

Kevin is 14 years old, but he doesn't know that. He should be in ninth grade, but instead he is in a dayroom of a state institution for mentally retarded children. He has lived here for 8 years and has had no visitors at all. The nurses and the ward attendants serve as his parents, and they like Kevin because, among other things, he makes them feel important and necessary. He smiles at them and his eyes dance with a magic that stays unexpressed by either his thoughts or his few words.

Kevin a teacher? C'mon—what could I learn from him? Permit me to share a special moment that remains a highlight in my career as an educator, thanks to Kevin.

It's Christmas morning: The 30+ ward residents are awakening to a fresh snow whose beauty is pockmarked by the heavy-gauge metal of our window screen. As the attendant on duty, I had placed one of the many donated gifts marked only *boy* or *girl* on the bed of each child. How special it was to watch the kids' eyes light up! Some *knew* it was Christmas, and surmised that Santa had paid a visit; others, like Kevin, just examined the bow, box, and ribbon as a special diversion from the usual day's schedule.

Kevin looked at his gift. He hugged it gently and then put it down. He looked at it again and, then, to no one in particular said, "Pretty." He then put his still-wrapped present back where he had found it and began the ritual of his morning routine.

After breakfast, he looked at his gift again. "Open it," I urged, but Kevin grabbed it from me and said "No!" This scene was repeated over the next few days, and by New Year's, the ribbon on Kevin's gift had become tattered and soiled to the point where it began shedding. Finally, when the wrappings were half off the gift, Kevin removed the shreds and opened the box. There was a truck inside. "Another present," he said and smiled.

For Kevin, the box itself had been a present and the truck inside was a second gift, kind of like the toy surprise in a Cracker Jack box (remember how special those were?). And for days—almost a week—the *wrappings* had been sufficient enough, special enough, to be called a "present."

Kevin did teach me. He taught me the value of appreciating the small things

Figure 6.1. Illustration by Maureen Canning Marshall. Reprinted by permission of the illustrator.

that happen each day: such as the child who says "aha!" after weeks of trying to learn a concept, or as my own son, who still feels special when we buy him his favorite cereal, Fruity Pebbles, even when we don't have a coupon for it.

Giftedness is just one end of the long, long continuum of human intelligence. Mental retardation, at the opposite end of this intellectual spectrum, may appear to be so different from giftedness that it lacks any similarity, any semblance of comparability. Yet as Kevin showed me—as he shows us all—insight and humanness span the scale of talents.

Given the opportunity educators have to learn from *all* of their students—gifted or not—it should be obvious that the strategies employed to benefit highly able students may prove positive in promoting the social, emotional, and intellectual lives of other students, too. As highlighted in Chapter 4, the work of Purkey and Novak is as important and effective in the regular classroom as in the gifted program class; as vital in college algebra as it is in kindergarten.

The following ideas, materials, and strategies are intended for use with intellectually gifted children. However, be forewarned: The strategies that are highlighted here may also be effective in other settings, with different populations of students.

UNDERSTANDING AND ACCEPTING PERSONAL TALENTS

Kurt Vonnegut's short story, *Harrison Bergeron,* begins in this way:

> The year was 2081, and everybody was finally equal. They weren't only equal before God and the law, they were equal every which way. Nobody was better looking than anybody else. Nobody was stronger or quicker than anybody else. All this equality was due to the 211th, 212th, and 213th Amendments to the Constitution and to the unceasing vigilance of agents of the United States Handicapper General. (Vonnegut, 1950, p. 7)

How easy life would be if human exceptionality was mythical! (How boring too.) Vonnegut's fantasy story shows just how different life would be if the wish of many gifted children, "Why can't I be like everyone else?" were granted. But as the adage goes, be careful of what you wish, for it just might come true.

Understanding and accepting personal differences begin with an acknowledgment that the differences actually exist. Educators of gifted students can use the following activities to provide opportunities for their students to note ways in which they differ from, and are similar to, their agemates.

Fill in the Blanks

Given the chance, children can take one word and give it multiple meanings. Starting with the word *gifted* (or *talented* or *smart*), ask your students to take each letter of the word and select *other* terms, ideas, or feelings that come to mind when they *hear gifted* or *talented* or *smart*. For example:

*G*reat	*G*ood at sports
*I*cky, sometimes	*I*nteresting
*F*un	*F*ascinated with everything
*T*eased a lot	*T*est anxious
*E*xcited about learning	*E*njoy my teachers
*D*oesn't mean perfect	*D*on't like being compared

Since no two people seem to agree on a precise definition of giftedness, it makes sense to allow children to describe themselves in ways that are personally meaningful to them. The above descriptions point out both the high points and hassles of having the term *gifted* applied to oneself. By allowing students to construct their own word pictures, they will have a vehicle through which they can discuss some of the benefits and drawbacks of this term.

The Gift of Many Colors

A 12-year-old boy, in describing the giftedness he noted in his family members, spoke to the issue of talents that transcend academics:

> Anybody could be gifted. It's just sort of like a special light or something. You've just gotta have the right match to light it. In a lot of people, that light stays dark their whole lives. For grown-ups, you don't have to go to college to be gifted. My grandfather? You give him spare parts from an old lawnmover and he can give you a lawnmower within twenty-four hours. He never went to college, but he's gifted.

Asking children to note gifts and talents in skills apart from academics, and in people separate from school, can get them to realize that "at present, there is no single expert or prevailing theory [of giftedness] on which to rely . . . you must expect ambiguity and diversity" (Eby and Smutny, 1990, pp. 14–15). Also, by noting specific talents in friends, family, and neighbors, students begin to learn that they are not unique in possessing exceptional skills in particular areas.

Ups and Downs

Gifted students are often bombarded with falsehoods disguised as truisms: "If you're so smart, school must be easy for you," or "I bet you *never* have to study for a test," or "Just because you're so smart you think you're a big shot."

When confronted with statements such as these (usually, by classmates), the gifted student's response is often *no* response—after all, why get into a verbal battle if you feel you are destined to lose? An 11-year-old girl noted, "Other people just expect me to do well and when I don't, they make fun of me. I wish I could be like everybody and be accepted by everyone" (Delisle, 1984, p. 29). To address this issue directly and to show students that every coin has two sides—every opinion an opposite version—try "Ups and Downs." As displayed in Figure 6.2, the hub of this activity is the term *gifted.* On the horizontal axes, students write something positive that comes to mind when they think of the term *gifted;* on the vertical axes, they write a negative aspect of the word. Then, for each initial reaction, positive and negative, the students consider an opposite feeling. Intended to show students the varying ways they can view a situation, "Ups and Downs" presents alternative ways of thinking about problems that may at first seem inherently bad or good.

Excerpted from the work of Betts and Niehart, "Ups and Downs" is one example of an activity that gives "students an opportunity to work together as a group, to learn about group process and interaction, and to learn more about the other people in the program" (1985, p. 3).

Invite the "Kids on the Block"

Sometimes, students are willing to listen to just about anyone except an adult. After all, for those of us who attended school while the earth was still cooling

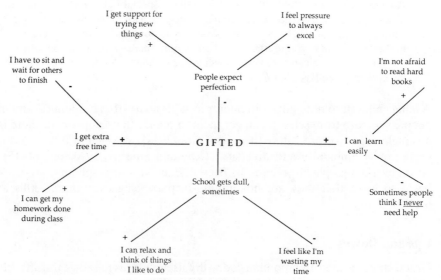

Figure 6.2. Ups and downs.

(in the eyes of children, that's anyone over age 25), what could we possibly know about today's kids, today's problems?

Enter the "Kids on the Block," a collection of child-sized puppets created by Barbara Aiello to teach children and adults about what it is like to be different. Over 30 separate puppets can be used to talk about topics such as deafness, spina bifida, epilepsy, child abuse, cultural differences, and giftedness. Each puppet is accompanied by scripts that present the audience, in a puppet show format, with realistic situations confronted by the individual "puppet with the difference." For example, Jinx Braxton, an outgoing 11-year-old girl puppet who spends part of her day in a resource room for gifted children, discusses the myths about giftedness, parental expectations, and friendship. At the end of the show, children can ask the puppets questions. To the children's delight, the puppets respond to the questions asked. Each script was developed by several experts in the education of gifted children. Here are some script summaries to give you an idea of how the puppets work.

The Gee Whiz Quiz Show

When Brenda and Jinx are competing on the Gee Whiz Quiz Show, it is Brenda who saves the day and wins for her school by coming up with the right answer to the final question. Renaldo is mystified that Jinx, the child identified as gifted and talented and placed in a special GT resource room, wasn't the one who knew all the answers. Jinx explains to Renaldo that having a special flair for learning doesn't mean that she's a "computer brain," and that she is a regular kid. (**Jinx, Brenda, Renaldo**)

Best Friends

When Brenda has trouble with the same assignments that were easy for Jinx to do she becomes upset and embarrassed. Jinx points out that everyone is smart, no one is gifted at everything and that the differences between them give their friendship a special flavor. (**Jinx, Brenda**)

The Family Letter

When Jinx returns from school she finds her mom at her desk composing a letter she plans to send to the entire family. As Jinx reads the letter aloud, she finds that her mom has focused on her schoolwork and on the fact that she's in a special class. Because Jinx feels that it is important that people see her as a regular kid, Jinx and her mother discuss rewriting the letter to reflect a more balanced description of family activities and other facets of Jinx's personality apart from the label "gifted and talented." (**Jinx, Mrs. Braxton played by an actor**)

Research conducted on its effectiveness shows increased positive attitudes among elementary children toward differences among people after use of "Kids on the Block." For example, Hawkins-Grider (1985) used "Kids on the Block" puppets with fifth and sixth graders to determine if the puppets were influential in changing attitudes toward children with handicaps. She found that the improvement in attitude change scores made by children who observed the puppet shows were preserved over time, as indicated by a delayed posttest. Powell (1985) conducted a similar study and found similar results amont third- through fifth-grade children. Further, Powell found that as children's attitudes toward disabled children improved, so did their knowledge of specific disabling conditions. Yet another study had similar results using "Kids on the Block" puppets (Haugland, 1986). It also found that there were no detectable differences in attitude according to gender. To date, no studies have been done using the Jinx Braxton puppet to determine children's attitude change toward gifted children, but this is due, no doubt, to the "newness" of Jinx's arrival on this very special block.

An exciting, innovative, and effective (though not inexpensive) option that has won awards from UNESCO, Easter Seals, and *Instructor* Magazine, among others, the "Kids on the Block" deserve to visit your neighborhood. *Their* neighborhood is *9385-C Gerwig Lane, Columbia, Maryland, 21046.*

Educational Psychology 101

Intelligence and achievement tests remain mysteries to many students who are required to take them. Some students may know the basic purposes of these tests, but just as likely, other students are apt to place too much importance on the results of these assessments. An IQ of 115, as measured in third grade, will not keep a child out of Harvard any more than a 1500 composite score on the SAT will guarantee a place in the Crimson's next freshman class. Students need to know that.

In order to debunk the myths and mysteries surrounding standardized tests and their interpretation, it is helpful to provide students with information that is generally not provided until college. This "Introduction to Educational Psychology" can help interested students learn the ins and outs of test construction and interpretation. Some possible items to review or define include the following:

> *Achievement versus aptitude:* The former provides data on how well you have learned your lessons; the latter gives clues as to your overall mental muscle. Put simply, achievement tells you "what is"; aptitude, "what may be."
>
> *Battery:* It does more than power a radio, it also indicates (in the electrifying world of school) a series of related tests that give an overall picture of one's achievement.
>
> *Ceiling effect:* Just as rooms have ceilings and houses have roofs, tests have uppermost limits, too. And just as a house built with midgets in

mind is likely to frustrate a 6'2" star center of the basketball team, so too will an easy test be inadequate for someone whose skills far surpass the level of the content being measured. This ceiling effect can do strange things to the psyche, for if you're a smart kid who has always done well in classes that appear too easy, you might begin to question your abilities when you finally confront a text, a test, or a teacher that is challenging.

These and other terms—*reliability, validity, pre/post,* and so on—can be explained to students in language that is neither technical nor threatening, and the end result could be a new understanding of the purposes behind and limits to intellectual and academic assessment. One especially helpful resource for explaining tests and testing to students is *Fighting Invisible Tigers,* a book designed for teenagers that lists positive and practical ways to understand life, school, and self (Hipp, 1985).

A Matter of "Terman"ology

Go ahead, find even one child who likes the term *gifted* when it is applied to him or her. In various studies related to children's perceptions and acceptance of the word *gifted,* the one point of agreement seems to be the blanket disapproval of the word (American Association for Gifted Children, 1978; Delisle, 1984; Coleman and Fults, 1982). It seems other-worldly to some, too burdensome to others, and just plain "geeky" to the majority. To some, the brain–nerd connection is reinforced merely by the use of a word that carries so much baggage: *gifted.*

If such is the case with your own students or the students you will teach some day—and I guarantee that it is or will be—have them describe why the term is so offensive. Further, since we must use *some* word to describe people whose abilities are higher than those of agemates, ask your students to suggest alternative terms. Then, probe further as to why the term(s) they've selected are more appropriate or meaningful than the one they've just discarded.

Each of these suggestions is designed to help gifted students understand and accept their individual talents. The intent is not to isolate students from their classmates by pointing at the ways in which they differ from the girl next door or the boy who sits behind them in English class. Rather, by honest discussion of the differences *and the similarities* between gifted children and others, it is hoped that gifted students can come to appreciate that *different* does not mean *detriment,* and that being better than a classmate *at* something does not imply that they are better *than* anyone else who shares their planet. (I realize I've beaten this point to death since Chapter 1; repetition, to me, indicates importance.)

TAKING CHARGE OF ONE'S OWN EDUCATION

It was the first semester of my PhD program, a time when piling up credits was *de rigueur.* I was sitting in day 2 of a summer course, "Introduction to Educational Administration," and I had read the previous night's assignment. Anticipating a lively discussion to ensue, I had written down several questions and comments that had come to mind. Eagerly, I awaited a dialogue.

The professor began. He lectured us all, and the 20+ students around me began to take notes feverishly and to ask for clarification on the spelling of certain last names. "But it's in the textbook," I thought to myself. "Why is everyone writing?"

This was how the first day had passed, and then the second, and the third. With a lot of time in class to think (since I didn't have to listen to the lectures), I figured that I had two options:

1. Be like my classmates, *don't* read the assignments, and be surprised by the content of the professor's lecture, or
2. Take charge (after all, it was *my* tuition dollar!) and meet with my professor to discuss alternate ways of fulfilling class requirements.

I chose the latter and was able to complete all readings and written assignments independently, needing to show up for class only on the morning of the final exam.

It worked; I earned it all: an *A* on my assignments, an *A* for the course, and the respect of a professor who admitted that no student had ever approached him with a dilemma *and* a solution.

Years later—PhD now earned—I wrote a prototypic dialogue on this event, the first in my life when I challenged authority from within "the system's" structure. That dialogue, reproduced in Figure 6.3, is written with students in mind—school-age students, not adult ones such as myself, who waited until I was 27 to take charge of my education.

The key point I learned—better late than never—was that if I was not the guardian of my own personal educational rights, then whatever happened to me was deserved. If my needs were not being met in a certain way, then it was up to me to make my needs known, for most teachers are not mind readers and they take silence or acquiesence from their students as signs that all is going well. Thus, if changes are to occur, it is often up to the student to take the first step.

Here are some other hints as to how that might happen.

A Lesson Learned

Many of life's important lessons are learned through the sometimes awkward approach of trial and error. We try something once and if it works we repeat it;

How To Talk To Almost Any Teacher (And Be Heard)

By Jim Delisle

Jim Delisle is associate professor of special education and gifted education at Kent State University in Kent, Ohio. He is the author of Gifted Kids Speak Out *and coauthor with Judy Galbraith of* The Gifted Kids Survival Guide II *(both Free Spirit Publishing, 1987).*

You have a school-related problem. You need help. The best person to ask for help is your teacher. So you decide to — what?

And here's where most students freeze. They don't know how to talk to teachers, especially not about a problem. Maybe they try, and the conversation is a bust. Or maybe they decide to just forget it and hope the problem will solve itself.

The good news is, you *can* talk to teachers, if you go about it the right way. After all, most teachers are reasonable creatures. Like the rest of us, they want to be treated with respect. Like the rest of us, they want their intelligence to be respected. Like the rest of us, they do not enjoy being kept waiting.

Following are eight tips that can help you talk to almost any teacher, about almost anything. They are illustrated here with an example. But once you learn the basics, you can write your own script.

The Problem: Sandy feels that her teacher is assigning too much of the same kind of classwork and homework.

She feels it's redundant and is wasting her time. So she stays after class one day and . . .

Sandy: Ms. Tyler, I was wondering if you would have a few minutes to talk with me about your class.

Ms. Tyler: Well, Sandy, now is not a good time — I've got another class in ten minutes.

Sandy: I know how busy you are; could we schedule a time to meet later? I figure we'll need about 15 minutes.

Tip #1: Be respectful of busy schedules and tell how much time you'll need.

Ms. Tyler: How about after lunch tomorrow — about 11:45?

Sandy: Sounds good — thanks. See you then.

At 11:45 the next day . . .

Tip #2: Be on time!

Sandy: Thanks for meeting with me, Ms. Tyler, I appreciate it.

Ms. Tyler: What's on your mind, Sandy?

Sandy: Well, I feel kind of awkward talking with teachers sometimes, but I have a concern about our class and I wanted to discuss it with you.

Tip #3: State your feelings to help "set the tone."

Ms. Tyler: . . . Specifically?

Sandy: I feel that some of the worksheets I'm doing in class, and some of the homework, too, covers concepts that I already know. For instance, this math sheet I did last week on equations has 50 examples, and I got 48 of them right. And last night's homework was similar. I finished it, and I think I did pretty well on it.

Tip #4: Offer specific examples and evidence of accomplishments.

Ms. Tyler: What's your point, Sandy?

Sandy: I was wondering if you would be willing to cut down on my homework assignments if I could prove to you that I already know how to do the work.

Tip #5: Provide a possible solution. Don't just state the problem.

Ms. Tyler: But Sandy, the homework is meant to reinforce basic skills — to give you extra practice.

Sandy: I know how important that is. My suggestion is not to forget about the homework entirely. I thought, instead, that we could compromise — maybe I could do half of the assigned problems, and if I got no more than two errors, then I wouldn't have to complete the other examples. Also, I'd be glad to redo any pages that I really mess up.

Tip #6: Show that you see the other person's side of the problem, and be willing to compromise.

Ms. Tyler: I haven't done this before, and I'm not sure it's fair to the other students who have to complete all the assignments given. I'll have to think about it.

Sandy: All I know is that it would really help me, because I do have a lot of other homework plus chores at home. So I appreciate your willingness to consider my idea.

Tip #7: Tell why and how a change would affect you.

Ms. Tyler: Thanks, Sandy. I'll get back to you.

Sandy: Thank you too, Ms. Tyler.

Tip #8: It pays to be polite.

Will Sandy get what she wants? Hard to say. Was the talk she had with her teacher successful? Very. And next time will be even easier.

✿

Figure 6.3. (*Source:* "How to Talk to Almost Any Teacher (and Be Heard)," by James R. Delisle. Excerpt from *Free Spirit: News and Views on Growing Up,* Vol. 3, No. 2. Nov/Dec 1989. Reprinted by permission of Free Spirit Publishing, Inc. Copyright © 1989. All rights reserved.)

if it fails, we try anew, using a new tactic. This pattern is used in social settings (where students attempt to gain entrance into a certain clique, for instance), but it is also used in other forms of communication, say between students and teachers.

A more synchronized approach to personal contact is presented in Table 6.1, in which students learn both the hows and whys of effective, efficient communication. By using a positive approach and a respectful tone, students will more likely than not be listened to by their teachers.

TABLE 6.1. 10 TIPS FOR TALKING TO TEACHERS

Are you having a problem with a class or an assignment? Can you see room for improvement in how a subject is being taught? Do you have a better idea for a special project or term paper? Don't just tell your friends. Talk to the teacher!

Many students have told us that they don't know how to go about doing this. The following suggestions are meant to make it easier for everyone—students *and* teachers.

1. **Make an appointment to meet and talk.** This shows the teacher that you're serious *and* that you have some understanding of his or her busy schedule. Be flexible—and don't be late! The teacher will appreciate that you took the initiative.

2. **If you know other students who feel the way you do, consider going to the teacher together.** There's strength in numbers. If a teacher hears the same thing from four or five people, he or she is more likely to do something about it.

3. **Think through what you want to say *before* you go into your meeting with the teacher.** Write down your questions or concerns. Make a list of the items you want to cover. You may even want to copy your list for the teacher so both of you can look at it during your meeting.

4. **Choose your words carefully.** For example, instead of saying, "I hate doing reports; they're a waste of time," try, "Is there some other way I could satisfy this requirement? Could I do a video instead?" Strike the word "boring" from your vocabulary. Boring is a buzzword for teachers.

5. **Don't expect the teacher to do all the work or come up with all the answers.** Be prepared to make suggestions, offer solutions, even recommend resources.

6. **Be diplomatic, tactful, and respectful.** Teachers have feelings, too. And they're more likely to be responsive if you remember that the purpose of your meeting is conversation, not confrontation.

7. **Focus on what you need, not on what you think the teacher is doing wrong.** The more the teacher learns about you, the more he or she will be able to help. The more defensive the teacher feels, the less he or she will *want* to help.

8. **Don't forget to listen.** This may seem obvious, but many students need practice in this important skill. The purpose of your meeting isn't just to hear yourself talk.

9. **Bring your sense of humor.** Not necessarily the joke-telling sense of humor, but the one that lets you laugh at yourself and your own misunderstandings and mistakes.

10. **Finally: If your meeting isn't the success you hoped it would be, get help from another adult**—a guidance counselor, the gifted program coordinator, or another teacher you know and trust—who is likely to support you and advocate for you. Then try again. (1989).

Since this open communication is bound to be awkward for the student to initiate, it is helpful to role play a situation or two in a "safe" environment—perhaps between the teacher of gifted students and a student, or between two students. Other class members can observe, noting strategies or techniques that seemed especially effective.

Should this strategy be used by all students with all teachers? Probably not. Yet if communication and honesty are goals of education espoused by the people in charge (that is, the teachers), then this type of face-to-face contact should be preferable to the backbiting that could take place if the conversation were not allowed to happen.

Three-Dimensional Learning

Sometimes, the materials of education can make or break a good lesson. While it is true that good learning can occur with even meager resources and that a boorish teacher can deflate the power of even the splashiest curriculum material, it often helps to have the proper tools for the job.

An especially good (and inexpensive) collection of classroom materials is available under the title of *The Brown Paper School Book Series,* published by Little, Brown and Company. The series consists of 15 (at present) books, each about 125 pages. Designed by "a good group of California teachers, writers, and artists who get together every now and then to work on stuff for kids and to have a good time" (Robertson and Robertson, 1971), *The Brown Paper School Book Series* is adaptable for use with children in primary grades through junior high school. Each book invites creative responses from both students and teachers, for example, in "Blood and Guts" students use paper towel rolls and balloons to construct arms and help explain how muscles work in pairs.

Books within the series include the following:

Blood and Guts: A Working Guide to Your Own Insides. Would-be physicians team up to learn about anatomy and bodily functions through real-life (and safe) experiments on self and others.

The "I Hate Mathematics" Book. For students (and teachers) tired of back-to-basics workbooks, this volume shows the applicability of math in everyday situations, such as sports, music, and gambling.

The Book of Think. Combining the use of logic with interpersonal relations, this book helps students tackle such problems as "coping with a friend who always tries to get you in trouble." Creative and logical thinking are explained through exploring child-size problems.

I Am Not a Short Adult. An effective guide for dealing with students who want to know how to react when someone tells them to "act their age, not their hat size."

Other titles—*The Night Sky Book, Beastly Neighbors: All About Things in the City, Make Mine Music*—concentrate on the arts, sciences, and social studies in such enticing ways that students won't even notice the learning taking place until the deed's been done, the lesson's been learned.

A Secondary Sourcebook

Did you ever notice how educators blame the individuals who immediately preceded their grade level for all the woes of education? College professors accuse high school teachers of ill-preparing their students. Secondary educators look askance at junior high teachers who should have "shaped up the kids before sending them to us." Seventh-grade teachers blame elementary educators for too much coddling, and the primary grade teachers get criticized for not teaching the basics when they "had the time to do so." The poor kindergarten teacher, with no colleague left to blame, points the finger at parents or (to complete the cycle) at college professors, who "should get out of their ivory towers once in a while and tell us how to teach in the *real* world." With all these bucks being passed, where is Harry Truman now?

In gifted education, the reverse of this pattern is true, as the lower-grade-level educators accuse their higher-level (so to speak) colleagues of not following through on the firm foundation set in the early grades. High school teachers get the worst rap of all, with such comments as "we *do* have a gifted program, *except* at the high school" or "the resource room model works prefectly well for us, but these high school teachers want nothing to do with one."

Perhaps that's because secondary-level educators know something that they don't often share: that a comprehensive secondary school already offers a multitude of options for gifted and talented students. LeoNora Cohen (1988) lists a variety of programs that can (and do) exist in grades 7 through 12. This roster is highlighted in Table 6.2. Two points are worth mentioning about Cohen's list:

Many of the options are open to, and valuable for, many students, not just those with gifts and talents.

Some of the best options—mentorships, internships, summer programs—take place outside of both the school walls and the school calendar.

Secondary options for gifted students need not take a back seat to the sometimes flashy counterparts that exist in earlier grades. Indeed, the diversity that is a natural part of most high school curricular and extracurricular activities can continue to benefit even the most highly able students.

TABLE 6.2. NATIONAL SECONDARY OPTIONS FOR THE GIFTED

Many successful programs for the gifted are in operation throughout the country. Listed below are the various national options available to gifted students in the school districts of our country. Gifted students are using these options to gain high school credit, college credit or placement and enrichment, depending upon the stipulations and regulations determined by the individual school districts.

A great variety of program and service options are used to meet the needs of secondary gifted and talented children across the nation. You may be surprised to find that your district is already utilizing one of more of these options.

In developing plans to comply with our state's new mandate, review this list to see what your district already has in place. These can form the base for your planning.

Advanced Placement

Admission to college with advanced standing as a result of the Advanced Placement Test scores.

CLEP—College Level Examination Program

Examinations testing student's college level competencies no matter where or how information was acquired.

Externship or Field Experience

Half of the school day or other periods of time are spent in career-oriented job or apprenticeship or in cultural education.

Correspondence Courses

Provides enrichment, independent study, and early entrance to college.

Exchange Courses

Encourages educational exchanges between students in schools in the same districts, neighboring districts, states, and countries.

After-School or Saturday Programs

Allows for educational experience and credit through field trips, discussions, seminars, and special interest clubs.

Combination of Grades

Completes two years of high school in one (or other grades).

Seminars and Tutorials

Allows time for gifted students to exchange ideas and concepts with other gifted students or hear guest speakers.

Accelerated Classes

Courses with a faster pace that move to higher levels than others at the same grade.

Independent Study

Designed to meet the needs of an individual rather than a group. Student contracts to do a specific project according to agreed upon guidelines.

College Courses

Students take college courses (usually on campus) when they have exhausted high school offerings. These may be taken for high school or college credit or both.

Interdisciplinary Programs

Courses from various disciplines are focused around a common core or theme, such as humanities. Emphasis is on finding relationships and generalization across disciplines.

IEP—Individual Educational Plan

Designed for the specific needs and interests of the student. It utilizes existing school offerings and seeks ways to meet needs if they cannot be met in the classroom, providing a flexible approach.

Mentorships

Students are paired with a person who has expertise in a field of mutual interest who guides the development of that student on projects or research.

Study Skills—Metacognition

Special courses offered in thinking and research skills, study skills, and understanding of one's own learning strategies and creative potential.

OM, Future Problem Solving, Young Writers

National competitions based on creativity and team work.

Radical Acceleration

On a tutorial basis, with specific testing and monitoring, a student can accelerate extremely rapidly through a sequence of courses, such as Math or English. Up to 4 years of work can be compressed into one.

Future Studies

Courses that deal with life in the future to prepare students for the change to come.

TABLE 6.2. (continued)

Specialized High Schools	**"Ologies" Model**
Schools or parts of schools with special emphasis in science and engineering, international studies, performing arts, or other areas which serve as a magnet for interested students.	Students (Middle school/Jr. High) take role of methodologist, technologist, and communicator.
Counseling	**Compacting**
Students meet one to one or in groups to deal with careers, underachievement, awareness of self as a gifted/creative individual, and concommitant problems.	Reducing the amount of time normally required for a topic or subject in order to free the student for other activities or courses. This can be done through a "testing out" of classes, conferencing, contracting, or other arrangements.
Special Classes	**International Baccalaureate**
Courses not usually offered in the school, such as Japanese, photography, or marine biology.	A comprehensive program incorporating problem-solving and the interrelationship of knowledge with an international slant (2 foreign languages and focus on social sciences).
Star Classes (or other names)	International standards of achievement allow the student to enter US universities at the sophomore level.
Homogeneous grouping of gifted students with greater depth or breadth of coverage.	

Source: Cohen, L. M. (1988). National Secondary Options for the Gifted. *Illinois Council for the Gifted Journal,* 8, 42. Reprinted with permission.

Sentence Completions

Setting reachable and appropriate expectations is a goal that many gifted students find elusive. Too often, they begin to see themselves in relation to what they have not accomplished rather than the goals they have achieved.

The following activity is offered in hopes that students will relax their self-expectations as well as those they perceive others have for them.

Ask each student to complete the following sentence stems:

1. When report cards come out . . .
2. Sometimes my teachers . . .
3. When I think about school . . .
4. The best teachers . . .
5. When someone compliments my work . . .
6. Within the next week . . .
7. Within the next year . . .
8. I like school when . . .
9. No one expects me . . .
10. If I fail a test . . .
11. When my friends think about me . . .
12. Whatever happens to me . . .
13. When I think back to first grade . . .

Once the activity is completed, ask your students to exchange lists (the lists should be submitted anonymously). Allow time for reading and sharing and ask the students to group the responses into categories that emerge from the completed sentence stems (for example, reachable versus unreachable goals; pleasant versus unpleasant memories). Follow up by having students devise their own sentence stems and posting some of their responses daily or weekly.

Intellectual differences are invisible, at least to the untrained eye or ear. Yet the owner of talents knows well the frustration of engaging in activities that offer little challenge or substance; what he or she may not know is that the situation does not have to be that way. If given the opportunity, and the skills, to take charge of their own education, gifted students begin to feel empowered. They grow to realize an important truth: Education is a partnership, not an oligarchy; their experiences as students can provide valuable insights into ways of improving their careers in elementary or high school. With a little luck, a dose of tact, and a lot of perseverance, gifted students will not have to wait to hit the legal age (as I did) before making their education work for them.

RELATING TO VARIOUS PEER GROUPS

As a gifted high school student once said to me, "I don't know what's more difficult about being gifted—living up to the label for my parents and teachers or living it down in front of my friends."

Being gifted means that you possess certain traits that are neither common to nor appreciated by all: heightened intelligence. If a student is lucky enough to inhabit a social milieu where any and all individual differences, both visible and invisible, are accepted, the presence of a superior intellect is a nonissue. However, I'm afraid this is more rare than common. Instead, the majority of young people live in the same world we do, where discrimination against particular races, ethnic groups, handicaps, lifestyles, and ideologies intrudes on the harmony that would exist were these negative attitudes not present.

Giving gifted students the opportunity to discuss the sensitive and relevant issues related to acceptance by agemates will allow them to see that others, too, may experience problems similar to theirs. Even if these discussions do not lead to a marked increase in either the number or the quality of friendships, they may still help to clarify a gifted student's place in the real world of individual differences.

Rational-Emotive Therapy

Albert Ellis, in his many articles and books, addresses the connection between how we think and how we act (Ellis, 1961, 1971, 1977). Hansen, Steyic, and Warmer explain this connection, called rational-emotive therapy (RET,) in the following way:

> RET is an approach to counseling that is based on the assumption that most people in our society develop many irrational ways of thinking. These irrational thoughts lead to irrational or inappropriate behavior. Therefore, counseling must be designed to help people recognize and change these irrational beliefs into more rational ones. (1977, p. 209)

Getting students to see the linkages between thoughts and actions is the first step toward social self-acceptance. Rational-emotive therapy is a cognitive approach to dealing with the often emotional barriers that gifted students perceive set them apart from others. This cognitive method meshes well with gifted students' verbal facility, but the astute educator can get beneath this surface-level talk and probe the thoughts that accompany the words. Then, through "questioning and challenging, even confrontation tactics, contracts, suggestions, and persuasion," the educator/counselor can encourage gifted students to challenge their personal views of reality (Gibson and Mitchell, 1981, p. 271). Some irrational beliefs worth discussing include these misconceptions:

1. Everyone must like me.
2. I must like everyone.
3. There's nothing left to learn and no one around who can teach me anything.
4. If I'm not popular then I'm a social outcast.
5. The majority is always right.
6. The majority is always wrong.
7. If I'm so smart I should be able to make friends easily.
8. No one will find me physically attractive enough to want to date me.
9. Friendship doesn't matter as long as you like yourself.
10. Boys are supposed to be smart, girls are supposed to be popular.

In using this list with your students, begin by having them highlight, anonymously, those irrational beliefs that affect their lives. Then, collect and tally their responses and begin a classroom discussion around the item(s) that most students cite as problematic. Also, invite them to add their own irrational beliefs to this list and use these, too, as a basis for group discussions. By doing so, you will show your students that others share their interpersonal concerns, and you will provide a "safe harbor" for discussion of feelings that, though important, can also be awkward to reveal.

Discussion with Near-Peers

How often have we started to console our students with such dependent clauses as the following:

"I know just how you are feeling . . ."

"When I was your age . . ."

Generally, these comforting words fall on deaf ears, as students often turn off anything that sounds similar to advice from or affiliation with an adult. In trying to be helpful we are, instead, defeated; our words are a generation too late.

However, if the same nuggets of advice are given by students just a few years older than the children who are listening, their words are considered golden, not gratuitous. These "near-peers" are old enough to be thought of as reliable, but not so far removed from the social scene that their ideas are passé. Here are some suggested uses for near-peers:

1. Ask gifted students from the sixth grade to describe to newly identified third-grade gifted students "what this gifted/talented program is *really* like."
2. Ask senior high students to relate to their seventh- and eighth-grade counterparts the differences in socialization patterns "once you get used to adolescence."
3. Ask college freshmen to return to their high school to talk about what current juniors and sophomores can do *now* to better adjust to college later.

In the process of discussion, it will be hard to discern who benefits more: the pane*lists* or the pane*lees*. Both sets of students find solace and fulfillment by reviewing the high points and hassles of growing up gifted.

Bibliotherapy

There are few occasions more self-assuring than finding out that some of your favorite fictional characters, if their lives had been real, would be suffering the same growing pains as you. Bibliotherapy allows this to happen, and *The Bookfinder: When Kids Need Books* 1989) is the prime resource for locating young adult literature that addresses particular social problems (Spredmann-Dreyer, 1989). With a subject index characterized by such diverse headings as "sibling rivalry," "friendship," "intellectual talents," "obesity," and "death of a loved one" (among hundreds of other subjects), this superbly cross-referenced volume provides lengthy synopses of books that address virtually any dilemma that children between the ages of 5 and 18 might experience.

Also, the editor was kind (and efficient) to provide a short paragraph for each of the 700+ entries that warns the educator of any questionable language or situations that might be no-no's to particularly sensitive school districts or families. As an inexpensive resource that is a gold mine for the busy educator, *The Bookfinder* is an essential reference work.

Allowing Multiage Grouping of Students

Except in grades K through 12, social clusterings are determined by interest, not age. For example, my wife and I are best friends with a couple who are 15 years older than we, but age doesn't matter, as we share other commonalities: a love of the ocean, a weakness for therapeutic massages, and philosophies of life that are congruent. We enjoy one another because . . . well, because we *just do*. Imagine how odd we would have been considered in high school, if our best friends were already out of college. Yet still, even then, I believe if we had all found each other, we would have been pleasantly surprised at how well we got along. Life philosophies don't appear, they develop.

Following this line of reasoning, it is logical to assume that children who differ from their agemates—gifted children—will enjoy, benefit from, and desire experiences with children who differ from them in age but who parallel them in interests or abilities. Setting up play groups and work groups that allow this to happen can occur in many ways, including the following:

1. Allow an especially creative writer to perfect her skill in a higher grade, with students more aligned with her expressive talents.
2. Permit a child in second grade to enjoy recess with older youngsters, if desired, so he or she gets to play games by established rules of conduct or order.
3. Suggest to gifted high school students that they might enjoy taking a college course—to their intellectual and social benefit.

These suggestions do not assume that all gifted children are so uniformly capable that they should be placed full-time with students who are older than they (Remember Amy? twinkies and milk). However, to deny unilaterally the opportunity to interact with multiage groups is to repress the reality that differences among agemates *do* exist; that gifted children *can* handle, intellectually and otherwise, the challenges and pleasures shared by children who may be "soulmates," if not "agemates."

CONFORMITY AND PHILOSOPHY OF LIFE

In discussing the problems encountered by students whose ideas burst forth openly like so many sparks on the fourth of July, Hollingworth wrote, "It is hard for them to maintain silence when ideas are pressing for utterance" (1942, p. 277). Conforming to group standards, such as waiting one's turn to speak, going along with a decision that one finds distasteful, or respecting adults because they are older, is a skill seldom perfected early by gifted children. Instead, they demand both to be heard and to be listened to, and they often give respect only when it is earned, not just in deference to age or position.

These social graces—adults collectively call them "tact"—are distinguishing features separating leaders from despots, politicians from demagogues, and up-and-comers from has-beens. The following sections contain suggestions for introducing students to methods for understanding how to use the fine art of compromise.

The Clash of Opposites

1. Aloneness/loneliness
2. Giving in/giving up
3. Knowledge/wisdom
4. Being smart/being bright
5. Friendship/popularity
6. Age/maturity
7. Happiness/contentment
8. Confusion/uncertainty

Each of these pairs represents terms that are commonly mistaken as synonyms. Used interchangeably at times by students, the words actually are very different in meaning, yet the nuances that separate one word from the next often are lost.

The educator's role is to allow open discussion of the definition of these terms and to allow students to give examples from their own lives of times or situations when the distinction between particular word pairs became clear. For example, a student might consider these subtle shadings:

Being *smart* means being able to answer questions and dates, but being *gifted* means having an imagination and a spirit, and being able to think creatively.

Being *confused* is an uncomfortable feeling, as it implies you don't really understand whatever it is you're trying to learn or decide, but being *uncertain* means that, despite knowing all the facts, you've not yet determined a course of action.

When students comprehend and verbalize the distinctions between terms that appear at first to be synonyms, they begin to appreciate the importance of gray areas. Thus, the next time they defer to a group of agemates who would rather see *Friday the 13th, Part Zillion* than the latest Woody Allen flick, they begin to realize that they are not necessarily violating their own principles. Instead, they are putting a situation into its proper social perspective. (Besides, this same student could probably find another time, another person, with whom to share a movie with subtitles or subtleties.)

Tippy-Tippy-Tap-Tap

Here it is, another cartoon (see Figure 6.4).

Going along with the crowd may result in changing a view, attitude, opinion, or behavior that was once held dear. This can create some inner turmoil. As seen through the facial expression of the fourth elf from the left, giving in to others' wishes can hurt:

> **Frame 1:** "I'm different, but nobody notices."
> (Ignorance is bliss.)
> **Frame 2:** "A few others pick up the fact that I'm different. I'm not sure how I feel about this."
> (Peer pressure is setting in.)
> **Frame 3:** "Uh oh. It looks like they're ready to hit me on the head with their hammers."
> (Minority-of-one status attained.)
> **Frame 4:** "Oh well, maybe they're right. What do I know anyway."
> (Who I am takes a back seat to how they expect me to be.)

Figure 6.4. "Tippy, Tippy, Tap, Tap," by Lorenz, appearing in *The New Yorker*, December 6, 1976.

Discussing this cartoon in the abstract (that is, "Why would the elf change his way of making shoes?") leads quickly into a discussion of times particular students "tippy-tippied" when they really wanted to "tap-tap." Also, other students will relate situations when they opted *not* to acquiesce to group norms, which probably resulted in a myriad of reactions and responses by others. *Discuss* these times and reveal occasions that you, too, were put in these social binds (we all have been at one time or another). Then, lead into more general questions regarding the factors used to determine when it's okay to tippy-tippy, and when one should stand his or her ground. (Generally, these determining factors include safety, morals, personal preferences or fear of punishment.) The "Tippy-Tippy-Tap-Tap" exercises open the door to discussion of topics both trivial and vital in one's development as a social creature.

Breaking the Sex-Role Barriers

"Which of you boys could help me move these desks into a circle?" the teacher asked.

Four boys volunteered.

"Now, who would like to take notes in our small group discussion?"

A young girl is selected.

The teacher begins the lesson or, at least, that is the assumption. For some students, though, the lesson has already started. Sex-role stereotyping has begun to run its course once again: boys are furnitures movers, girls are note-takers.

An overblown example? An isolated incident? Perhaps, but also, perhaps not.

> Gifted girls usually know what they need to do in order to fit in. Commonly, this means that they will read girls' magazines [and] will participate in feminine play activities. . . . Gifted girls will readily participate in traditional feminine activities, even if they aren't crazy about them, simply because they are usually cheerful, friendly and compliant little people. (Kerr, 1985a, p. 93)

Sex-role stereotyping has, in recent years, focused on the specific needs of gifted females (Callahan, 1980; Horner, 1972; Kerr, 1983). Authors now have begun to note that the gender-related expectations affecting girls can also stifle gifted boys from reaching their fullest potential.

> Gifted boys have problems, too. . . . Highly creative or sensitive boys raised primarily with "macho" values can experience extreme frustration and insecurity when they're expected to conform to the "tough guy" image. . . . Boys are expected to succeed in life—to have a career, for example—and

> are believed to have more opportunities to succeed than girls. . . . Boys cannot *not* succeed. (Alvino, 1989, p. 23)

Limiting one's aspirations on the basis of one's sex is a most extreme example of conformity in action. A male nurse still raises as many eyebrows as does a female marine, for our society has yet to reconcile itself to the fact that "different strokes for different folks" is more than a jaded expression of 1960s liberalism.

To address this issue of gender conformity with gifted students (and their parents and teachers), a concentrated effort must begin early. Kerr (1985b) suggests modifying everything from toddlers' toys and playclothes to allowing teenagers to interact with mentors who work in careers or avocations that differ from what is typical or expected from each respective gender. The Girls Clubs of Santa Barbara, California, have published two self-help guides that address issues related to physical, emotional, and social growth in direct, nonsexist ways (Bingham, Edmondson, and Stryker, 1983).

The education of gifted students is complex and multifaceted. Yet if the issue of gender expectations is not addressed early and often, our most able students might limit their options to those that are safe, expected, and culturally biased in favor of timeworn societal standards.

Developing a Satisfying Philosophy of Life

How many of humanity's philosophical and moral dilemmas could be solved if only each person could enter this world with a rulebook—a set of guidelines that takes into account all of life's lessons learned through previous generations! Alas, life's journey is not that straight, that focused; instead, we often travel down the path of greatest resistance or follow lines of thought or action that lead nowhere but in circles.

The quest goes on, from year to year, life to life. Each person, ironically, on a *personal* quest for a *universal* ideal.

Gifted students, who seldom shy away from questions related to *why,* need help in understanding that the ability to ask questions, to see gray areas, or to notice contradictions is even a greater talent than being able to *solve* these existential dilemmas. That is not to say that the path to enlightenment is easy; however, that path is well-trodden, and knowing who and what has come before you may make the travels both easier and more meaningful. Here are some ways in which educators can help.

The Luxury of Existential Thought. A hungry child, a cold child, a child without a home or family: What they share is a "basic need for basic needs" (Maslow, 1970). This theory, related to the hierarchy of needs, places personal comfort and a sense of belonging at the foundation levels of human satisfac-

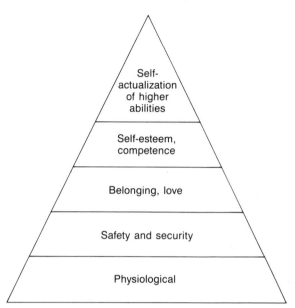

Figure 6.5. Hierarchy of needs. (*Source: Motivation and Personality,* by Abraham H. Maslow. Copyright 1954 by Harper & Row, Publishers, Inc. Copyright © 1970 by Abraham H. Maslow. Reprinted by permission of Harper & Row, Publishers, Inc.)

tion (see Figure 6.5). Without the presence of these fundamental human conditions, questions related to the bigger picture seem meaningless and void of purpose: "Who *cares* about the plight of third world countries when *I* don't even have a dumpy roof over my head to keep me warm and dry?"

As cultured and secure as most of you, dear readers, may be, it would probably be hard to differentiate you from savages if environmental conditions pitted you head-to-head against others in a battle for survival. When push comes to shove, life or death struggles preclude the meaning of existence; we react viscerally, instinctively, to protect ourselves and our own.

By explaining Maslow's theory to students and providing examples from literature, current events, and history that attest to its universality (the novel and film *Lord of the Flies* comes to mind here), gifted students may come to appreciate as luxuries the essentials of life that must be attained before global awareness or existential thoughts can emerge. Further, Maslow's work may help students understand more clearly that not all people (classmates included) have the essentials of life that allow consideration of issues that transcend the personal.

We are all, individually and collectively, members of the family of humanity. But just as one person differs from the next in the nuclear family in a comfortable American suburb, the same is true on a universal scale. Understanding and accepting this truth are vital first steps in appreciating the reasons that people act and think as they do.

Dendrochronology. The issue of "What I want to be when I grow up" has been around for countless generations, each of which has been just as enamored as we are with our own futures and those of our children. In addition, our society reinforces this by seeming to value what will be as much or more than what is. Too often the focus of our thinking about our own personal futures is on jobs and careers, not lifestyles. Gifted children, whose employment options are numerous and varied, may need help in seeing the interconnectedness of career and lifestyle. *Dendrochronology* is but one small way to offer that help.

Dendrochronology: the determination of the approximate dates of past events and periods of time by a study of the growth rings on trees. With only a little imagination, gifted children can use the principle of dendrochronology to work forward instead of backward, predicting what will happen in their lives at certain ages and stages. An example follows in Figure 6.6.

By examining the events listed on each child's chart, educators can begin to discuss the various passages through which each person travels—personal and professional, sad and happy.

Empowering the Innocents. A catastrophe strikes—a hurricane, earthquake, or famine—and even young gifted children feel sadness for people they will never meet. As the nightly news dramatizes the destruction of a piece of our world or the spirit of a people, young eyes are focused on problems, the extent of which cannot be fully grasped by even the brightest children. Still, the pain is very much there, and gifted children, sometimes more than others,

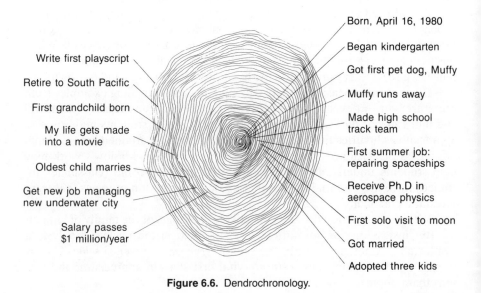

Write first playscript

Retire to South Pacific

First grandchild born

My life gets made into a movie

Oldest child marries

Get new job managing new underwater city

Salary passes $1 million/year

Born, April 16, 1980

Began kindergarten

Got first pet dog, Muffy

Muffy runs away

Made high school track team

First summer job: repairing spaceships

Receive Ph.D in aerospace physics

First solo visit to moon

Got married

Adopted three kids

Figure 6.6. Dendrochronology.

want to know, "How can we help?" Often, the adult response is one that tries to minimize the reality that the children see. Comments such as "Don't worry, dear, the Red Cross will help them" or "There's really nothing you can do, you're just a child" are said by well-intentioned (yet misguided) adults who believe that by dismissing a child's problem they have conquered it for him or her. But the children don't buy it; they know that the pain remains long after the news is over and the headlines have gone on to yet-another crisis.

This ability to see beyond one's years is one of the bittersweet aspects of giftedness. How special it is to be able to identify with the suffering of a stranger, yet how sad that you're too young to make a difference in that person's life.

But some educators know the secret of *empowerment*. A new buzzword in educational circles, empowerment puts children in the proverbial driver's seat, so that they can make a dent in the problems faced by their global neighbors. Two examples of empowerment in action follow:

> Chip, age 7, saw the loss of property caused by killer hurricane Hugo in 1989 and decided he could help by sending a stuffed animal to a child who lost all toys during the storm. Chip's mom, knowing a good idea when she saw it, asked friends and colleagues for other stuffed animals. The result? More than 1,000 stuffed toys were sent to Charleston, South Carolina, compliments of Chip.
>
> The fourth-grade class of Forrestdale Elementary School in Rumson, New Jersey, grew tired of the ocean pollution dirtying their shore. They developed a calendar that helped explain the problem and made suggestions for improving the situation (see Figure 6.7). The money earned from the calendar sales went into an environmental protection fund, sponsored by the children.

Each day, in every community, at least one child is empowered by an adult who takes time to tend to the very real problems faced by the world. By allowing children a voice in seeking solutions, we show them that we respect their abilities to face adult-sized issues and are giving them a chance to alter their world for the better—a lesson too seldom (if ever) learned by some adults.

The Courage of Conviction

> How did the world begin?
>
> Is there a separate God for each religion, or one "overall" God?
>
> Why do people say they believe one thing and then act in the opposite way?

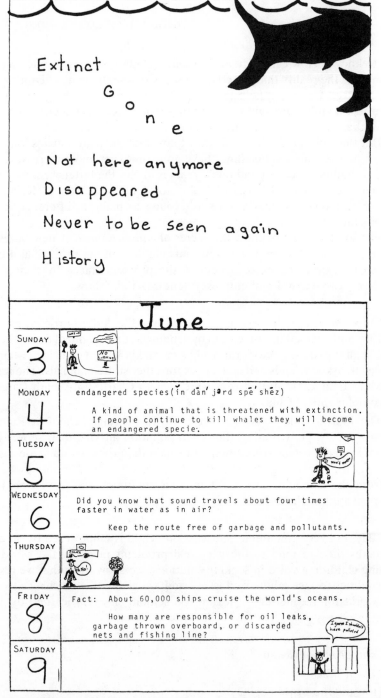

Figure 6.7. Environmental calendar. (*Source: "Helping the Ocean 2gether (H₂O)"* by the Fourth Grade Class of Forrestdale School, Rumson, NJ. Reprinted by permission of Rumson Public Schools.)

Heavy issues, heady questions—ideas, philosophies, and theories that have been bandied about for centuries in this game called life.

In *The Courage of Conviction,* Joan Baez notes the difficulty of holding to one's beliefs.

> I have had to discipline myself in whatever I've done all my life because I have not taken to other people's disciplines. I guess what I'm saying is that if something could force a discipline on me and I liked it, it would just make life easier. (Berman, 1986, p. 18)

The Courage of Conviction is a motherlode of global and personal philosophies. In it, prominent contemporaries—Mario Cuomo, Lech Walesa, H. H. Dalai Lama, Jane Goodall, and others—discuss their beliefs and how they put them into action in their daily lives. Useful with adults and senior high students, this resource helps people put their philosophical houses in order, as the realms of politics, religion, ecology, and other issues are exposed and dissected.

"People are like teabags," Rita Mae Brown writes. "You never know how strong they'll be until they're in hot water" (Berman, 1986, p. 23). Acting in accordance with one's own belief structure is easier said than done (most things are), but *The Courage of Conviction* will help thoughtful adolescents and adults make this important connection.

CONCLUSION

To tell you the truth, I thought this chapter was *never* going to end. Intended to be written in a terse 15 or so pages, it has extended far beyond that—but not so far, I hope, as to have hit the point of diminishing returns.

If the length of this chapter leaves me with any one feeling (other than relief that it is finished), it is this: Addressing the specific social and emotional adjustment concerns of gifted students could encompass a full year *each year* in the goings-on of an education program for gifted children. Also, I am left with the impression (as are you, I hope) that it is myopic to view affective education as a discrete curricular component. Indeed, it underlies every language lesson, every social studies worksheet, and every math concepts test that we use with our students.

To go to school is to be socialized; to learn content is to be left a more educated person than before; to discuss issues and problems is to learn to respect and value both our individual differences and our collective similarities.

Carry on, good teacher, and after a rest, begin Chapter 7. There is as much ahead of us as there is behind.

CONTINUING QUESTS AND QUESTIONS

1. What happens in our schools, and in our world, when the only types of gifts for which we provide special programs are intellectual and athletic ones? Does the vocationally gifted child or the grandfather who fixed lawnmowers (remember him?) get relegated to "second best status" by default? How can we, as individuals and as a society, channel our efforts toward the protection of those gifts that may not fit into the typical interpretation of *gifted?*

2. Students who become activists in their own education scare people—especially teachers. Visions of 1960s-era sit-ins and protests come into the minds of educators who think that teaching is something best left to educators, and learning is something uniquely applicable to students. How can we convince our colleagues that gifted students have a legitimate right to question the value of their own education? Even if students approach their teachers in a logical, respectful manner, what are the next steps that *we* must take if they hit a brick wall of illogical opposition?

3. As the reality of yet-another teacher shortage looms nearer, individual states are allowing persons not trained as educators to become classroom teachers, especially in the secondary grades. Generally, some form of internship and several education courses are required of these individuals, yet these experiences are often very brief. Investigate your own state's regulations regarding alternative certification programs and, based on your findings, consider the possible impacts—positive and negative— that could result. What advice would you give state legislators as regards the essentials that these newly certified educators must possess?

4. If you were to plan an inservice presentation to your colleagues on the social and emotional components of giftedness, what specific topics and format would you choose? How would you address audience comments or stares that imply, "if they're so smart, why can't they take care of themselves?" In what ways could you link together the cognitive and affective needs of gifted students so that teachers would feel able and willing to address these issues in their interactions with gifted students?

OUT OF THE WAY/OUT OF THIS WORLD
RESOURCES

The Autonomous Learner Model, by George Betts and Jolene Knapp (Autonomous Learner Publishing System, Greeley, CO, 1985).

This book includes a rationale, a program model, and many activities based on the *Autonomous Learner Model*—a junior–senior high school program for gifted students which involves many aspects of guidance and counseling. The activities suggested by the authors can also be used in a "free-standing" manner, as a series of sequential opportunities for gifted students to better understand and use their talents.

Project RISE: A Program for the Vocationally Gifted (sponsored by Careerline Tech Center, Holland, MI, 1989).

Project RISE, a secondary school program for students with such outstanding talents as auto mechanics, child care workers, advertising designers, and industrial electricians, is based on the Betts Autonomous Learner Model (Betts and Knapp, 1985) and contains goals, objectives, and evaluation methods that would match any found in a program for academically gifted students. Based on the belief that "a person's dream is not important because it does or does not happen, but because it could happen" (George Betts), Project RISE is an exemplary plan for designing programs for vocationally gifted adolescents.

Becoming a Master Student, 5th Edition, by David Ellis (College Survival Press, Sioux Falls, SD, 1986).

Written originally as a self-study guide for college students who needed help with time management and organization, this book can be a powerful addition to the library of books for younger gifted students who are having trouble, literally, "getting their acts together." When the issue is *managing* one's talents rather than *locating* them, this is the book to buy. (A teacher's/parent's manual is also available separately.)

Frederick, by Leo Leonni (Farrar, Strauss and Giroux, New York, 1967).

While all the other field mice gather nuts and berries for winter storage, Frederick collects colors, sunshine, and warmth. Other mice call Frederick lazy, and they get very upset that he is not contributing to their winter cupboard. Only when winter drags on and Frederick brings out his "contributions" do the other mice understand the benefit of gathering "nonessentials" such as beauty and rainbows. This is a fine picture book to use with any age group, and the implications are clear as to the author's intended messages.

CHAPTER 7

Underachievement and Nonproduction

The intent of this chapter is to

Review literature and research on what has historically been called "underachievement" in the professional literature

Distinguish between the identification and treatment of two types of low performance by gifted children: underachievement and nonproduction

Present a paradigm of underachievement that is behavioristic in nature

Suggest strategies for reversing patterns of underachieving and nonproductive behaviors through curricular and counseling interventions

MATT

When I met Matt he was a fifth grader and I was a first-year teacher. To Matt, school was *irrelevant,* and he told me so every day by writing that very word—in red crayon—across the top of any worksheet he found either distasteful or unrelated to the needs he perceived he had. More often than not Matt then formed a paper airplane out of his worksheet and sent it nonstop to my desk. Thanks to this behavior, among others, Matt spent much time in the hall, at the principal's office, or (horror of horrors) off-task.

Then, one day, a miracle: Matt got sprayed by a skunk in his back yard—a common occurrence in our northern New England setting. Actually, Matt's spraying was a harbinger of good things to come. You see, skunks emerge from hiber-

Figure 7.1. Illustration by Maureen Canning Marshall. Reprinted by permission of the illustrator.

nation in early spring to seek mates. Also, maple sap starts to flow as the days get warmer but the nights remain cold. Matt, I learned, was a maple sugar farmer, and his unfortunate and smelly meeting took place when, in the process of tapping a tree, he interrupted a couple of amorous skunks. The rest is smelly history.

Matt and I talked (downwind, at his suggestion) and decided that maple sugar farming would become a part of his curriculum. Thus, his math assignments evolved from rote drill to making change and converting quarts to pints. Reading and writing assignments involved completing invoices and making posters and flyers to advertise his product—he made $65.50 after expenses. Matt's social studies assignment became a photo essay of his newly honed skills of maple sugar farming. He even spoke at a Rotary Club luncheon, where, truth be told, he listened to old war stories and contributed a tasteless joke or two of his own to the colorful discussion.

Was Matt an underachiever who suddenly came to appreciate school under the guidance of his skilled first-year teacher? No, I think not. I believe, instead, that Matt was "selective," not "turned off," regarding his education, and his learning never stopped, even during our most difficult moments. Matt needed a reason to learn, a purpose, and he was not finding that purpose in his Scott-Foresman reader. Rather, like Dorothy in the *Wizard of Oz,* Matt found the magic of learning—and living—to be in his own backyard; not in a Kansas cornfield but in a New Hampshire sugar maple grove.

I'm glad he gave me visitation privileges to his learning environment.

UNDERACHIEVEMENT: A MATTER OF DEFINITION

Both early researchers and more recent authors have defined underachievement in terms of a discrepancy between a child's school performance and some ability index, such as an IQ score (Raph, Goldberg, and Passow, 1966; Davis and Rimm, 1989). But such "discrepancy" definitions, though clean-cut and precise, are actually quite limiting; for when underachievement is seen from the vantage point of test scores versus daily performance, it becomes associated exclusively with academic, school-based endeavors. Yet as Maple Sugar Matt clearly has shown us, underachievement in particular subjects is often more a symptom of another concern (in Matt's case, an inappropriate curriculum) than it is a problem in and of itself.

The issue of defining underachievement is important because the term itself—*underachievement*—is a buzzword among educators. The mere mention of the term releases many images (all of them negative) about the child in question. We picture the underachiever as belligerent, difficult to work with, smart but not motivated, or a "poor me" student who could "come up to snuff" but just doesn't want to. These mental *images* can transform quickly into mental *blocks,* as the teacher may begin to resent the apparent unwillingness of the student to perform on cue and may accuse the student of creating problems that could be resolved with a little extra effort.

The bottom line is this: Where underachievement is concerned, the name of the game is *blame.* Everyone involved in the dilemma (including the student) tries to attribute its presence to being someone else's fault and therefore someone else's problem.

A NEW AVENUE OF APPROACH

If underachievement is too limited when defined by a discrepancy formula, then how else might it be described? I'm glad you asked.

There are several useful ways to consider the phenomenon of underachievement without getting overly precise about defining it. A warning though: to some educators, this solution might not be good enough. After all, there is safety in numbers, and in "number crunching," and for folks who feel secure only when a specific, numerical line of demarcation exists, the suggestions I'm about to offer just won't fit the bill. Still, if I had the choice of believing exact numbers that may have no validity or more amorphous indicators of underachievement that get at the heart of the problem, I would choose the latter. I'd rather be imprecise in describing a real problem than fully secure with numbers that skirt around the central issue. Warning having been stated, here is a new way to "define" underachievement.

Underachievement is first and foremost a behavior and, as such, it can change over time. Too often, underachievement is seen as a problem of attitude ("He's just being stubborn; he can do the work") or work habits ("If she wasn't so lazy, she could pass that course"). However, neither habits nor attitude can be modified as directly as can behaviors. Thus, to speak of "underachieving behaviors" is to pinpoint those parts of childrens' lives that they are most able to alter: actions.

Underachievement is content and situation specific. Gifted children who do not succeed in school are often successful in outside activities—sports, social events, after-school jobs, maple sugar farming. Also, even children who do poorly in *most* school subjects often display a talent or interest in at least *one* school subject. Thus, when we label a child as an underachiever, we disregard any positive outcomes or behaviors that child displays. Since it is better to label the student's *behaviors* rather than labeling the student, we should identify a child as "underachieving in math and language arts" rather than as an "underachieving student."

Underachievement is in the eyes of the beholder. For some students (and educators), as long as a passing grade is attained, underachievement does not exist. "After all," this group would say, "a *D* isn't failure!" To others, a grade of *B*+ constitutes underachievement if the student in question was "expected" to get an *A*. Indeed, when it comes to academic grades, we all have different thresholds of pain; thus, the same grade of *B* might elate one student, while a classmate of equal ability might be devastated by such a low grade. Recognizing that the definition of underachievement varies with each person is the first step in understanding this complex phenomenon.

Underachievement is tied intimately to self-concept development. A child who learns to see himself or herself in terms of failure eventually begins to place self-imposed limits on what is possible. Thus, any academic success experiences are written off as "flukes," while low grades or achievement serve to reinforce the negative perceptions one holds about one's self. This self-deprecating attitude often results in such comments as, "Why should I even try? I'm just going to fail anyway" or "Even if I *do* succeed, people'll say it's because I cheated." The end product is a low self-concept, in which the student sees himself or herself as weak in academics. Under this assumption, a child's initiative to change or to accept a challenge is limited, as expressed by an 11-year-old boy who sees the link between feeling and thinking (from Delisle, 1982, p. 17):

> *Teachers told me I was rude,*
> *Bumptious, overbearing, shrewd.*
> *Some of the things they said were crude*
> *I couldn't understand.*

And so I built myself a wall,
Strong, solid, ten feet tall.
With bricks you couldn't see at all.
So I couldn't understand.

Underachievement implies that adults disapprove of a child's behavior.
Underachievement is a problem for children because it is recognized as
such by adults. Likewise, students who are labeled as "underachievers"
suffer the pangs of knowing that they are disappointing significant
others—parents and teachers. Thus burdened, these children learn to
assess their abilities relative to what they *have not* accomplished instead
of what they are capable of doing (Bloom, 1977). Similar to the frustration felt when attempting to deepen a hole in wet sand, the underachiever
sees each victory squelched by the collapse of other unmet goals.

Underachievement is a learned set of behaviors. Underachievement can be
learned by gifted students for whom school and education are in separate
spheres. In two national studies of education, published a decade apart,
criticism was leveled at curricula that are designed strictly by grade-level
norms with little regard for individual rates of learning. "The boredom
that results from discrepancies between the child's knowledge and the
school's offerings leads to underachievement and behavior disorders affecting self and others" (Marland, 1972, p. 25). And, in 1983, the National Commission on Excellence in Education published *A Nation at
Risk,* the first of many national critiques of the practice of education in
America. Speaking specifically to the education of gifted students, the
commission concluded:

"Over half the population of gifted students do not match their tested ability
with comparable achievement in school." (p. 8)

Only 31 percent of high school graduates complete intermediate algebra; 13
percent complete French I; and calculus classes, though available in 60
percent of US high schools, are completed by only 6 percent of the students
(pp. 18–19).

Textbooks are too easy for able students, and rigorous texts remain unavailable because of the "thin market" for sales that is perceived by publishers (p.
28).

The ultimate irony is that gifted children, whose education is unchallenging, have come to be perceived as handicapped, emotionally incapa-
ble (in some cases) of performing to their inherent potential.

Too often, the name of the game is blame; but before we place too much
of it on the shoulders of the students themselves, it is best to look also at the
curriculum with which they are presented. Perhaps, in the final analysis,
underachievement is *learned* because it is *taught* so well, and so often.

MORE CLOUD COVER:
THE DIFFERENCE BETWEEN
UNDERACHIEVEMENT AND NONPRODUCTION

As discussed previously, the problem of underachievement begins with its definition; there is no consensus regarding an overall concept of what underachievement actually is, where it starts, and at which point the metamorphosis to achievement occurs. Another stumbling block is this: Any child who is not working up to potential—however that potential is defined—can be dubbed an underachiever. Too seldom, though, do the people who attach that label actually consider the root cause—the source—of the problem. They see the *result*—the lack of achievement—and scurry to label the student as something she or he may not be. In many cases, the child in question is not an *underachiever* but is, instead, a *nonproducer;* the differences in etiology, treatment, and rate of success in reversing the patterns are subtle to the untrained eye, but obvious to the careful observer.

Let's examine two case studies, Stephanie and Mark, to pinpoint the distinctions between underachievement and nonproduction.

Stephanie is a fifth grader whose report card comments read like a list of missed opportunities: "Stephanie is bright, but seems insecure about her ability to do well"; "Stephanie would be more successful in school if she only gave herself a chance"; "Stephanie's perfectionism prevents her from pursuing new topics or projects." In class, Stephanie seldom causes trouble—in fact, you hardly know she's there. She pursues her work with caution, and when her teacher hands her an assignment, Stephanie's out-loud comment is "this is too hard for a stupid-head like me." Often, she is her own worst enemy, for when she receives a high grade on a project she attributes it to "being lucky," and when she doesn't do well, she internalizes the failure and calls herself "dumb." Socially Stephanie fits in with one or two friends who she has had since first grade, but most students don't know her well; it's not that she's totally withdrawn, but she is—well—very quiet. Stephanie would like to do better in school, but she claims she can't. She says that she's not as smart as everyone says anyway, and she can prove it by showing you all her low grade and bad papers. To the *casual* observer, Stephanie is a nice, quiet girl who just lacks confidence. To the *careful* observer, Stephanie is a sad girl who seems to have little hope of ever being anything more than she is right now: self-critical, self-deprecating, and unable to chart her own course, socially or academically.

Mark is a student most teachers hear about before they ever meet him. This reputation precedes him because Mark is the source of constant teacher-lounge banter: "You've got to approach him just so, or else he'll walk all over you"; "He's a smart kid, and he knows it—*that's* his biggest problem"; "He can do great work one day and no work the next." In class, Mark's performance and behavior are sporadic. On some days he is the most animated discussant in a review of current world events. Other days, he just sits there completing seatwork when he feels like it, and turning in homework when the mood strikes him to do so. Mark dislikes "busy work" and teachers who assign it, and although he can and does succeed on projects that pique his interests, he often concentrates solely on this work to the exclusion of other tasks. This, of course, makes it difficult for teachers to assign grades; they *know* that Mark understands the concepts of his lessons, but if he refuses to turn in all of his required work, how can they possibly reward him with high grades? It wouldn't be fair. Socially, Mark has few problems and some students even see him as a leader—a rebel with a cause, an agent with a mission: to take the best from school and leave the rest behind. Most everyone is frustrated with Mark's sporadic performance, except for one person: Mark. He *does* know he's smart and he realizes, too, that if he "played the game by the rules," he could be a straight-A student. Somehow, though, getting high grades isn't necessarily one of Mark's personal goals; he's into learning, but it doesn't naturally follow that school is the place where lots of learning occurs. To the *casual* observer, Mark is rebelling for the sake of rebelling, and if he isn't willing to change his attitude then "he can just sit there and get Fs." To the *careful* observer, Mark is a selective consumer of education. He knows what he knows, and he doesn't want to have to keep proving it through homework and "dumb" assignments that do little more than serve as time fillers. Mark could improve his social performance markedly and almost overnight: He knows what the hoops are, but he's just not willing to jump through them.

If you were to compare the report card *grades* of Stephanie and Mark, the similarities would outweigh the distinctions. If you were to compare their report card *comments,* you would find teachers have very different impressions of these two underachievers. In fact, Mark *is not* an underachiever, despite grades that indicate otherwise. He *is* however, *nonproductive:* a student very much in touch with both himself and the world of learning but unwilling to do much of his assigned work. Stephanie *does* display underachieving behaviors. She is a lost soul in the academic miasma called school, who desperately wants to do better—and feel better—but is at a loss as to how she might begin to do either.

NONPRODUCERS VERSUS UNDERACHIEVERS: A COMPARISON

The similarities and distinctions between students with underachieving and nonproductive behaviors are presented in Table 7.1.

As is true with any such side-by-side comparison, it must be remembered that each trait or behavior listed is etched in soap, not stone. That is, a particular student may seem to fit one pattern more than another, but it is still likely that some of the items listed under that pattern will not apply. Table 7-1 is provided more as guidance than gospel and should, therefore, be regarded

TABLE 7.1. NONPRODUCERS VERSUS UNDERACHIEVERS: A CASE OF COMPARING ACADEMIC APPLES AND ORANGES

Nonproducers	Underachievers
Mentally healthy	Psychologically at risk
Can explain both the problem and possible solutions	Does not understand causes or cures
Independent and proactive	Dependent and reactive
Tends to rebel	Tends to withdraw
Sees teachers as adversaries; contentious	Respects or fears authority figures
Counseling needs minimal	Strong counseling program needed
Requires little structure; needs "breathing room"	Needs both structure and imposed limits
Performance varies relative to teacher and/or content	Performance uniformly weak
Can be dealt with within school resources	Requires family intervention
Change may occur "overnight"	Change is long term
Frequently satisfied with accomplishments	Often perfectionistic
Sees self as academically able	Poor academic self-concept

Commonalities
Socialization may be impaired with classmates
Prefers "family" versus "factory" classroom atmosphere
Needs to change both behaviors and attitudes

more as relative than absolute. Nonetheless, the overall idea that some so-called underachievers are actually nonproducers in disguise seems legitimate and is worth exploring further.

For example, in a review of 30 years of research studies on underachievement (1931 to 1961), Raph and Tannenbaum (1961) report that the findings of the 90+ empirical studies they analyzed did not support any one unified explanation of the phenomenon of underachievement. Asbury (1974) and Ziv (1977) concur with this finding that no specific psychosocial factors seem consistently associated with underachievement.

What is the problem here? How can decades of research show so little direction toward understanding a phenomenon that everyone agrees does exist? It is my contention that a major part of the conundrum exists because of the unresolved issues previously described in this chapter: the unfocused definitions of underachievement and the lack of recognition of the distinctions between underachievement and nonproduction. Rimm (1986), in her extensive review of underachievement as a multifaceted set of behaviors, alludes to this distinction between underachievers and nonproducers, though she does not use those exact terms. Rather, she creates caricatures of specific (but fictional) children such as "Manipulative Mary," "Rebellious Rebecca," "Taunted Terrence," and "Torn Tommy." The attribute that distinguishes the varieties of underachievement within these children is their unique levels of *dependence* and *dominance*. Seen from another vantage point, these children could represent the characteristics of underachievers versus those of nonproducers—same tune, different lyrics. Rimm goes on to explain the circumstances and environments that prompt the emergence of the "Depressed Donnas" and "Dramatic Dicks" of the world, including school climate, inflexible and competitive classrooms, negative expectations, and an unrewarding curriculum (Davis and Rimm, 1989).

In her review of 21 research studies related to underachievement, Clark (1988) arrives at 21 characteristics of children with underachieving behaviors. Some of these characteristics in Table 7.2 show a resemblance to the items previously listed in Table 7.1—with one big and important exception: Clark's list does not differentiate between those that are behaviors (for example, items 4, 7, 8, and 10) and those that are less visible, yet still debilitating (for example, items 2, 3, 11, and 14).

It seems important at this point in our knowledge (or lack thereof) about the issue of underachieving behaviors to take a few steps back before we try to take any more steps forward. That is, before we begin to offer solutions to reverse the patterns of underachievement, educators need to reexamine—for the umpteenth time—what they mean by that term. It is my suggestion, based on both my clinical experiences as a teacher and counselor and my review of pertinent research, that underachievement be subdivided as described in Table 7-1. Once it is acknowledged that some so-called underachievers have nearly total control of their academic lives but merely *choose not* to perform, while others *could not* change their behaviors because of a lack of personal power or inner resources, then the general strategies that are used to address the specific behaviors will become more on-target and focused.

When approaching any problem, there are two general lines of attack: the "shotgun" approach, where strategies are applied willy-nilly in hopes that something will hit its target, and the "spotlight" approach, where a sharp, precise beam is focused on a specific situation or problem. In issues as complex as underachievement and nonproduction, time and effort spent in locating the target will result ultimately in more effective and efficient treatment strategies.

As a final comparison between underachievement and nonproduction, let me offer two analogies. The child who chooses not to perform up to academic snuff—the nonproducer—reminds me of the adage "you can lead a horse to water but you can't make him drink." In the case of nonproduction, just a little editorial license is needed to apply this proverb to such a case: "You can lead a child to knowledge but you can't make him think."

On the other hand, the child with underachieving behaviors, who has little control over or understanding of his or her depressed performance, is reminiscent of Narcissus, the Greek mythological character who, upon seeing

TABLE 7.2. CHARACTERISTICS OF UNDERACHIEVERS GLEANED FROM RESEARCH STUDIES, 1947–1980

1. A finding repeated in most studies is the low self-concept of underachievers. They are negative in their evaluations of themselves. Their feelings of inferiority may be demonstrated by distrust, indifference, lack of concern, and even hostility toward others. They believe no one likes them.
2. They often feel rejected by their family; they feel that their parents are dissatisfied with them.
3. Because of a feeling of helplessness, they may take no responsibility for their actions, externalizing conflict and problems.
4. They may show marked hostility toward adult authority figures and general distrust of adults.
5. They may have an autonomous focus, resistant to influence from teacher or parent.
6. They may feel victimized.
7. They often do not like school or their teachers and choose companions who also have negative attitudes toward school.
8. They may seem rebellious.
9. Weak motivation for academic achievement has been noted, and they may lack academic skills.
10. They tend to have poor study habits, do less homework, frequently nap when trying to study, and leave more of their work incomplete.
11. They are less intellectually adaptive.
12. They are less persistent, less assertive, and show high levels of withdrawal in classroom situations.
13. They hold lower leadership status and are less popular with their peers.
14. They are often less mature than achievers (e.g., lack self-discipline, procrastinate, show unwillingness to complete tasks deemed unpleasant, have high distractibility, act highly impulsively, and are unwilling to face unpleasant realities).
15. They often show poor personal adjustment and express feelings of being restricted in their actions.
16. They may not have any hobbies, interests, or activities that could occupy their spare time.
17. They are often test phobic and have poor test results.
18. They tend to have lower aspirations than achievers and do not have a clear idea of vocational goals.
19. They are not able to think of or plan future goals.
20. They tend to state their goals very late and often choose goals that are not in line with their major interests or abilities. Often the goals they adopt have been set for them.
21. In choosing a career, they show preferences for manual activities, business, sales occupations, or anything with a strong persuasive trend, over more socially concerned or professional occupations.

Source: Reprinted with permission of Merrill, an imprint of Macmillan Publishing Company, from *Growing Up Gifted: Developing the Potential of Children at Home and at School,* 3e by Barbara Clark. Copyright © 1988 by Merrill Publishing Company.

his reflection in a pond, pined away for the lovely creature he saw. In his case, Narcissus was longing for something that he already had, so his was not a problem of attainment, but of realization. And just as Narcissus was eventually transformed into a beautiful flower, so might the child with underachieving behaviors come into full bloom, given the proper mix of support and nurturance.

STRATEGIES TO REVERSE NONPRODUCTION AND UNDERACHIEVEMENT

Since both underachievement and nonproduction are noted especially in academic situations, it makes sense to look toward the roles played by schools in the treatment of these problems. This is not meant to either deny or downplay the important influences of the family (more on that in Chapter 10), but rather to focus attention on the situations and structure most amenable to change by educators: school.

Although many strategies work better with nonproductive behaviors than they do with underachieving behaviors—and vice versa—there are some common denominators that apply to both groups. Classified into three clusters by Whitmore (1980), these collective forms of reinforcement are the following:

1. *Supportive strategies:* These "affirm the worth of the child in the classroom and convey the promise of greater potential and success yet to be discovered and enjoyed." (p. 256)
2. *Intrinsic strategies:* These are "designed to develop intrinsic achievement motivation through the child's discovery of rewards available . . . as a result of efforts to learn, achieve, and contribute to the group." (p. 265)
3. *Remedial strategies:* These are "employed to improve the student's academic performance in an area of learning in which (s)he has evidenced difficulty learning, has experienced a sense of failure, and has become unmotivated to engage in learning tasks." (p. 271)

These three families of strategies all focus around one central theme: putting the child back in charge of his or her own education. Only when students feel academically capable and internally motivated to learn will school success occur. And, since success is more likely to breed additional success, the child who learns early on that he or she has a good degree of power in determining learning outcomes will be more ready to absorb knowledge independent of adult supervision once the structured parameters of school are in the past.

To explain the distinctions between the use of Whitmore's strategies with nonproductive and with underachieving behaviors, let's return to two students you have already met: Mark and Stephanie.

MARK

Some people would surmise that Mark doesn't need much in the line of supportive strategies—"Surely, his cockiness is a sign of a strong self-concept," they'd say. But, just as looks can be deceiving, so can bravado: Mark's rebellious attitude toward authority may be a well-disguised "front" to cover for the inadequacies he fears he might have. Mark probably does need support—who doesn't?—to show him that it is okay to show a vulnerability; a need for others to like and accept him for himself, not for someone he is trying to be. Therefore, a supportive teacher would acknowledge and thank Mark whenever he showed a glimmer of cooperation or whenever his independence was demonstrated in a positive or helpful way.

Intrinsically, Mark already knows that he is the "real teacher" in the sense of controlling when and if he learns, and he needs to be rewarded for these insights. At the same time, Mark and his teacher need to come up with some type of "pact" that agrees to the following accord: As long as Mark learns what he *needs* to learn (by the teacher's standards) via his own methods, the teacher will not interfere. However, if Mark's method falls short, or he is at a loss as to how to proceed, then his teacher will intervene on Mark's behalf—by mutual consent.

Mark may have few areas in need of remediation, but if they do exist, they should be approached in an up-front manner by his teacher: "I *know* you don't like to write notecards before doing a report, but I need to see one set from you just so I know you have that skill—then, I'm off your back." This gives Mark a chance to demonstrate a skill he says he has, and it satisfies his teacher's need to know how close Mark's perception is to reality.

STEPHANIE

One minute, one hour, one day at a time, Stephanie needs to hear that she is a valuable person, regardless of the grades she attains. Comments such as "It's so special to have you in class, Stephanie. When you smile it lights up the whole room!" need to be interspersed with accolades for Stephanie's attempts (not necessarily successes) at academics: "I saw you practicing spelling with Julie—thank you for helping her out." In subtle and obvious ways (for example, words *and* smiles), in both one-on-one and in group settings, Stephanie needs to be reminded that she is able, valuable, and responsible.

Intrinsically, Stephanie's need is to feel that she is an active participant *in* rather than a passive recipient *of* her education. When she does a good job on a project or paper, the teacher should ask Stephanie how and why she thinks she succeeded. If Stephanie claims it was due to luck or fate, a few words of rebuttal will help: "I bet you studied—even a little" or "The way you put this report together shows me that you have fine organizational skills." The more specific the comments, the better, as it is harder to deny direct statements than it is to dismiss as trivial a general "Good job, Stephanie!"

If there is any remediation to be done, Stephanie needs to know that it is okay to be better at some things than others. The catch phrase to apply to Stephanie should be "Less than perfection is more than acceptable." So, should she need help with handwriting, research skills, or any other area related to school success, Stephanie needs to be told that even she—a gifted child—isn't expected to know everything.

Stephanie cares about and respects school a great deal—it is the prime source of her attitudes toward herself and learning. Knowing this, the concerned teacher will take great care in acknowledging Stephanie's efforts and will support her both directly (through words) and indirectly (through gestures) so that Stephanie's attempts to succeed are noted as the brave efforts they certainly are.

Specific distinctions in using supportive, intrinsic, and remedial strategies to address nonproductive and underachieving behaviors are noted in Table 7-3. As this chart shows, the strategies suggested for use in reversing nonproductive behaviors take on a different tenor than those to be used in addressing

TABLE 7.3. STRATEGIES TO IMPROVE ACADEMIC PERFORMANCE

	Nonproductive Behaviors	Underachieving Behaviors
Supportive Strategies	Eliminating work already mastered Allowing independent study on topics of personal interest Nonauthoritarian atmosphere Permitting students to prove competence via multiple methods Teach through problem-solving techniques over rote drill	Daily class meetings to discuss student concerns Directive atmosphere, to show the student that the teacher is in charge and is competent Daily, written contracts of work to be completed Free time scheduled each day, to show importance of relaxation and free choice
Intrinsic Strategies	Students help determine class rules Assigning specific responsibilities for classroom maintenance or management Teacher practices reflective listening—comments to students serve to clarify statements, not evaluate them Students set daily goals, with approval of teacher	Daily review of new attempts and small successes, done individually Allow students to evaluate work prior to the teacher assigning a grade Frequent and positive contact with family regarding child's progress Verbal rewards for any self-initiating behaviors
Remedial Strategies	Self-selected, weekly goals for improvement determined between student and teacher Private instruction in areas of weakness Use of humor and personal example to approach areas of academic weakness Familiarize students with learning styles research and its personal implications for classroom performance	Programmed instruction materials, where students grade their own papers immediately on completion Peer tutoring of younger students in areas of strength Small group instruction in common areas of weakness (e.g., spelling, sequencing, phonics) Encourage students to work on projects which do not involve a grade or other external evaluation

underachieving behaviors. In both instances, the teacher is a supportive partner in the learning process, yet he or she is more directive, more in control, when working with students who underachieve. When nonproductive behaviors among students are addressed, the teacher adopts a more "laid back, how-can-I-help-you-learn-best?" approach. Under both circumstances, the teacher is fully in charge of the events transpiring in the classroom and the conditions under which learning is most likely to occur for specific, individual students. However, the approaches used to attain success give new meaning to the phrase "the ends must justify the means." In this case, they do, as students who may appear on first glance to be similar because of the commonality of their poor academic performance are, in fact, very different from each other. Thus, the strategies used, the demeanor displayed, and the degree of autonomy provided by the teacher may (and should!) differ considerably from student to student.

This idea of individualizing curriculum and instruction for different students is hardly revolutionary. Even the most staunch traditionalists would agree that since children learn at different rates, some degree of consideration must be given to the possibility that what works for one pupil will score a big, fat zero with another child. What *is* revolutionary—or at least novel—is that nothing in the research literature—at least, nothing *I* could find—suggests treating low-achieving gifted students differently from high-achieving gifted students based on variances in their *ability* and *willingness* to change, their degree of *dependence* versus *autonomy,* and their attitudes toward the *school environment* and the *professionals who teach and guide them.* Yet these very factors—invisible variables—may help to explain why the overall problem of academic underachievement has vexed parents, educators, and researchers ever since the term itself was coined. If you recall, at the beginning of this chapter, the work of Abraham Tannenbaum was cited; one can almost see the disappointment in the words he used to summarize the three decades of research on underachievement: "Added together, the studies yield a tangle of conclusions that are more puzzling than revealing" (Tannenbaum, 1983, p. 210). There is no way a phenomenon such as underachievement—and its reversal—could be that elusive for so long except for one reason: The term itself was (and is) too ill-defined. Even in a more recent study, the authors define *underachievement* as the bottom quartile of achievement test scores for participants in two school districts' program for gifted students (Laffoon, Jenkins-Friedman, and Tollefson, 1989). This translates into a mean standardized achievement test score of 87th percentile. Thus defined, Laffoon, Jenkins-Friedman, and Tollefson label these students as *relative underachievers*—a term that might work in a research study, but bears little resemblance to what *most* of us would consider a threshold of underachievement in a real classroom. (And, to boot, these researchers labeled this group as underachievers with no regard to the students' daily academic performance—curious . . . erroneous, but curious.) Alas, this study goes on, as do others before it, providing prescriptions and proscriptions that, in the end, do little more than contribute to an already large pile of already suspect information.

Dowdall and Colangelo (1982), in their review of research on underachieving gifted students, conclude that "the inescapable result in definitions is of a magnitude that makes the concept of underachieving gifted (students) almost meaningless" (p. 179). With a single exception—Whitmore's analysis of underachievers based on years of classroom intervention and research—it is my belief that it might be best to throw out what we think we know and begin again with a *tabula rasa*, a clear slate, on which we might draw conclusions based on new research, new beginnings, and a new set of guidelines regarding *underachievement*.

A clear distinction must be made between underachievement and nonproduction, as explained in this chapter.

Studies must look at student behaviors over a span of time, not merely over one school term or one testing situation.

Underachievement must be defined specifically and painstakingly by individual researchers, so that everyone and his brother will not generalize a study's findings to other groups of similarily labeled (yet very different) students.

You, dear readers, forge ahead with strategies that work for the particular students in your class whose behaviors are not up to snuff, be they underachieving behaviors or nonproductive behaviors (which, by now, you can distinguish quite clearly).

CONCLUSION

Perhaps you were hoping for a nice, tight definition of underachievement to end this chapter.

Not a chance.

Underachievement and nonproduction are constructs that take on personal interpretations—always. Like other collective nouns—justice, beauty, respect—the definition of *underachievement* and *nonproduction* cannot be fully appreciated on paper. Like beauty, they are in the eye of the beholder; like justice, they seem to vary depending on the surrounding circumstances; and like respect, you know it when it's there, though explaining exactly what makes it so remains elusive.

Still, having difficulty *defining* beauty does not diminish our enjoyment of seeing it in a painting, a person, or a relationship. And not being able to accurately pinpoint what we mean by justice in no way keeps us from interpreting the latest Supreme Court decision.

So must it be with *underachievement* and *nonproduction*. For even if I cannot define them each to *my* own and *your* own satisfaction, that does not diminish my responsibility to Matt, whose passion to make maple sugar is surpassed only by his ability to do so, or to any other student who "does not go to school well" and is, therefore, labeled as something that no one wants to be.

CONTINUING QUESTS AND QUESTIONS

1. Consider, in your own life, those occasions in which you did not perform up to the standards that either you or others expected. Analyze the conditions under which this low achievement occurred—was it a new task or one with which you were familiar already? Was the task completed (or attempted) under competitive or noncompetitive conditions? At which point did you realize that the level of performance you hoped to attain would not be reached, and what happened to your desire to continue with the task beyond this realization? After you have critiqued this incident, write down your thoughts so that you might be able to share them with other persons—colleagues or students—who may be experiencing their own bout with low performance.

2. For many gifted students, a certain level of classroom performance is expected to be maintained in order to receive program services. For example, a gifted elementary student might be required to keep up with regular assignments in order to be eligible for inclusion in the resource room designated for the program for gifted students. Likewise, a high school student might be expected to maintain a *B* average in order to take advanced-level courses. What are your views on policies such as these, and what potential impacts could they have on students with nonproductive or underachieving behaviors? If you disagree with such achievement-based policies, what alternatives can you suggest that would satisfy both the students' high abilities and the mainstream teachers' wish to see students maintain at least minimal performance standards?

3. What types of educational interventions should be used with children who underachieve or underproduce? Given that these two groups are very dissimilar in their outlook towards self, school, and teachers, would it be advantageous to combine such students into the same class? Also, whatever educational placements or strategies you would suggest, how would you go about instilling self-confidence in these students? Last, in a regular classroom setting, how could you address the needs of these students without making it appear to other *achieving* students that you are rewarding poor work habits and school attitude?

4. How would you convince a caring but frustrated colleague that the nonproducing student is not totally at fault for his or her low performance or output? In a world that is filled with either/or scenarios ("Either she does the work or she flunks. Period."), how can we work together toward addressing the issues raised in this chapter? What emotional barriers may *educators* have to get beyond before real changes are made in changing students' outlooks and/or performances?

OUT OF THE WAY/OUT OF THIS WORLD RESOURCES

Get Off My Brain: A Survival Guide for Lazy Students, by Randall McCutcheon (Free Spirit Publishing, Minneapolis, MN, 1985).

Although I'm a bit "put off" by this book's title—"lazy students" exist in the eye of the beholder—the content of this book would be very helpful for highly able students whose school experiences have been less than stellar. Humorous and insightful, *Get Off My Brain* gives specific and usable advice.

The Gifted in Socio-educational Perspective, by T. Ernest Newland (Prentice-Hall, Englewood Cliffs, NJ, 1976).

Out of print, yet available in libraries, this text is among the best ever written in education for gifted students in terms of the social/emotional needs of this population. Further, the author takes a no-nonsense approach to psychological and philosophical issues related to gifted education and highlights the still-existing gaps between theory and practice.

Invitational Learning for Counseling and Development, by William W. Purkey and John J. Schmidt (ERIC/CAPS, University of Michigan, Ann Arbor, MI, 1986).

Similar to Purkey's other books, but focusing specifically on the field of counseling, the authors give examples of invitational learning and its positive effects in seven different school settings.

Internships 1990, by Brian Ringsley (Writer's Digest Books, Cincinnati, OH, 1990).

This book, issued annually and usually by a new editor each year, highlights over 35,000 school-year and summer experiences that could benefit gifted adolescents and adults. If you work (or live) with a student who "underachieves" only in school, this book will provide internship opportunities, both paid and unpaid, in business, conservation, human services, and other endeavors.

CHAPTER 8

Specific Concerns of Gifted Adolescents

The intent of this chapter is to

Propose to you that adolescence is a complex, though not necessarily turbulent, developmental period

Cite several concerns that confront gifted adolescents at an earlier time and/or at a more emotionally intense level than is typically expected

Propose six "realities" which, when understood by gifted adolescents and the adults who care for them, can result in a smoother transition into young adulthood

Suggest specific activities and materials that can be useful in working with gifted adolescents who are concerned about their own social and emotional growth

MY TEACHERS

My students (my teachers),
I learn so much
from you,
Things of great value, which touch
my heart.

You, the best hope for a wounded world
(my generation was once the best hope)
perhaps together . . .

You, with your social consciousness
and your heart on your sleeve,
Idealism over cynicism
Vulnerability and strength
Gentle wit, laughter, joy.

In your wildest dreams you do not
Imagine your great worth—
unlimited potential—

So, together now,
let us agree to learn.
Back to the basics:
Such things as:

> *Not to make an issue of the trivial.*
> *Never to trivialize the real issues.*
> *To push back further and further*
> *the limits of what we perceive as possible.*
> *To reach out to all, in love,*
> *To accept responsibility for our own life.*
> *To find joy in the moment.*

I have only this one time in this life
to be "middle-aged" an "authority figure"
with all its advantages and disappointments.
Just as you have only this time to be
A teenager.
Life is not a dress rehearsal.
But by sharing our lives a little,
we can peek through each other's perspectives
and teach and learn.

For this I thank you,
My students (my teachers).

Rita Sellers Hoffman
Mountain Home, Idaho

FIFTEEN-LOVE

If life was simple, there would be some unassailable groundrules, such as "teachers educate, students learn." However, nothing important is ever absolute, and little that is relevant gets its meaning from dogma. Instead, the pesky gray areas—the "what ifs?" the "has anyone ever considereds?"—are the incubators of knowledge and personal growth, for both students and teachers.

Students and teachers: Which is which when? Who does what to whom? As expressed so eloquently in the poem that opens this chapter, the roles we assume are not always the ones to which we have been assigned. Children and teens, if we allow them the chance, can become our guides as surely as we can become their mentors. Call it what you will—"give and take," "repartee"— students and their teachers are involved in an educational tennis match where, at different times, each serves the other. Unlike tennis, though, both parties can score simultaneously; both can serve and return "aces" to the other, gaining important points on the scoreboard of life.

Adolescents—teens and preteens—are probably more able than younger children to teach life's lessons to adults. It is not that their 7-year-old counterparts cannot perform the function of "teacher"; rather, adolescents are simply more consciously aware of their influence than are younger children. In effect, adults must constantly seek out the nuggets of knowledge these innocents (arbitrarily, below age 10) provide through their words or deeds. On the other hand, adolescents inform us openly of talents and insights they possess. In fact, instead of being actively alert for signs of the knowledge adolescents hold, adults *may* need to be reminded to *overlook* certain overt behaviors (which might be read as arrogance or pomposity) that tend to distort or disguise the acuity, the insight, the seasoned judgment that is within the repertoire of many adolescents.

So, dear reader, as you peruse this chapter, keep your mind open to the possibility that adolescence is more than a series of random changes and traumatic stopping points on the route between childhood and adult maturity. In some ways, adolescence is a time filled with constancy and assurance; a time that is volatile only when the adults "in charge" expect it to be so.

ADOLESCENCE: A BRIEF HISTORY

If popular movies and television shows were our sole indicators, most people would agree that adolescence is a turbulent developmental period. But as a Yiddish proverb reminds us, " 'For example' is not proof."

Early adolescence (ages 11 to 15) is generally accompanied by a gradual but *decreasing* dependency on parents and other adults. Now, these youngsters seek to define themselves in relation to a new set of standards: one imposed by a peer group. Later adolescence (ages 16 to 22) is frequently accompanied by a gradual but ever-*increasing* reaffiliation with the adult world. As the external trappings of societal independence are made legal and available—for example, the license to drive, the privilege to vote, the right to drink alcohol, the opportunity for employment—older adolescents often become *a part of* an adult culture which, several years prior, they had been trying to be *apart from*.

Over the course of this decade-plus of adolescence, some potential dilemmas accompany the physical, social, emotional, and intellectual changes that are occurring in these young people (Montemayor, 1984). The key word here in discussing particular dilemmas is *potential,* for nowhere is it written that adolescence *must* be a time of rebellion, nonconformity, and blatant rejection of anything that even bears a tinge of acceptability by adults. Peter Blos (1979), a neo-Freudian psychiatrist, proposed that the so-called rebellious behaviors noted in adolescence are actually oriented toward the attainment of goals appropriate for this developmental period. These goals, highlighted by Buescher (1986) and reproduced in the following list, may help to explain how some adolescent behaviors that might seem irrational from an adult perspective are actually very much in concert with the adolescent's search for self-identity.

Prominent Needs of Most Adolescents[1]

1. Opportunities to experience real independence
2. Concrete experiences of successful self-direction
3. A variety of adult and leadership models to emulate
4. Ability to cope while building real-life skills
5. Successful avenues for defining oneself beyond the options suggested by adults
6. A desire to be taken seriously by peers and adults
7. Predictable space where one can safely explore acceptance and rejection by peers
8. A factual basis for understanding the process of adolescence

Thus, when a 15-year-old ("who should know better") stays out past curfew and gets punished for doing so, she or he may retort, "You always tell me I'm responsible enough to take care of myself and *now* you treat me like a baby." This push–pull bind that accompanies a developmental stage as transitional as is adolescence may appear to be full of contradictions to teenagers, especially intellectually capable ones. Searching for a link, a congruency between word and deed, gifted adolescents who "rebel" against adult authority may be doing so out of a quest for justice and equity, not merely to see how quickly they can turn their parents' hair prematurely gray.

Not always, of course: Some talented adolescents *do* rebel for no reason that either they or we can explain. Still, the likelihood that "rebellious" behaviors exist (as does giftedness itself and underachievement) in the eyes of the beholder is definitely within the realms of both reason and possibility.

Csikszentmihalyi and Larson (1984), in their study of adolescence, pose the following view: "A community needs people who are self-confident, motivated to achieve yet respectful of others, who are adaptable, original, and at peace with their own selves, more than it needs students who score high on

---

[1] From "Prominent Needs of Most Adolescents," adapted from E. Williams (1978) appearing in T. Buescher *Understanding Gifted and Talented Adolescents.* Evanston, IL: Center for Talent Development, Northwestern University. Reprinted by permission.

tests" (p. 199). Pie-in-the-sky? Perhaps not *that* extreme, but certainly this goal cited is one that is easier said than done; more readily written than carried through. Piechowski (1989), in reacting to Csikszentmihalyi and Larson, questions how such confidence and composure can exist within the mind of intelligent, insightful adolescents: "Is it possible to be original, adaptable, and at peace with oneself, yet at the same time be a sensitive barometer of the undercurrents, conflicts, future trends, and tensions in society? Hardly" (p. 87). This tension between "what is" and "what should be" is one factor that could play an important role in the gifted adolescent's willingness to accept a system, a world society, that seems inherently contradictory. The intensity with which able adolescents *notice* and *judge* life's absurdities and inconsistencies also helps determmine the degree to which they are willing to address societal dilemmas face-front; to try to make changes that bring the "real" even a little closer to the "ideal."

As cited throughout this text, the ability to perform well on school-based tasks is a very different gift from being able to see the possibilities of a world that is cohesive and free from strife. Peck and Havighurst (1960) describe the development of the former in their case study of Ralph, an adolescent whose intelligence is in the superior range, but whose vision of the world is one of acceptance. Ralph's rational–altruistic stance helps him to assess each new action and its effects realistically (rational) while being aware of and interested in the welfare of others (altruistic). For example, when asked what he would do if his family could not support him financially, Ralph responded, "Why, I'd get a job, I expect, and help the folks out till things got better" (p. 74). This altruistic response was given by only one out of ten young people of Ralph's age. Still, there remains a gnawing suspicion that Ralph will follow the existing system rather than trying to change it; his thirst for knowledge and equity is limited, respectively, to his own backyard and his small community of friends. He has, according to Peck and Havighurst, a "strongly practical, realistic outlook, which pervades even his mild fantasy. When he daydreams, it is almost always about real problems" (1960, p. 75).

Arthur, on the other hand, is highly intelligent and perceptive, but is also a pain in the neck. Verbally abusive as a child, Arthur is described by Peck and Havighurst as hostile, emotionally immature, poorly socialized, and highly unstable. The character type to which he is assigned says it all: amoral. Yet as much as Arthur's behaviors can be criticized as immature (he would often tell relatives who gave him presents that they did so only because it was Christmas, not because they cared for him), his insights into the human condition, as described by Peck and Havighurst, cannot be so labeled. For example, although Arthur was a difficult student to have in class, Arthur was especially sensitive toward those who were rejected (as he was) by classmates, parents, or teachers. Arthur had "begun to appreciate, just a little, the virtues of honesty and kindness [even though] he now receives little of them. He now is more actively kind . . . to younger children, with whom he identifies and feels safe" (Peck and Havighurst, 1960, p. 46). Perhaps in a family structure less chaotic than his, Arthur might have developed his potential to see inequities and to then act upon them in socially responsible ways.

Ralph and Arthur: two sides of a very odd coin. Both capable of more, yet both in need of adult guidance so as to be able to fulfill some of their unrealized potential.

. . . Which, as a lead-in to the next section, isn't all that bad.

ADOLESCENCE: GROWTH THROUGH DEPENDENCE

Few of us readily admit our dependency on others. We like to see ourselves as entities, complete and fulfilled. Sure, we acknowledge the roles people have played in our personal development—family, friends, colleagues—but we generally recognize these contributions retroactively: "I'm the person I am today because of so many who have helped me in the past." Rarely, though (except at testimonials where we are lauded publicly for our accomplishments), do we admit our dependency as existing in the present tense. We prefer to think we can function on our own; that we are strong enough to fend for ourselves. External support was something we needed earlier, before, or "way back when." How myopic we can be when we view our own *present* stage of development.

Adolescents, by definition, are undergoing a process of intense and rapid change (*adolescere,* the Latin root word, translates into "to grow up"). Yet like their adults role models, they often don an air of bravado when it comes to dependency. "I'm an individual," they think. Or, "I'm not like those other guys—*I* know who I am!" Cloaked in this apparently protective shell, they may think themselves immune to trauma, disappointment, or confusion. Yet just as a nylon windbreaker is only effective on days when you need it least, the thin coverup of independence is sapped of its strength during a real downpour of fear or contradiction.

The adult role in helping adolescents who may not believe they require any outside help begins with accepting this attitude of independence as a natural state of affairs. The next step, once this mindset is reached, is understanding some of the particular areas of concern that affect most adolescents, at least temporarily. Each of these areas, though not necessarily unique to gifted adolescents, may influence them to a greater degree because of the heightened awareness they have of these personal and life issues (Seeley, 1984). Dealing with these issues in a realistic matter-of-fact manner and using examples and resources that will be seen as credible by the adolescents themselves require skill and commitment from counselors and other educators.

Buescher (1984) lists some of the dynamic issues specifically related to giftedness that occur during adolescence:

1. *Ownership:* "Who *says* I am gifted anyhow?"
2. *Dissonance:* "If I'm as smart as everyone says, why is my work, and my life, imperfect?"
3. *Risk-taking:* "Should I be taking new risks or seeking secure situations?"
4. *Others' expectations:* "What's more important? Others' expectations of me or fulfilling my own needs?"
5. *Impatience:* "I have to know the answers right now!"
6. *Identity:* "What counts is who I am *now,* not who I'll be in ten years!"

SIX REALITIES FOR SUCCESSFUL TRANSITIONS: THE ADULT'S ROLE IN GUIDING GIFTED ADOLESCENTS

Reality 1: Remember That the Real Basics Go Beyond Reading, Writing, and Arithmetic

Lorin Hollander, a child prodigy who entertained his kindergarten classmates by playing the two-part inventions of Bach on "circus day" at school, challenges our societal concern with early intellectual pursuits. The real basics, he contends, revolve around those practices that are written in 4/4 time, sketched onto canvas, or found in the sandbox or the Crayola carton:

> Creativity, the beautiful, delicate, God-given gift of all human beings, is being stifled in many of our classrooms. We watch helplessly as our children, born so playful and curious, who hate to go to sleep because there is too much adventure to living; whose creations are so imaginative, multidimensional and symbolic; grow increasingly more concerned with the approval and marks of the grown-ups, and their work less poetic, systematically more analytical, shallow and predictable. We turn playing with crayons, movement, and building blocks into homework. (Hollander, 1987, p. 29)

The societal call to "get serious," especially to gifted adolescents who are about to inherit a harsh, often uncompromising world, seems so pervasive. They are given the message that the days of childhood, daydreaming, and foolish pursuits such as painting, dance, and play are activities for the young and immature, and that algebra, chemistry, and advanced placement English are legitimate pursuits for an able teenager.

Rubbish.

To convince gifted adolescents of the importance of downtime, play, and quiet reflection, we need look no further than Lorin Hollander, who grew up to be a pianist of world renown. Or to Graham Wallas who, in 1926, wrote that the seeds of creative productivity often occur in an *incubation* stage, a period of "relaxation from all conscious mental work" (in Davis, 1986, p. 63). Or at the Water Rat, in Kenneth Grahame's *The Wind in the Willows,* whose life's credo befits a deep thinker: "Believe me, my young friend, there is nothing—absolutely nothing—half so much worth doing as simply messing about in boats. Simply messing . . . messing-about-in-boats; messing . . . (Grahame, 1981, p. 5).

Reality 2: You Can Be Good at Something You Don't Enjoy Doing

. . . Another example from the arts.

MiDori, a 16-year-old Japanese violinist who is widely acknowledged as the most talented prodigy the world of classical music has seen in the last quarter century, envisions a personal future that might not include music. She dreams of becoming an archeologist or perhaps a writer. Already, she writes for a Japanese magazine aimed at adolescents, composes essays on her life in America, and writes surrealistic short stories about such topics as "epic battles between the 'pretty' cockroaches and the 'ugly' ones" (Roberts, 1988, p. 70). She reads Emily Brontë, Jack London, and Arthur Miller, takes karate classes, and considers herself a has-been gymnast—"I used to be flexible," she says.

And, in fact, she still is flexible. Open to life's possibilities and the many options they provide, MiDori states unequivocally that "I don't want to do something I don't want to do" (Roberts, 1988, p. 70). Understanding a lesson understood by too few—that being good at something doesn't imply that it must become your life's sole or primary focus—MiDori will, no doubt, encounter her share of nay-sayers, people who won't allow her to pursue interests outside of a very limited range of options. Still, if she is to achieve her life's ambitions, MiDori will need to keep her attitude of individuality (which some will misread as defiance) and will need adults around her who also support whatever choices she makes.

This internally based decision to pursue projects and topics where success is a *goal* not a *given* does not happen upon a person at the age of 16. Rather, it is important for the idea that it is okay to pursue multiple and varied interests to be introduced in the early years, by parents and teachers who are committed to broad-based exposure instead of narrowly focused refinement. Further, this attitude of *generalization* versus *specialization* needs to be continued throughout the high school years, when pigeonholing young people into various "camps"—jocks, scientists, musicians, writers—becomes increasingly more pronounced.

Will MiDori become the greatest adult violinist the world of classical music comes to know in the *next* quarter century? Perhaps. The choice is hers to make—and hers alone.

We should wish her well, ask how we can help, and follow through with words of encouragement.

Reality 3: You Can Be Good at Some Things That Are Unpopular with Your Friends

If there is one thing that the typical teenager wants from peer relationships, it is to *not* stand out in any way that is "uncool." Football players seldom need worry about this, nor do basketball stars. And top academic achievers (especially if they are also athletes) often have enough elan to get through the rough interpersonal spots they might run into because of their reputation for being a "brain." But what about being a member of the chorus, or president of the math club, or chair of the local Students Against Drunk Driving (SADD) chapter? Whether *these* positions are socially acceptable depends very much on the ethos of the individual school that the students attend. And what if *my* favorite activity, as a teenager, guarantees me a place in "The Outcasts' Hall of Fame"—do I give up on or deny my talents so that others *like* me more, or do I pursue my passions with no regard to the potential barbs from others? So many questions, so many options, so much confusion!

And no easy answers. Leta Hollingworth (Chapter 1) would ask teens to practice her concept of "suffering fools gladly"—playing along with established group norms just enough to get by, while pursuing individual preferences in the privacy of one's own mind or with others who have similar interests.

But suffering fools—gladly or otherwise—is easier said than done, often requiring a social agility as refined as the sense of balance needed by tightrope walkers. Too, some adolescents refuse to budge, even a little, believing that such acquiescence is tantamount to total defeat at the hands of the masses. "Besides," such students think, "if other people are so concerned about how I'm living *my* life, what does that say about their own?" A good point—but still, hard to live with day in and day out.

How can adults help? Only tangentially, yet perhaps this is still good enough. For one, they can connect the students with others—near peers— who recently lived through the same fears of social ostracism that feel so unique to the adolescent who is experiencing them (Newland, 1976). As detailed in Chapter 6, the best teachers of social skills are those who have recently been through the same types of experiences.

Second, adults can encourage young artists, activists, and chess champs to surround themselves with others of their own ilk; for in a group of "weirdos" connected by the same focus, differences diminish and defenses dissolve.

Third, these adolescents can be reminded that life changes, that things do get better. In fact, by college age, the questions of "who does what?" and "with whom?" are more trivial than vital. So yes, patience, that most elusive of adolescent virtues, does pay off.

Last, we can remind gifted adolescents to be on guard against their own half-buried stereotypes, as illustrated both in Figure 8.1 and in the following excerpt from a 17-year-old girl's diary:

I used to be completely against football players. I had this stereotyped image of them, so that was how I judged them. Then my uncle died. He was a football coach at a Catholic high school in the area. During calling hours at the funeral home, I saw hundreds of football players, present and past, from his school and even two or three other public high schools file past his casket and cry. I realized at that moment that it is completely unjust to judge anyone before knowing them as individuals. (DeSalvo, 1988, p. 18)

Funny thing, stereotypes: They're multidirectional. And just as wrong as it is for the "jocks" to make fun of the "geeks," so, too, is it wrong for the "brains" to criticize the "heads." Even talented musicians from Juilliard, if not aware of their own possible prejudices, might inflict the same pain onto others that they sometimes feel themselves.

Figure 8.1. "The Bullies of Juilliard." (Source: The BIZARRO comic feature by Pirard. San Francisco: Chronicle Features, 1985.)

Reality 4: Life Is Not a Race to See Who Can Get to the End the Fastest

According to a T. S. Eliot poem, "April is the cruelest month." Obviously, Old T. S. never lived through an adolescence filled with SAT tests, college application deadlines, and academic and athletic competitions. If he had, he would have realized that April is often an emotional anticlimax, after the rigors of a winter full of commitments and life-changing choices.

William Glasser, in his book *Positive Addiction* (1976), considers children and adolescents prime candidates for performance anxiety—exemplified by the types of behaviors in adults that media have hyped as "type A personalities": persons always on the go, moving on the fast track toward accomplishments and deadlines. Gifted adolescents often fit this type *A* mold to a *T,* as they register for the hardest courses, overcommit themselves to extracurricular activities, and try to maintain an academic intensity that allows no room for a grade of *B*. The result can be physical or emotional stress or even a breakdown or a sustained effort to do even more—only faster, better, and with more assurance. Whatever the end result, what often gets sidetracked is the noncompetitive, amorphous goals of adolescence: blowing money on Nintendo, pining away for the kid next door, or "vegging out" in bed until your parents threaten you with eviction unless you activate some brain cells. Yet, as adults, what are our fondest memories of our teen years: preparing for the SAT or listening to that special song (for the twentieth consecutive time) that reminded us of that long-lost love whose name we *still* recall?

Yeah . . . I thought so.

Adults—educators and parents—can promote free-time activities in many ways, the most effective of which is to emulate it in their own behaviors. (Haven't taken a *real* vacation in 5 years? Then *this* speaks more loudly than any of your advice to slow down or take things more casually.) Specifically, they can also encourage adolescents to do the following:

> *Play "mental health hooky." Take* that course in photography instead of your umpteenth elective in math. You will learn something about lenses—and life—that cannot be gleaned from texts.
>
> *Spend time on yourself.* Whether you like your pizza with pepperoni or smothered in anchovies, find someone else with whom you can share a slice or two and then enjoy. Even the staunchest type A's need to discover (and rediscover) the simple pleasures of just living.
>
> *Pursue a goal where success is not guaranteed.* William Purkey once wrote that "anything worth doing is worth doing poorly"—not "well," but "poorly"—for if persons only choose activities where success is assured, their repertoire of behaviors will be quite limited. There's nothing wrong with success, of course, but neither is there anything wrong with a grade

of *B,* or a mediocre performance at something that proved to be tons of fun. (In my own case, for example, volleyball.)

Besides, the difference between doing something poorly and doing it well is sometimes only the little word *practice,* which you'll never get to do if you limit yourself to just those activities in which you excel.

Listen to the masters. In an interview with gifted adults who were reviewing their own life accomplishments, the most frequently cited source of achievement and pleasure involved family and personal matters, not work-related tasks (White, 1990). This should not be too surprising; it was a lesson learned well centuries ago (MacCurdy, 1939):

> *Every now and then go away.*
>   *have a little relaxation,*
>   *for when you come back*
>   *to your work*
>   *your judgement will be surer;*
>   *since to remain constantly at work*
>   *will cause you to lose power*
>   *of judgement . . .*
> *Go some distance away*
>   *because the work appears smaller*
>   *and more of it*
>   *can be taken in at a glance,*
>   *and a lack of harmony*
>   *or proportion*
>   *is more readily seen.*
>
>   **Leonardo da Vinci**

"Nothing succeeds like success," claims an old adage (are there any *new* adages?). But for type A adolescents embarking on a life path that will bear a strong resemblance to the patterns they follow later, perhaps we can change the wording slightly: "Nothing succeeds like attempts."

There it is—a *new* adage.

Reality 5: You Have the Ability to Ask Questions That *Should* Have Answers but *Don't*

Why must life be?

What will I be 10 years from now?

How can so much pain exist in a world that is supposed to be beautiful?

Why was I born to my parents and not others in southeast Asia?

These issues, these questions cannot be answered on IBM bubble sheets; "fill-in-the-blank" does not apply here.

As reviewed earlier in Chapter 5, life's most important lessons are learned best by active doers and thinkers, not by the passive recipients of whatever fate chooses to toss one's way. Unfortunately, the lessons one learns are not always pretty or fair. As adolescents encounter the realities of religion, politics, ethics, and morals, they learn abruptly that the individual differences that make us unique can also put us at odds with each other on both a one-to-one and a global scale. As the naivete of childhood gives way to the sophistication of adolescence, once-cherished beliefs and impressions shatter: Parents *do* make mistakes, teachers *aren't* always right, friends *can* stab you in the back, politicians *sometimes* lie and lie again.

The chorus bellows: "Life isn't fair! Life isn't perfect! It's not supposed to be this way!"

But it is, and always has been, and until cloning becomes common and mind control universal, always will be.

This reality—that life has its unfair moments—need not be a depressing or dead-end issue when discussed with students. Two ways that adults can help to address these grown-up issues take the form of childhood reminders: *look* and *listen*.

Look. Biographies and autobiographies (both abbreviated and extended forms) are essential in the development of self-worth. Compilations of brief biographies, as found in *Creative Encounters with Creative People* (Gudeman, 1986), *Cradles of Eminence* (Goertzel and Goertzel, 1962), *Three Hundred Eminent Personalities* (Goertzel, Goertzel & Goertzel, 1978), and *Scientists Around the World* (DeBruin, 1988), are useful in "priming the pump" with younger adolescents, who may later choose some longer books, such as *The Diary of Anne Frank, Manchild in the Promised Land,* Hermann Hesse's *Siddharta,* Isak Dinesen's *Letters From Africa,* Lewis Thomas's *Lives of a Cell,* Robert Pirsig's *Zen and the Art of Motorcycle Maintenance,* or Margaret Mead's *Blackberry Winter.*

Some purists among you, I'm sure, have already noted that the aforementioned books are not all biographies—some are essays, others are adventures. Still, I'll take learning wherever I can get it, and if it is true that fine writers can bring even fictional characters to life for their readers, then even these unreal people can have real questions and quests.

Listen. No, I'm not talking here about the kind of listening that effective counselors do ("I hear what you're saying"); rather, I refer to the type of listening you do when you tune to a radio station. On a recent trek down the FM dial, here's what I heard:

Phil Collins singing about "Another Day in Paradise," a story of homeless folks and the simple pleasures they are denied by being people of the street.

The Jeff Healey Band singing about "Angel Eyes," a beautiful girl who falls in love with a boy who is neither good-looking nor popular. "How did I ever win your love?" he asks in innocence and joy.

Billy Joel, who reminds listeners that "We Didn't Start the Fire"; that many of the world's sorrows (and triumphs: "Brooklyn's got a winning team") came before us, and that life goes on and on and on and on.

'WE DIDN'T START THE FIRE'[1]

'49: "Harry Truman, Doris Day, Red China, Johnnie Ray
  South Pacific, Walter Winchell, Joe DiMaggio"
'50: "Joe McCarthy, Richard Nixon, Studebaker, television
  North Korea, South Korea, Marilyn Monroe"
'51: "Rosenbergs, H-bomb, Sugar Ray, Panmunjom
  Brando, *The King and I* and *The Catcher in the Rye*"
'52: "Eisenhower, vaccine, England's got a new queen
  Marciano, Liberace, Santayana goodbye"
Chorus: "We didn't start the fire
  It was always burning
  Since the world's been turning
  We didn't start the fire
  No we didn't light it
  But we tried to fight it"
'53: "Joseph Stalin, Malenkov, Nasser and Prokofiev
  Rockefeller, Campanella, Communist bloc"
'54: "Roy Cohn, Juan Peron, Toscanini, Dacron
  Dien Bien Phu falls, *Rock Around the Clock*"
'55: "Einstein, James Dean, Brooklyn's got a winning team
  Davy Crockett, *Peter Pan,* Elvis Presley, Disneyland"
'56: "Bardot, Budapest, Alabama, Khrushchev
  Princess Grace, *Peyton Place,* trouble in the Suez"
(Chorus repeats)
'57: "Little Rock, Pasternak, Mickey Mantle, Kerouac
  Sputnik, Chou En-Lai, *Bridge on the River Kwai*"
'58: "Lebanon, Charles de Gaulle, California baseball
  Starkweather, homicide, children of thalidomide"
'59: "Buddy Holly, *Ben Hur,* space monkey, Mafia
  Hula-hoops, Castro, Edsel is a no-go"
'60: "U-2, Syngman Rhee, payola and Kennedy
  Chubby Checker, *Psycho,* Belgians in the Congo"
(Chorus repeats)
'61: "Hemingway, Eichmann, *Stranger in a Strange Land*
  Dylan, Berlin, Bay of Pigs invasion

---

[1] *"We Didn't Start the Fire"* by Billy Joel © 1989 Joel Songs. All Rights Controlled and Administered by EM1 Blackwood Music Inc. All Rights Reserved. International Copyright Secured. Used by Permission.

'62: "*Lawrence of Arabia,* British Beatlemania
Ole Miss, John Glenn, Liston beats Patterson"
'63: "Pope Paul, Malcolm X, British politician sex
JFK blown away, what else do I have to say"
(Chorus repeats)
'64–'89: "Birth control, Ho Chi Minh, Richard Nixon back again
Moonshot, Woodstock, Watergate, punk rock
Begin, Reagan, Palestine, terror on the airline
Ayatollah's in Iran, Russians in Afghanistan
Wheel of Fortune, Sally Ride, heavy metal, suicide
Foreign debts, homeless vets, AIDS, crack, Bernie Goetz
Hypodermics on the shores, China's under martial law
Rock and roller cola wars, I can't take it anymore"
Chorus: "We didn't start the fire
It was always burning
Since the world's been turning on us
We didn't start the fire
But when we are gone
Will it still burn on, and on, and on, and on . . ."

Billy Joel

These songs, by the time you read this page, will have dropped from the charts into the netherland of "oldies." That's okay, because other songs, other artists, will have replaced these, and the messages contained in their lyrics are as important now as was Billy Joel "then."

Listen to these songs—your students do—and use their themes as contemporary vehicles through which to explore universal questions, conditions, and issues that are alive in the minds of the adolescents you teach.

The next stage, following *input* from books and music, is *output:* specific actions that adolescents can take after understanding and discussing the messages in the work and words of others. These actions are addressed fully in Chapter 9, so look there now if you need immediate assistance. Otherwise, let's move on to a final reality of adolescence.

Reality 6: It's Never Too Late to Be What You Might Have Been

This reality, culled from the wisdom of author George Sand, gives hope eternal to those adolescents who feel that their mistakes to date have either sentenced them or limited them to a particular career, life, or lifestyle.

Case in point: Keith. A musically talented 17-year-old (he played saxophone in a jazz band), Keith had ambitions to become a journalist. His first step was getting accepted at his college of choice, Northwestern University. However, a big problem confronted Keith in fulfilling his aspirations: his poor performance in ninth and tenth grades. During those years, girls and free time were more important than grades and studying (you *could* say he took Reality 4 just a tad too far), and his cumulative grade point average was a whopping 2.1—a very low *C*. However, once eleventh grade hit and college loomed closer, Keith refocused himself on academics, and by the time he was two months into his senior year he was buzzing along with the potential that everyone earlier claimed he had. Still, his early high school performance clung to him like lint on a sweater; since he could not rid himself of his past, Keith thought he could never get on with his future: "Why would they want me at Northwestern? They've got 4.0s applying from all over the country."

True enough, which made the selling job he had to do to the admissions officers that much more important.

So, armed with arguments for why he should be accepted at a university whose standards exceeded his scholastic performance, Keith approached Northwestern with a frontal attack of his strengths. He talked of his *recent* performance in high school, showed impressive SAT scores, shared articles he had written for his school and hometown newspapers, brought along strong recommendations from counselors and editors who knew both "the new Keith" and the old one, and he even mentioned (before they did) his lack of ambition in earlier grades.

The rest, as they say, is history; for $4\frac{1}{2}$ years Keith enjoyed Northwestern, and the local jazz clubs benefited from the young man who wasn't afraid to blow his own horn.

Keith is one example of an adolescent who refused to allow the common logic—"Go to a state school for a year and then see if you can transfer into Northwestern later"—to alter his dreams. Importantly, he had help along the way from parents, educators, and others, but even *more* important, Keith had the inner drive to become what he had long wanted to be: a journalist. In the truest sense, Keith exemplifies the person Franklin Delano Roosevelt had in mind when he said, "The ablest man I ever met is the man you think you are."

College planning and career guidance are as basic for gifted adolescents as sandbox play and drawing are for gifted preschoolers. Too often, though, these basic skills are sidestepped in deference to a more academic pursuit. Sandra Berger (1989) presents a coherent scheme for college and career planning that is based on the gifted adolescent's abilities, interests, values, and needs as they relate to educational, career, and lifestyle opportunities.

> College planning should be a positive, growth-promoting experience. . . . It is an opportunity for (students) to learn more about themselves and their special skills, interests, and learning styles and to heighten self-confidence. If they go to a college or university that is appropriate for them, where they achieve academic success, they are more likely to contribute to the school and set career goals designed to provide a satisfying life. (p. 3)

Based on the research of career and college planning experts, Berger presents a thorough, step-by-step guide for helping gifted adolescents—in fact, all college-bound adolescents—educate themselves about their many and varied options (Gysbers and Moore, 1987; Marshall, 1981). Beginning with a *Student Needs Assessment Survey* (see Figure 8.2), Berger provides specific advice and resources available to gifted adolescents, their counselors, and their parents. The *Student Needs Assessment Survey* is merely the first step in documenting the many facets of career and college guidance.

FIGURE 8.2. STUDENT NEEDS ASSESSMENT SURVEY. (*Source: River City High School: High School Student Services, A Conceptual Model,* 1982, The American College Testing Program. Adapted with permission. This Student Needs Assessment Survey may be duplicated for limited use. Berger, S. L. 1989. *College Planning for Gifted Students,* Reston, VA: The Council for Exceptional Children.)

DIRECTIONS: Ask student to rank each of the following on a 5-point scale:
1. Not important to me
2. Important to me but I need no further assistance
3. I would like a little assistance
4. I would like medium assistance
5. I would like a lot of assistance

CAREER DEVELOPMENT

_____ 1. To explore how various jobs could affect my life style.

_____ 2. To become more aware of my career interest areas.

_____ 3. To know more about job opportunities in my career interest areas.

_____ 4. To know more about training requirements for jobs I might like.

_____ 5. To become aware of training offered in my career interest areas.

_____ 6. To talk with people employed in my career interest areas.

_____ 7. To get some job experience in my career interest areas.

_____ 8. To understand the changing patterns of careers for both men and women.

_____ 9. To have help to obtain part-time and/or summer work.

_____ 10. To know what jobs are available locally.

_____ 11. To know how to apply for a job.

_____ 12. To know how to interview for a job.

_____ 13. To get my parents interested in my career planning.

_____ 14. To know how important people influence my career choice.

_____ 15. To know how to prepare for careers that interest me.

_____ 16. To have actual on-the-job experience; to know what it is like to be employed.

_____ 17. To know where and how to start looking for a job.

_____ 18. To have counseling about my career plans.

_____ 19. To know more about possible careers and the world of work.

_____ 20. To explore in detail careers I might like.

_____ 21. To understand the impact of my sex on career plans.

_____ 22. To know how the courses I am taking relate to jobs in my career interest areas.

_____ 23. To understand how my values relate to my career plans.

_____ 24. To know how my personality and preferred method of learning relate to my career plans.

_____ 25. To know how important people influence my career choice.

LIFE SKILLS DEVELOPMENT

_____ 26. To improve my study skills and habits.

_____ 27. To develop my test-taking skills.

_____ 28. To learn how to handle pressure from friends, teachers, family, or myself.

_____ 29. To learn how to make decisions and solve problems.

_____ 30. To learn how to set goals in my life.

_____ 31. To learn how to manage my time better.

_____ 32. To learn how to spend money more wisely.

_____ 33. To learn how to stay healthy, both mentally and physically.

_____ 34. To understand better the effects of alcohol, drugs, and medicines.

_____ 35. To learn how to deal with community problems.

_____ 36. To learn how to participate in government.

_____ 37. To learn how to get more out of my life through leisure time activities.

KNOWING MYSELF

_____ 38. To identify my strengths and abilities.

_____ 39. To develop more confidence in myself.

_____ 40. To understand my personal values.

_____ 41. To know how to stay in shape.

_____ 42. To understand my achievement and ability test scores better.

_____ 43. To know how to handle things that worry me.

_____ 44. To learn more about grooming and personal care.

_____ 45. To accept my own views as OK.

_____ 46. To get over my shyness.

_____ 47. To understand the way I learn best.

_____ 48. To know more about my position on social issues of the day.

_____ 49. To know about how the expectations of others affect my life.

_____ 50. To have a better understanding of my achievement test scores.

_____ 51. To develop my musical abilities.

_____ 52. To develop my artistic abilities.

_____ 53. To discipline myself for better study habits.

EDUCATIONAL PLANNING

_____ 54. To understand why I am in high school.

_____ 55. To understand the importance of graduating from high school.

_____ 56. To know more about high school graduation requirements.

_____ 57. To get help in selecting the right courses for me.

_____ 58. To become more aware of my educational options after high school (college, voc-tech, military, etc.).

_____ 59. To know more about financial aid available for continuing my education after high school.

_____ 60. To learn how to evaluate and choose an educational or training program that will be right for me.

_____ 61. To learn more about college entrance requirements.

_____ 62. To know how and when to select a college major.

_____ 63. To know how to earn college credit without taking a particular course.

_____ 64. To have counseling about my educational planning.

_____ 65. To know the proper steps for a campus visit.

_____ 66. To know how to decide which college is right for me.

_____ 67. To talk to college admission counselors about my career plans.

_____ 68. To talk to college students about my college and career plans.

_____ 69. To select more school courses by myself.

_____ 70. To find more courses relevant to my future.

_____ 71. To understand and accept what I can realistically achieve.

GETTING ALONG WITH OTHERS

_____ 72. To be able to get along better with teachers.

_____ 73. To be able to get along better with other students.

_____ 74. To know how to work with my counselor/advisor.

_____ 75. To be able to get along better with my parents.

_____ 76. To be able to get along better with my brothers and sisters.

_____ 77. To learn how to make more friends of my own sex.

_____ 78. To learn how to make more friends of the other sex.

_____ 79. To understand more about love and sex.

_____ 80. To learn more about marriage and family living.

_____ 81. To understand the changing roles of men and women in today's society.

_____ 82. To gain a better understanding of people of different races and cultural backgrounds.

_____ 83. To know about places in my school and community where I can get help with my problems.

_____ 84. To understand the needs of elderly people.

_____ 85. To accept people who feel or think differently from me.

_____ 86. To have someone listen to me when I have problems.

_____ 87. To be able to tell others how I feel.

_____ 88. To learn to get along better with my job supervisor.

OPTIONAL NEEDS ASSESSMENT ITEMS

_____ 89. To learn more about summer opportunities.

_____ 90. To learn more about mentor relationships and how to find a mentor.

_____ 91. To learn more about internships.

WRITE YOUR OWN GOALS WITH WHICH YOU WANT HELP

_____ 92. _____

_____ 93. _____

_____ 94. _____

_____ 95. _____

In a similar vein, Delisle and Squires (1989) provide justification for career guidance for gifted adolescents based upon the special needs of this population including the following:

> *Multipotential:* The interest and ability to succeed in so many vocational areas that choosing one career path becomes problematic.
>
> *Societal expectations:* Selecting a career that is based on personal strengths and interests, rather than a vocation that significant others consider sufficiently challenging for "someone so bright."
>
> *Societal "payback":* Confronting the issue of whether or not gifted adolescents must return an "extra measure" to society due to their academic potential.
>
> *Career investment decisions:* Realizing the financial, temporal, and personal commitments involved in extended career preparation, especially for professions, such as law or medicine, requiring extensive years of study.

The bottom-line purpose of career and college planning for gifted adolescents is to provide them with information and guidance that is often lacking because of the misconception that able students can make these decisions on their own (Sanborn, 1979). Such planning is an organized, long-term commitment that should begin at home and extend throughout the school years (that is, it does not begin in eleventh grade, as with Keith). When done well, such planning helps gifted adolescents realize fully their individual talents and the impact these talents may have in shaping the course of our global society.

CONCLUSION . . . AND TRANSITION

It is not only the physical growth spurts occurring during adolescence that make for some awkward movements. Never a time of complete control—of one's body, or mind, or emotions—the "package" of adolescence is a time that creates "awkward moments" in all these spheres. Adolescence is particularly a time of testing. Often, the tests are paper-and-pencil, from SATs to Advanced Placement Qualifying Exams. Other tests are those of will—"Who says I *will* go to college?" "Who says I *will* finish my homework before I go out with my friends?" Still more tests are invisible, taking place within the unspoken thoughts of the adolescent who wonders if she or he is strong enough or capable enough to grow into a world that seems so big and often so uncompromising.

During this period of testing and change, adolescents need the advice and counsel of adults who appreciate the very real struggles that these young people face on a daily basis. Every decision—"Do I study for my exams or party with my friends?" "Should I have sex now or wait?" "Should I go to college or get a job?" "What college/job?"—is accompanied by risks and consequences. Gone are the days of plunging ahead without paying heed to the effect of one's actions. For adolescents, even the smallest of details—"Do I buy Reeboks or L.A. Gear?"—seem to be more difficult than the choices one faced during the innocence of childhood.

Yes, life becomes more complex during adolescence, and the unfair thing about that is that no one asks for these complexities to encroach on their personal space. It just happens.

Adults, thankfully, do not need to have all the answers. However, to be effective in their dealings with adolescents—at home and at school—they *do* need to accept the questions being raised as legitimate ones. Perhaps truer during adolescence than at any other developmental period, the need to be taken seriously is vital.

Throughout this chapter, I have tried to avoid using the terms *adolescent* and *teenager* interchangeably. The teenage years are just that—the years from 13 to 19. However, the period of years our society labels as adolescence stretches the bounds of an entire decade to include not just the teen years but also the preteen years of 11 and 12 and the early twenties, a time by which college graduation or entry into workforce has usually occurred. This extended adolescence is especially true for gifted youth, who often "think adult thoughts" from a very young age, while remaining in the financially dependent role of student into their mid-twenties, a time when most people have already entered the workplace on a full-time basis.

Fascinating, isn't it? What is often seen by adults as the most dreaded developmental period—adolescence, in the United States and other Western societies—has become longer today than it has ever been previously. Indeed, adolescence is a twentieth-century "invention," created by our increasingly complex culture when child labor laws originated early in the 1900s. No longer do most 10-year-old children go directly from sand lot baseball to sweat shops; today, they are more likely to go through an extended period of preparation before entry into the adult world.

Hope, though, does spring eternal—perhaps at no time more prominently than during adolescence. Is it a turbulent time for most adolescents? Of course (any change, unaccompanied by conflict, generally reflects only minimal growth). Is it a time of frustration? Again, it depends on the situation, yet it may do adults well to recall that the frustration *they* feel is also felt by those adolescents who are the basis of their frustration.

Mark Twain wrote: "When I was a boy of 14, my father was so ignorant I could hardly stand to have the old man around. But when I got to be 21, I was astonished at how much he had learned in seven years."

Adolescence: a unique developmental stage, a time period that does give way, eventually, to adulthood and its accompanying commitments and new understandings. Still it is very much an entity and, even if the young people going through this state of life seem in a constant search for their own sense of purpose, adolescence, as a state of life, has a collective identity all its own.

CONTINUING QUESTS AND QUESTIONS

1. When was the last time you learned something from one of your students? When was the time before that? Did you tell that student (or that group of students) that your own knowledge base was expanded because of their efforts? Reflect on specific incidents in which your students became your teachers and then go back and tell them how much you appreciated this interchange. The hardest part of communication is bridging those last few inches—face-to-face contact—so tell your students now of *their* impact on *you* before you forget. Remember, adolescents need to know that they are taken seriously by others, so inform them when this is the case.
2. Examine the discipline procedures that exist within your school relative to their developmental applicability to adolescents. If some or all of the following procedures exist, then you are probably operating in an environment that is developmentally inappropriate for the students you serve.

     Using writing exercises as punishments for minor infractions (for example, writing 100 times, "I will respect other people's rights.")

     Having a "group detention room" where all students with detentions, no matter the reason, are lumped together in a common punishment

     Allowing teachers to give failing grades to students who know their subject but who do not turn in homework or other assignments

   Examine those disciplinary strategies and, if necessary, convene a group of educators and students to evaluate their merits. Remember, if students are expected to behave in mature and responsible ways, adults must discipline with dignity, *not* with degradation.
3. Frequently, gifted adolescents are given the option of taking college courses while they are still enrolled in high school. In some cases, children as young as 11 years old take college courses in the summer or on a part-time basis during the academic calendar year. Under what conditions are these arrangements appropriate, and on which occasions would you disallow an able student this option? The benefits of acceleration (for example, skipping grades, entering college early) are extolled widely by researchers who propose this strategy for highly able students, but individual cases where students have accelerated often paint a less-rosy picture. Where do *you* stand, and why?

OUT OF THE WAY/OUT OF THIS WORLD RESOURCES

Respecting the Pupil, edited by Donald Cole and Robert Cornett (The Phillips Exeter Academy Press, Exeter, NH, 1981).

This gem of a book is virtually unknown to educators, since the publisher is housed within a secondary school in New Hampshire. Still, this book is especially valuable to high school educators who wish to better understand gifted and talented adolescents. Written as a series of "Essays on Teaching Able Students," the authors are all teachers. The book's title is a good description of the tone this volume takes with respect to teaching gifted teens.

All Grown Up with No Place To Go, by David Elkind (Addison-Wesley, Reading, MA, 1984).

A follow-up to his earlier book, *The Hurried Child,* in which he examined the too-rapid push to educate young children, this volume is written with a similar message, but for a different audience: parents of adolescents. Elkind examines the drawbacks to premature growing up and asks the same question repeatedly (though not in these exact words): Since you're in such a hurry to grow up—what are you going to do when you get there? The benefits of childhood and the many positive aspects of dependency are examined in this important book.

Breakfast in America, by Supertramp (A and M Records, Hollywood, CA, 1979).

This record album (tape, CD) is older than some of the young people who listen to its songs, but the fact that Supertramp's music is still played today tunes you in to its timeliness. Selections such as "The Long Way Home"explores the benefits of the road seldom taken; "The Logical Song" is a face-front encounter with the ifs, ands, and buts of life; and "Goodbye Stranger" is an introspective look at the new person you become when you are able to see life from multiple angles. A megahit upon its release, *Breakfast in America* continues to enjoy popularity today—and for good reasons.

National Center for Effective Secondary Schools Newsletter (University of Wisconsin, College of Education, Madison, WI, 1986–on).

Since the early 1980s, educators have been barraged with reports on how America's schools can be improved, test scores raised, students more internationally competitive, and so on. Few resources, though, suggest workable solutions to these and other dilemmas as well as does this newsletter written *by* educators *for* educators. "Skirting the Brain—Nerd Connection: How Bright Students Save Face among Peers" was a recent topic addressed. It is a *free* resource (actually, it's funded with federal dollars so we've *all* paid for it already) and well worth the effort to locate and read.

CHAPTER 9

Special Topics and Special Populations

The intent of this chapter is to

Introduce you to several populations of gifted students whose intellectual talents have been frequently ignored by gifted education researchers and practitioners

Review the incidence and causes of suicidal attempts among gifted students and provide examples of treatment strategies and materials to alleviate this problem

Focus on the lifelong impact of gifted abilities, as noted through the specific concerns of talented adults

Discuss the role of the gifted child as a contributing member of a global society

JASON

It was cold on the morning of December 23, 1988, when 11-year-old Jason Allen walked away from the Child and Adolescent Treatment Center (CATC) in Wauwatosa, Wisconsin. Described by juvenile officers as "very bright, but recently troubled and morose," Jason remained missing until January 12, 1989, when he turned himself in to his psychiatric social worker.

During the 21 days he was missing, Jason contacted family friends, and he also wrote letters to the local newspaper explaining why he had run away.

"If I go to CATC and they are successful in building my self-esteem or whatever, what happens when I am to return to the other world that

has their (sic) own philosophy? . . . I don't care to live in this world as
it is. Each day I care less." (Allen, 1989)

An accomplished artist, an ace in spelling bees, a self-taught musician, and almost
a straight-A student, Jason is a gifted young man who, at 11, has seen more strife
than many adults feel in a lifetime. "Oh, well, what do I know," writes Jason. "I
am just a kid . . . just one among thousands of others whose stories go untold."
   "Just a kid," Jason says. Yet his insights into himself, others, and the world
around him belie his youth, and they seem too heavy to be borne by Jason's 11
years and 80-lb frame.
   Jason represents a neglected minority *within* a minority: a gifted child at risk
both physically and emotionally. In our world of surveys, statistics, and probabili-
ties, it is helpful to remind ourselves that behind these data lie children in pain;
children afraid. Children such as Jason.

THE SWEET SCENT OF POTPOURRI

In developing a chapter-by-chapter book prospectus—as was done for this
text and for most others like it—authors put their best feet forward first. The
real "meat" of the book appears early-on (after the obligatory introduction)
and, as the prospectus progresses, the topics get more specialized and, at
times, more esoteric.
   Such is the case with this book. Few would agree concerning the importance of a review of underachievement or overall counselling needs of gifted
students in a book with the title of this one. But here we are in Chapter 9, and
the issues raised may appear to some as just so much filler. I mean really:
gifted students with handicaps? suicide? gifted adults? Isn't this stretching the
topic (and therefore, the size of the book) just a little too far?
   Let me put it to you this way: You, dear readers, are busy people, as am
I. So it does me no good to either belabor a point that is obvious or to invent a
topic to satisfy some editor's idea of how long a book-length manuscript
should be. And if the information provided were merely redundant, it would
do *you* no good to read my reiterations.
   No, this chapter is an important one, I believe. The topics addressed in it
might appear initially to be "fringe" issues, yet to the young people who are
traversing the turf covered within the topics presented here, the issues are
more front-burner than back.
   Observe, for example, a highly gifted young person so far advanced from
her classmates that, statistically speaking, she is one in a million. Or the able
fourth grader who doesn't understand how he can comprehend every word his
teacher speaks, yet seems unable to read even a simple text without difficulty.
Or the young woman whose prime career goal is to become a geologist, but
who hears from family and friends that "that's no job for a girl." Or the
emotionally troubled adolescent whose life circumstances have led him to

believe that death by suicide is acceptable, for at least it gives him a stake in choosing his own destiny.

Which chapter will they—or the people who educate them—turn to first? They couldn't care less about "who defines giftedness how"; their needs are more direct, more personal, and will probably be answered more in this fringe chapter than in all the others combined—at least that is my hope.

So, to those readers among you who are *beginning* this book with Chapter 9, welcome! We've been waiting for you.

As to the opening allusion to potpourri. In trying to think of a three-dimensional equivalent to the contents of this chapter, all I could think of was the basket of greens, rose petals, lavender seeds, and lemon plant leaves that graces our kitchen table. Each time I pass it, a cacophony of aromas benignly assaults my nose; and each time I pass it, the scent is just a bit different from the time before. The smell, always sweet, varies with my distance and direction from the table. Each aroma, in and of itself, is subtle and distinct. Yet taken together, the potpourri earns its very appropriate name and has its own unique essence.

As, it is hoped, will the topics covered in this chapter.

SUICIDE AMONG GIFTED ADOLESCENTS

In a society so advanced that we debate the right to life for both the unborn and the incurably ill, the idea of suicide is anathema. Add to this the fact that some suicides occur among young people, those "whose lives are just beginning," and the idea of suicide becomes even more unbelievable. Then, on top of our overall regard for life and youth, add the factor of giftedness, and we get a combination that seems totally unfathomable: an intelligent young person who seems to have "all options open" ending his or her own life voluntarily. Even in a society such as ours that has grown increasingly immune to tragedy, the pain we feel for the young victims of suicide grips us almost universally.

The problem of adolescent suicide is one that is generally addressed in schools only after a suicide occurs. For all manner of ill-founded reasons—"If we *mention* suicide, it'll put the idea of it into some kid's head," for example—educators elect to postpone discussion of this inherently sensitive topic. However, the incidence of adolescent suicide in the United States is such that to dismiss treatment of this topic in schools is to deny a startling reality: that between 5000 to 6000 youths per year take their own lives and that at least 10 times as many more make an unsuccessful attempt (Hayes and Sloat, 1990).

The number of these young people who would be classified as intellectually gifted is difficult to estimate, for various reasons. First, the varied definitions of giftedness prevent a precise description of which adolescent suicide victims would be considered as gifted or talented. Second, in the data that do exist regarding the demographic variables of the population of young suicides, intellectual ability is seldom mentioned. School *performance* is frequently cited (and a marked decrease in academic performance is often cited as a warning sign of suicide [Jones, 1987]), yet academic performance that is low can surely disguise high potential. Third, the reporting of suicide is inaccurate, as many incidences of suicide get recorded as accidents, thereby limiting our full understanding of the extent of this problem among *all* adolescents, including those who are gifted (Frymier, 1988). However, in a study of adolescent suicides occurring in southeastern Ohio, Seibel and Murray (1988) highlight six case studies, including the following:

> David was an honor student, star quarterback on his high school football team, and a perfectionist who gave 100% to everything he did. When he earned an athletic scholarship to a prestigious Midwest college, the community shared his family's pride. But by the beginning of his sophomore year, things were not going well. After he was cut from the college football team, friends began to notice his despondency and strange behavior. They urged him to sign himself into a hospital. Hours later, David slipped out of the psychiatric ward and made his last run. Dashing down the corridor, he plunged through a plate glass window to his death three floors below. (p. 51)

In three of the remaining five case studies, the authors use other terms— "capable of doing more," "talented," "highly educated"—that *imply giftedness,* although that term itself is never used.

In another study by Lajoie and Shore (1981), the incidence of suicide, depression, and delinquency among gifted students was investigated. Although the results could not establish a specific percentage of these behaviors among gifted versus nongifted populations, they did come to the following conclusion:

> Suicide statistics and theories about the causes of suicide are . . . most accommodating to the idea of overrepresentation of the gifted, especially at college age. . . . This review should dispel the notion that gifted youth require no special help, that they can make it on their own. At least some do not, and these may be more than are apparent now. (p. 141)

Perhaps the main question should not be trying to determine the precise number of adolescent suicides who are gifted or talented. Instead, the primary responsibility of researchers and educators should be the prevention of this life-threatening behavior among *all* adolescents, including those who are especially able.

Nonetheless, there are some aspects of giftedness that may impact on already distressed adolescents enough that suicide is seen as a viable alternative. These conditions, as well as some preventive strategies and resources that may be useful in addressing suicide prevention in schools, are reviewed in the following section.

Death with Honors: Understanding and Preventing Suicidal Behaviors

The pressure towards *perfection* is the most overlooked, yet influential, aspect of being gifted (Whitmore, 1980). When the striving to succeed becomes the struggle to continue, the perfectionistic person sees life as a series of missed opportunities: "I *should have* done better on that test"; "I *didn't live up* to my parents' expectations"; "I *could have been* so much more than I am." Often, a person who notes the failures instead of the successes is unlikely to risk new endeavors, new challenges, fearing that the end result will be yet another disappointment. This fear of failure among highly able youth often contrasts vividly with their excellent academic achievements, and Peck (1968) contends that the real pressure to succeed comes from the student's attempt to attain parental—*not* internal—standards of performance.

The importance of *perception* becomes obvious yet again; what others see as signs of success—a good report card, a well-paying job, a secure future— the perfectionistic person interprets as just average achievement. A teenager discussing personal interpretations of success wrote, "Just how good am I? Just how smart is smart? How do I become better than the bestest best? The questions constantly plagued me" (American Association for Gifted Children, 1978, p. 13).

Another factor that may contribute to suicidal behaviors in gifted adolescents is *societal expectations*. Tangential to perfectionism, *societal expectations* refers to the idea that gifted youth are often expected to become our "future leaders" or "the movers and shakers of the next generation." The implication is that gifted youth whose academic performance or chosen careers do not reach these high, high standards will have, somehow, missed the mark in contributing to their world. The frustration felt by adolescents who perceive society's goals for them as overly ambitious or unattainable often remains unstated, yet when the thoughts are voiced, the message sent is unmistakable:

> Being gifted, I have a strong sense of future, because people are always telling me how well I will do when I grow up. . . . My feelings fluctuate from a sense of responsibility for everything to a kind of "leave me alone—quit pushing." (American Association for Gifted Children, 1978, p. 7)

At times, the stress of living up to expectations that the adolescent perceives as unfair or unreachable overrides the desire to go on, and life becomes aimless and barren (Shneidman, 1972).

A third area of concern is *dyssynchronous development*. Gifted children— as all children—develop in a sequence of spurts. Their voices and bodies mature along established paths; logical and ethical reasoning proceeds as if on a well-planned itinerary. Yet when gaps exist between the maturation of the mind and the body, the adolescent is the first to notice. At a stage of intellectual development that *should* allow for individual differences, gifted youth often accept these idiosyncrasies in everyone but themselves (Webb, Meckstroth, and Tolan, 1982). In addition, the social acceptability of high academic talent diminishes during adolescence. Whereas gifted students are more popular than their less-able classmates in elementary school, this popularity diminishes significantly in high school, especially for gifted girls (Austin and Draper, 1981; Coleman, 1961; Tannenbaum 1962). "Here we go again," the able adolescent may feel. "Someone changed the rules on me and no one even asked my permission." The frustration of not fitting in—physically, socially, and/or intellectually—is too much stress all at once for some able youth.

A final aspect of giftedness that may cause at-risk adolescents considerable discomfort is being *philosophically astute, but pragmatically impotent.* When a gifted 12-year-old asks why famine exists in a world of plenty, or why our government can spend money to renovate the White House while it does not provide shelter for the homeless people who live across the street from it, the answers they often hear are "I don't know" or "Don't worry about such things; you're too young." These, of course, are nonresponses, and the astute child asking for answers is not satisfied by the complacency with which these real questions were treated.

Yet, the ability to perceive problems (and possible solutions) cannot be dismissed merely because the thinker is, presumably, too young to be concerned; to adopt this posture denies the existence of those very qualities that help define the youngster as gifted in the first place. Further, this attitude undercuts the able youth's perceptions of his or her ability to change the status quo; to improve the lot of a sorry, sorry world. When this occurs, the adolescent may begin to perceive all problems as catastrophic and all solutions as untenable. The solution may be to remove all the problems immediately, through suicide (Smith and Mauceri, 1982).

These four issues—perfectionism, societal expectations, dyssynchronous development, and impotence in affecting real-world change—confront every gifted adolescent to some degree. And, statistically, for every youth who sees these problems as insurmountable and unending, millions succeed without resorting to suicide. Still, the cost of the loss of even one young life—to the suicide victim, the family left behind, the society that is now just a bit less vibrant than it once was—is impossible to document. We never know what might have been if the suicide victim had lived.

Intervention Strategies and Resources

Just as there are those who at the least indisposition develop a fever, so do those whom we call suicides, and who are always very emotional and sensi-

> tive, develop at the least shock the notion of suicide. Had we a science with the courage and authority to concern itself with mankind . . . these matters of fact would be familiar to everyone. (Hesse, 1974, p. 55)

As stated so eloquently by Hesse, the prediction of suicide is, at best, imprecise. Despite years of research and mountains of data, we will still lose to suicide some adolescents who we thought were psychologically secure. And, ironically, some individuals for whom life circumstances seem intolerable will pull through with few emotional scars. Yet we must persevere to do what we are able and to live up to the Greek translation of *psukhe,* the root word for psychology which translates, literally, to "the study of life."

Until recently, few practical resources for adolescent suicide prevention were available to educators. Today, in response to an increasing need, new materials are being developed. The most comprehensive resource currently available, *Youth in Crisis: Seeking Solutions to Self-Destructive Behavior,* was created by the director of a school-based intervention project in Englewood, Colorado (Barrett, 1987). This comprehensive document includes chapters on the problem of suicide (that is, its incidence and causes), intervention strategies, and community networking. Compiled after a thorough review of existing research, and its direct application within a school district that experienced multiple youth suicides over a short period of time, *Youth in Crisis* was cited by Kim Smith of The Menninger Clinic as an important addition to the literature:

> While we are moving quickly in our use of education as a suicide prevention, intervention, and even postvention tool, the conceptualization of these endeavors has lagged behind. This book is the first comprehensive effort to remedy these deficits. (in Barrett, 1987, p. v)

The suggestions that follow are culled from *Youth in Crisis,* either directly or tangentially, and thus correspond with the current research and literature related to the phenomenon of youth suicide.

1. *Do not wait until a suicide or attempt occurs to implement a suicide prevention program.* It is commonly thought that suicide is a problem that happens in other towns or in other schools. If youth suicide has not touched your locale, then consider yourself lucky. For although suicide is a more common event in rural than urban settings, its incidence respects no geographic, economic, or ethnic boundaries (Frymier, 1988). Also, since at least 10 suicide attempts occur for every suicide completion, the problem of teen suicide in most communities, is, if anything, underrecognized (Hafen and Frandsen, 1986).

2. *Include a unit on suicide prevention as a part of the mental health curriculum, beginning in junior high school.* The topic of adolescent suicide is never a pleasant one, and due, in part, to the mistaken belief that the mention

of suicide to adolescents will prompt its occurrence, it is often neglected. While it is not helpful to romanticize suicide or its victims, a clinical discussion of the reasons for suicide and its effects on survivors must still be addressed. These discussions can take place within the structure of a health class, where other ecological problems of adolescence are reviewed—drug abuse, sexual behavior, and smoking.

3. *Provide inservice training on suicide prevention to school personnel and parents.* Even the most ambitious and well-intentioned plans for implementing a suicide prevention program can become mired in controversy and misperceptions; thus, it is imperative that educators and parents be made aware ahead of time of any curricular approaches to this topic. In developing *Youth in Crisis,* its author presented specific materials and strategies for use with both educators and parents. The results of the pre/post testing regarding the incidence of suicide and its prevention showed significant increases in both group's understanding of the problem and methods for lessening its incidence.

4. *Appreciate the crucial role that students play in recognizing other adolescents who are suicidal.* Verbal or written intent to commit suicide is given by nearly 75 percent of those who attempt suicide, and this message is given most frequently from one adolescent to another (Delisle, 1986). Expressions such as "The world will be better off without me," or "Don't bother to call me tomorrow, I'll probably be dead" may seem to be typical reactions to an adolescent crisis. However, they may be not-so-subtle clues that a suicide attempt is imminent. Teens need to be made aware of these and other warning signs that may indicate an impending attempt at self-destruction by a peer. It must be remembered, though, that "teenagers make very good diagnosticians, but they make terrible therapists," and that adults must take charge once the at-risk student is identified (Frymier, 1988, p. 293). For both moral and legal reasons, every verbal message of suicide must be considered legitimate, and any suicide attempt, regardless of its presumed "seriousness," must be taken as a gesture of pain.

5. *Provide resources on suicide prevention to teachers, counselors, and students.* A wide variety of low-cost, effective resources has become available on the growing problem of adolescent suicide. *Teen Suicide: A Guide to Understanding Adolescents Who Take Their Own Life* is inexpensive (under $2.00) and includes a solid introduction to the issue of suicide, including common myths, identifying suicidal teens, and reacting to suicidal gestures (Jones, 1987). *Empty Chairs,* a 30-minute video, is a play written and enacted by students dramatizing the effect of a teenage girl's suicide on her friends (Agency for Instructional Technology, 1988). Accompanied by a comprehensive guide, *Empty Chairs* has been recommended by the National Teen Suicide Prevention Task Force.

In addition, there are resources available for use directly by students. *Dead Serious: A Book for Teenagers about Teenage Suicide* uses many case studies to show adolescents both the seriousness of the teen suicide problem and ways to recognize the problem in their friends (Leder, 1987). Too, young adult literature includes selections which deal with the issue of suicide in a realistic, unromanticized way. Among these titles are *Tunnel Vision* which addresses the impact of a parent's suicide on the family survivors and *Triple Boy* which details a teenager's own struggle with self-identity following a suicide attempt (Arrick, 1980; Carlson, 1977). Other selections on related topics can be found in volumes 3 and 4 of *The Bookfinder,* in which more than 40 young adult books dealing with suicide are annotated (Dreyer, 1985; Spreddmann-Dreyer, 1989).

6. *Be prepared to act specifically should a suicide, or an attempt, occur in your school.* Although nearly 70 percent of adolescent suicides occur in the home, using implements readily available there, suicide attempts also occur in schools—even in schools that include suicide prevention within their curriculum (Husain and Vandiver, 1984). Should this event occur (and even if the suicide does not take place on school grounds but involves an enrolled student), school officials should have a detailed plan designed to address both the inevitable rumors that will arise and the very real pain that will be evidenced by some students. To act as if the suicide did not occur is to dismiss its importance altogether—a fault almost as grievous as extolling the praises of the suicide victim to such a degree that he or she gains status as a type of "folk hero" among the students.

A balanced, realistic response is needed that begins with a matter-of-fact announcement that the suicide did occur. Individual students should then be allowed to speak with counselors at any time during that day or subsequent days, as feelings of anger, guilt, fear, and other emotions will surely emerge (Worden, 1983). More elaborate information regarding communal responses to teen suicide are available and should be consulted as a part of planning a schoolwide response to student suicide (Hawton, 1986; Phi Delta Kappa Task Force on Adolescent Suicide, 1988; Smith and Mauceri, 1982).

Summary

> *In the depths of winter I finally learned that within me lay an invincible summer.*
>
> **Albert Camus**

The decision to end one's life is seldom made hastily. The human spirit, with its vast resilience, seeks reasons to go on; to live; to find a purpose in existing. It is only when the last hope for improvement has been destroyed that suicide becomes a viable alternative. Often, the decision to end one's life is not a conscious wish to die but, rather, a pronouncement that living has become too painful. When this occurs, even nothingness seems preferable to existence in a world so full of personal hurt.

Suicide among gifted students seems even more inexplicable than other suicides. There seems so much to look forward to, so many things to become and to do, so much potential and promise. All shattered by a gunshot, a jump, a vial of pills. "I don't care to live in this world as it is," Jason Allen's note said. "Each day I care less." Such feelings of remorse are not innate in children; they are learned and developed over time. Thankfully, they can also be reversed.

Educators of gifted and talented students need to be aware of how the problem of youth suicide meshes with the overall topic of mental health. They need to know the unique social and emotional needs of gifted students, and they need to offer guidance that legitimizes the students' right to see their world from a slightly different vantage point than most. They need to know suicide's warning signs and to be ready to act specifically to prevent the loss of yet another young life. Last, they need to realize the psychotherapeutic power of a listening ear, a guiding hand, a caring reaffirmation that despite differences in age, sex, color, or social class we all share the bond of humanness. And then on that superb day when our schools monitor mental health as carefully as they do achievement test scores, the problem of youth suicide may become a problem whose time has passed.

GIFTED YOUTH WITH HANDICAPS: "SPECIAL TWICE" CHILDREN

As a field of study matures, it often becomes broader in its goal or mission than was envisioned originally by its founders. This maxim holds true today in gifted child education, and the best indicator of this extended vision is noted in our recent attention to gifted persons with handicapping conditions; those who are "special twice," once for their gift, and once again for their disability.

June Maker (1977) and Merle Karnes (1979) were among the first to write about the needs of gifted children with handicapping conditions. Maker continued to write about this population and, in 1985, collaborated with Joanne Whitmore to produce an important but little-known book, *Intellectual Giftedness in Disabled Persons* (Whitmore and Maker, 1985). In this volume, the authors describe the conditions under which giftedness can coexist with physical disabilities, sensory impairments, and specific learning disabilities. One of the most insightful chapters includes an autobiography of "John," a PhD candidate in education:

> I have been a quadriplegic since I was 25 years of age, owing to a spinal cord injury that resulted from an automobile accident in 1972. I have no motor function and only partial sensory ability in my lower extremities. . . . My wife is also a quadriplegic owing to a spinal cord injury, although her functional ability is remarkably higher than my own. We live in our own more

than slightly mortgaged house in suburbia. . . . Through all efforts to attain my career and life goals as an individual with a severely handicapping condition, my needs have centered on finding effective ways to accommodate the disabling conditions, gaining control over my self and life, and receiving psychological support from others. These needs are not unique to me, or to any other disabled person; they are common to all human beings. (pp. 136; 144)

These comments point toward a reality that is often disguised due to its simplicity: that above all else, gifted persons with handicaps want to be treated as feeling and thinking human beings. Their handicaps, whether visible or unseen, take a back seat to their humanity; *cap*ability becomes more important than *dis*ability. As stated by Baum, Emerick, Herman, and Dixon (1989) in evaluating a program for gifted handicapped students, "Perhaps for the only time in their lives, they were singled out and respected for their gifts. Such attention, in the long run, may contribute more to their success in life than equal efforts to remediate basic skills" (p. 53).

In addition to Whitmore and Maker, other authors have written texts on the topic of gifted children with learning disabilities (Daniels, 1983; Fox, Brody and Tobin, 1983). Also, an entire issue of the journal for the education of gifted students, *Roeper Review* (September 1989), was devoted to the topic of gifted children with either visible or hidden handicaps.

Throughout each of these resources, some common threads emerge regarding the educational provisions that must exist if "special twice" children are to reach their fullest potential.

Giftedness and Other Handicapping Conditions: Overlapping Linkages

The curriculum is
Assumed to be the starting point from which differentiation must begin
Inappropriate "as is" and must be modified (inclusion and exclusion)
Altered to take advantage of individual strengths and interests
Unresponsive to developmental/conceptual lags in individual children
Presented at a pace that is inappropriate for other-than-average learners

The student is
Selected on the basis of other-than-average abilities
Dissimilar to agemates as regards social/emotional functioning
Aware of the intellectual distinctions that exist between him or her and his or her classmates
In need of a "peer group" that is responsive to her or his intellectual abilities
Expected to upgrade any obvious weaknesses

The teacher is

A specialist at meeting individual needs

Specially trained in alternate methods of instruction and in use of materials other than textbook basals

Allowed to experiment in approaches to instruction

Is expected to "prove" the worthiness of his or her professional existence

Is aware of assessment tools to measure student potential

Underlying all treatments, though, is a common attitude: Whatever the combination of their gifts and deficiencies, gifted children with handicaps are greater than the sum of their dual labels. That is, when providing instructional programs, educators must do more than just pile one existing provision on top of another. For example, a gifted child with a specific learning disability cannot be assumed to benefit from placement in an intact gifted program and a preexisting learning disabilities class. The content and structure of these special programs may need to be altered or refined so as to meet the specific needs of this twice-labeled child. Thus, if the gifted program is not adapted for a student with a written expression disability, then the amount of work due and the content of the program may be inappropriate. Likewise, if the learning disabilities program stresses rote drill and repetitive activities, then the child's specific talents might be given short shrift.

Educational provisions that take into acccount the multiple needs of gifted children with disabilities are as varied as they are individualized. However, the following set of suggestions gives some specific ideas provided in the research literature.

Programmatic Suggestions for Working with Gifted–Handicapped Students

Gifted Students with Hearing Impairments

Establish some form of oral and/or manual communication system as early as possible (Maker, Redden, Tonelson, and Howell, 1978).

Encourage early reading and read aloud to the children while using manual communication (Yewchuk and Bibby, 1989).

Establish contacts with successful hearing-impaired adults (Maker, Redden, Tonelson, and Howell, 1978).

Assist the child to develop alternative plans for reaching goals when a barrier is encountered, rather than suggesting that the goal be changed (Whitmore and Maker, 1985).

Frequent home–school communication so that parents are aware of, and can assist with, specific projects. Also, parents should inform school personnel of a child's strengths, which may serve as a basis for enrichment and extension activities (Maker, Redden, Tonelson, and Howell, 1978).

Provide interpreters for easier integration into regular school classes (Antia, 1985).

Gifted Students with Vision Impairments

Look for concrete evidence, rather than abstract understanding of concepts, to identify young gifted children with vision impairments (Johnson, 1987).

Use instruments adapted for use with visually impaired children (for example, the Perkins Binet) to assess intelligence (Davis, 1980; Johnsen, 1988).

Use technology that is becoming increasingly available to visually impaired persons (the *Optacon* and the *Visualtek,* for example) for instruction and independent study (Porter, 1982).

Encourage active, independent exploration of one's environment; avoid overprotecting the child (Whitmore and Maker, 1985).

Encourage interaction with sighted classmates to promote cognitive and social development (Simpkins and Stephens, 1974).

Place visually impaired gifted students in existing gifted programs, providing hands-on, exploratory experiences as well as supplemental services, such as instruction in braille and the use of specialized equipment (Whitmore and Maker, 1985).

Gifted Students with Severe Physical Impairments

Provide adaptive equipment and aids that allow children to participate safely in as many activities as possible (Melichar, 1978).

Purchase books and toys that the child can use independently, teach the use of communication devices as early as possible, and, instead of restricting the child from certain risky activities, discuss the possible dangers with the child, but allow participation (Whitmore and Maker, 1985).

Do not "talk down" to a physically impaired child—cerebral palsy or a speech impairment does not imply mental inferiority (Maker, Redden, Tonelson, Howell, 1978).

Locate physicians who understand and appreciate the child's talents and can "see beyond" the impairment (Obringer, 1984).

Parents, educators, and colleagues must become "watchdogs" to ensure that the physically impaired gifted adult or adolescent is provided with appropriately challenging and enjoyable academic and social experiences (Robertson, 1985).

Gifted Students with Learning Disabilities

Use curriculum materials that are meaningful, interesting, and intellectually appropriate, even if these materials seem to be "above" the student's current reading level (French, 1982).

Plan activities that demand active and task-oriented student responses and ask students to generate relationships between the information they are learning and their personal experiences (Whitrock, 1979).

Psychologists and educators need to look less at global measures of intelligence and more at patterns of scores that reflect unique cognitive processing qualities; education commensurate with these talents should follow (Barton and Starnes, 1989).

Establish self-contained or resource programs that offer both a cohesive educational program and a chance to interact with children who have similar strengths and deficits (Daniels, 1983).

Specific learning disabilities can be remediated, but not in lieu of offering gifted program services monopolizing strengths and emphasizing self-concept instruction (Nielsen and Mortorff-Albert, 1989).

Provide a "home plan" with a structured timetable of the student's responsibilities that is reinforced by parents, in order to improve students' organizational abilities (Sah and Borland, 1989).

Involve children in activities based on their levels of interest and expertise and provide them outlets for sharing these talents with others (Baum, Emerick, Herman, and Dixon, 1989).

Gifted children with handicapping conditions provide a unique challenge even to the most energetic and innovative educators. At some times, it will appear that for every step forward, these students take two steps back. Yet the growth that *can* be achieved by providing programs and provisions that attend to strengths while not ignoring weaknesses is surely greater than the growth that would occur were such options not to be offered.

More so, perhaps, than with any other subcategory of gifted children, those students with both identifiable gifts *and* handicaps need educational modifications that are very much individualized. An easy task? You bet it isn't, but just listen to one young adult who experienced two kinds of educators: some poor ones, and some educators who, true to the Hallmark tradition, "cared enough to send their very best." Zannet Coleman, a graduate of Gallaudet College and currently an instructional counselor at the California School for the Deaf, reflects on her experiences in seventh and eighth grades:

> I attended seventh grade at a public junior high school, where I experienced a damaging defeat to my personal self-esteem—removal from the fast learner "bright kids" class. Everything went wrong. The teacher was new to the school, and he was a rapid lecturer with very little movement. Exams were given orally and answers were to be written within a specified time

limit. The teacher never repeated anything twice and had very little patience. No matter how hard I tried, I couldn't lipread him. I couldn't follow without the help of visual aids, and he considered me an impediment to the progress of the class. I was transferred to a slower class. Of course I was hurt. Somehow it didn't diminish my positive attitude toward learning, but I didn't have too much admiration for that teacher.

Now 13 years old, I was the only deaf child in the entire junior high. My new teacher went out of her way to make me feel welcome by *everyone* in the class. I was placed in the front row at her favorite location in the room. She had eyes like a hawk, and I can recall her saying so often, "Zannet, you must pay attention so you can read my lips." I understood everything she said because she cared and took time to be repetitive and to use visual aids.

Even though I felt I was a favorite, I didn't experience any resentment from my fellow classmates. I was often used as an example for others to follow because I was quick to learn and completed assignments with a minimum of errors. I seemed to fit into that class perfectly. I kept contact with this teacher for many years. She is one of the many people who made an impression on me and motivated me to do my best. (Coleman, 1983, pp. 43–44)

GLOBAL AWARENESS

> *The future . . . seems to me no unified dream, but a mince pie, long in the baking, never quite done.*
>
> **E. B. White,** *"One Man's Meat,"* 1944

The awareness of our earth as a fragile planet, susceptible to all forms of mistreatment by its inhabitants, is not a new notion. Respect for the land that feeds and sustains us is a fundamental tenet of Eastern philosophies that date back centuries. And one need look no further than Henry David Thoreau's backyard—Walden Pond—to locate within our own history and culture individuals who call for compassion when it comes to tending to the needs of a defenseless friend: our planet earth.

Until the twentieth century, though, the earth's inhabitants saw themselves more as a collection of entities than as an interdependent family. Separated by land forms and oceans, yet united by common water and air that respect no political boundaries, the family of humanity is now linked in ways that were never before so obvious. Acid rain from America's Rust Belt kills lakes hundreds of miles away in once pristine Canadian wilderness. The destruction of rain forests in the remote Amazon affects the quality of air available to us all. The explosion of a Russian nuclear plant obliterates life for generations to come near Chernobyl and kills fish in coastal Norway. Although these connections are not new, our awareness of them has been enhanced by our technological "advances" and our instantaneous communication with all parts of the world. Where once our news came on the heels of a messenger on horseback who rode between distant locales, we now travel between cities, countries, hemispheres—even outer space—with the speed of light and sound. Each day, it becomes more difficult to remain culturally isolated and unique. A Korean peasant may never get to Dallas, but will know all about it by watching a television show of that same name.

Inherently neither bad nor good, this global awareness is merely a by-product of an ever-changing, increasingly complex, global society. But today's generation of children is the first one in history who receive good or bad news about our planet's condition at the same time that it is being broadcast to world leaders; no longer is the populace told only weeks after an event occurs that it has, in fact, transpired. (As stated by Cordell Hull, "a lie goes halfway around the world before truth has time to get its trousers on.") Rather, with a flash of a news bulletin, 10-year-olds learn about a crisis at the same time that our country's president is informed; undigested, raw material is laid before the eyes and minds of children who may be left on their own to consider its ramifications. One student presented her view among many others prompted by today's headlines, showing a child's concern for the planet on which she lives.

PORTRAIT OF AN OIL SPILL[1]

"What does an oil spill look like?" asked a child of her mother.
"An oil spill looks like an otter struggling for breath, and warmth, and life that was once his own."
"What does an oil spill sound like?" said the child.
"It's the breath of a dying bird, the cry of a lark that can breathe no more.
Isn't it appropriate that he should wear black to his own funeral?"
"Mommy, have you even seen the effects of an oil spill?"
"No, daughter, I cannot hear silence nor can I view emptiness."

Laura Bird, seventh grade
P.K. Yonge Laboratory School
Gainesville, FL
(from *Creative Kids,*
December 1989, p. 9)

For gifted young people—or any youth who are sufficiently cognizant of the world they inhabit—this awareness can breed concern, anxiety, fear, or

---

[1] From: L. Bird, "Portrait of of an Oil Spill." Mobile, AL: *Creative Kids, 8* (3), December 1989. Reprinted by permission.

helplessness—"What can *I* do? I'm just a kid!" For this reason, it is imperative that educators take time to explain to and explore with students both
some of the earth's problems and possible solutions.

A number of education advocates of gifted children have offered rationales and suggestions for involving youth in global awareness activities. Whaley
(1980) highlighted six areas of emphasis in the study of global futures:

1. *Systems theory:* instruction that examines the functional interdependence
   of seemingly disparate fields of study, for example, religion, economics,
   and history
2. *Cultural analysis:* review of nationalism versus a global viewpoint; cross-
   cultural communication and barriers to communication; and study of the
   development of third-world nations
3. *Conflict/Power:* discussions and simulations that expose students to the
   various violent and nonviolent ways that individuals and governments
   resolve conflict and gain power
4. *Communication:* explores various types of verbal and nonverbal communication and the influence of these forms on different cultures
5. *Interdependence:* review of the benefits and detriments caused by our
   ecological connectedness, and the political and economic ramifications
   of this interdependence
6. *Futuristics:* acknowledgment of the impermanence of everything and the
   transient nature of knowledge in an ever-changing world (pp. 28–29)

Brandwein (1987) proposes similar ideas in his analysis of structuring
elementary-level science, humanities, and social science curricula along conceptual schemes that are global in nature. He deals with theses such as *a
living thing is the product of its heredity and environment, economic behavior
depends on the use of resources,* and *individuals seek and express the ideas of
justice.* The rationale for the importance of this thematic structuring is this:
"Full minds do not develop on restricted experience and an indifferent environment . . . ours is not simply a developing post-industrial world; it is
showing all the signs of becoming one world" (p. 40).

Many other educators and researchers have contributed ideas and resources for global awareness and education, also. Passow (1988) admonishes
educators of gifted children to nurture consciousness, concern, personal responsibility, and commitment so that these able students will not ignore the
ever-present threats to humanity and dignity. Through such instruction, able
students will feel equipped to use their creative talents toward the resolution
of global problems. Alexander (1989) provides a comprehensive, annotated
listing of books, newsletters, organizations, and media kits that can show
students how we are all "one planet, one human tribe, an interdependent
global village" (p. 1). And Shannon (1989) provides yet-another related aspect of global education: the opportunity for students to do "apprenticeships
in caring," wherein they perform acts of volunteer service within their schools

and communities in order to experience first-hand the unity of all facets of their environment (p. 185).

. . . And on and on. The number of resources available to practice global education is outnumbered only by the number of reasons that it is important to do so. Yet amidst all of the individuals who have suggested strategies and rationales for global awareness, no one single person has even come close to the depth which two individuals, George and Anne-Marie Roeper, have provided. The Roepers, having escaped the Nazis to establish a new home, a new family, in America, know too well what happens when "obedience" is misinterpreted as "responsibility," and when "basic skills" become equated with "life skills":

> (Our experience in Nazi Germany) makes it easy to remember that mutual respect and nonviolence come before everything else. A child's difficulties in school with spelling and reading are only a small part of learning about life. . . . Global education means that all children should have a view of the whole world as a community. All people have to relate to each other. Gifted children, as conceptual thinkers, need to learn this as a part of their education. (Williams, 1988, pp. 53–54)

"A mince pie," E. B. White called the future, "long in the baking." For today's gifted children, that future is as uncertain as futures have always been, yet through the introduction of global awareness strategies, the foundation on which they will build their future—our future—will be firm and steady.

SPECIFIC NEEDS OF GIFTED ADULTS

It happens to every educator eventually: While walking down Main Street or shopping at A&P, you meet a former student. An adult, now, perhaps with a tot or two in tow, this young person still retains a bit of the child that you knew back when you first met. You talk, you reflect, you catch up on old times; then, as he or she says goodbye, still calling you "Mr. Smith" or "Mrs O'Hara," you begin to feel your age.

And you begin to wonder, too, about the hundreds of other children whose lives you have touched. Instinctively, like a protective parent, you wish them all well and hope they have achieved (or eventually will achieve) the dreams and goals that seemed so vivid when they were your students. Also, you make a silent wish that you have left a positive impact; you want to have made a difference.

Gifted adults surround us, and often, these persons have intellectual and emotional needs that parallel those of gifted children. More intense, perhaps, or better refined, these needs can remain unmet. Similar to their younger counterparts, the needs for challenge, social acceptance, and emotional stability are vibrant, and if these needs are suppressed artificially, the personal and societal loss can be great. Whether it is the sonata unwritten, the curative drug undiscovered, or the absence of political insight, our society is less than it could have been if those persons had been fully functioning individuals (Gallagher, 1985).

David Willings (1985) reviewed several areas of adult development that must be addressed if the full potential of gifted adults is to be realized. Extrapolating these ideas from his longitudinal follow-up study of 15 former university students identified as gifted, the areas of concern are as follows (Willings, 1983):

Frustration in intellectual and creative areas due to the university experience. Expecting intellectual challenge and stimulation following an often bland high school experience, gifted college students are disillusioned by "more of the same" when confronted by easy courses, unchallenging professors, or students ambivalent about their own learning needs.

The perceived need, especially in females, to suppress talents to achieve social acceptability. The remnants of the adolescent desire for social acceptance at all costs remain a concern to some able young adults who may suppress their intelligence to better fit in with classmates.

Unfulfilling marriages and personal relationships due to role conflicts or intellectual boredom. In Willings's sample, 11 of the 15 individuals were married, but only two described their marriages as fulfilling or happy. Boredom with one's spouse or that one partner felt overwhelmed or "swamped" by the other were the main contributors for dissatisfaction.

Unsatisfying careers in which conformity and maintenance are prized more than innovation and excellence. The majority of the sample made several radical career changes, such as a teacher who became a monk and later a professor of anthropology or an accountant who became a social worker. As in social and marital relationships among this sample, lack of intellectual stimulation was cited as the main source of dissatisfaction.

Lack of personal satisfaction from achievements which are attained too easily, even if external reaction is positive. Guilt, depression, anger, and contempt for people or institutions giving the accolades were cited as the reason for this false sense of satisfaction.

The gnawing perception that you are not a valuable person unless achieving perfection consistently. The perfect job, the perfect family, the perfect social life: If one is not performing on all eight cylinders at all times, then the individuals felt as if their lives were void of purpose.

Reading these reactions of gifted adults to their own lives may make you want to do one of two things: Stay a child forever or wish you never were identified as gifted in the first place. It is important to remember, though, that not *all* gifted adults experience the sense of social and intellectual frustration expressed by the "Willings 15" and that even if some pain is present, there are strategies that can help guide gifted adults toward paths of personal fulfillment and societal success.

Bibliotherapy—the analysis of eminent persons' lives for purposes of self-reflection; interaction and discussion with people of like mind and abilities; formal counseling with a trained therapist; and realistic goal setting that allows for errors in judgment or action are all avenues that can lead gifted adults toward both satisfaction and happiness.

Actually, the areas of affective development of importance to gifted adults correspond with those of gifted children; the differences, where they exist, are in matters of degree, not kind.

Once again, it appears that we have come full circle. Able and willing to recognize the special needs of gifted children, we often assume that gifted adults can "make it on their own," without external guidance. Analogously, would we stop watering a full grown plant just because it is no longer a seedling? It is doubtful. Do we stop doting on our pets when they outgrow their stages as puppies or kittens? Of course not. Do we delete our love, caring, or concern for any living thing merely because it has matured? No, we don't; for we are aware that development never ceases or slows, it merely changes focus.

Such a mindset, if carried through into actions with gifted adults, may help them to see the full merits of their own potentials.

HIGHLY GIFTED CHILDREN

David Huang, as a college sophomore, was enrolled in 16 semester hours of organic chemistry, biology, calculus, and microcomputer graphics. His A− grade point average as a college freshman was an impressive beginning for a university career—especially for someone such as David, who was 9 years old at the time he achieved this success. Graduating from high school when he was 8, reading at age 2, and instructing his father (a chemical engineer) in BASIC computer language at 4, David is a child who is so rare that his talents inspire awe in the adults who observe him. Still, his after-school activities do not inspire any awe, just some smiles: "I have friends of all ages," David says, "but the ones I ride bikes with are 5 or 6." He also likes cartoons, especially "Woody Woodpecker" and "Scooby-Doo."

David, and other children like him, are the stuff of science fiction novels and hokey made-for-television movies. Unless you have observed, taught, or lived with one of these highly gifted children, you might assume they exist only in myth, for as adults, we sometimes do not want to believe that such extreme intelligence can exist in a child so young. As stated by J. David Smith, "social myths are constantly in the making—compelling in their simplicity and alluring because we want to believe them" (1985, p. 9).

Yet such highly gifted children *do* exist, whether or not you have met one; whether or not you believe that such extreme intellectual talents *should* be present in 5-, 6-, or 10-year-olds. And, if we put stock in some research on this population, the incidence of extreme giftedness is more prevalent than would be expected statistically (Gaunt, 1989; MacLeish, 1984; Silverman and Kearney, 1989).

But we're getting ahead of ourselves. Exactly who *is* the highly gifted child, and what is the line of intellectual demarcation that separates these children from the "generic gifted" children who are more typically found in the population? In virtually all definitions of highly gifted children—and there are several definitions—intelligence test scores are used to distinguish this group from their less-able agemates. Terman and Merrill (1973) and Whitmore (1980) use a score of 140 IQ to qualify a child as highly gifted. McGuffey, Feiring, and Lewis (1987) use IQ 164 and above as "extremely gifted," and Hollingworth's study of highly gifted children used 180 IQ and above as the point at which giftedness is manifest in an extreme form. These various definitions differ by as much as 40 IQ points—which is the same range that differentiates moderately retarded from average children (60 to 100 IQ) or average from moderately gifted children (100 to 140 IQ). This is certainly too large a spread to assume that the children who fall within this 40-point range (140 to 180 IQ) are a cohesive group. One point of agreement, though, is this: The higher the score used to define *highly gifted,* the sparser the literature base. As stated by Feldman (1987): "I puzzled long and hard over an explanation for such incredible neglect of what seemed to me to be some of the most fascinating facets of giftedness. I was unable to suggest a plausible explanation" (p. 72). Ironically, although a precise definition of extreme giftedness is lacking, most researchers agree on common traits and characteristics that are present in this group (Kline and Meckstroth, 1985; Kearney, 1988; Tolan, 1989). These include

A preference for adults or children older than they with whom to share interests and activities

An intensity and persistence in accomplishing self-set tasks

High energy levels, combined with a lessened need for sleep than children their same age

A high tolerance for clutter and acceptance of what appears to others as chaos

Marked discrepancies between intellectual and other areas of development

An aversion to regular school placements, resulting frequently in behavior and/or achievement problems

An exceptional knowledge base—outstripping that of parents and teachers—in particular areas of strength or interest

An intense ability to perceive injustices and moral wrongs, resulting in the idea that "everything matters, and it matters that it matters" (Kline and Meckstroth, 1985, p. 25)

Extreme expressions of joy, grief, sorrow, and other emotions

A susceptibility to embarrassment and self-doubt, sometimes interfering with social relationships

The need for specialized academic services that are frequently unavailable in public schools

As expressed by Tolan (1990), the difficulty with highly gifted children can be summed up in three words—*they don't fit.*

Yet all is not negative, all is not turmoil, in the lives of highly gifted children, their parents, and their teachers. In a comparative study of the perceptions of parents of highly and moderately gifted children, Gaunt (1989) found that there were as many similarities as differences between these groups of children as regards learning characteristics, school experiences, and social/emotional needs. Where differences did exist, parents of highly gifted children often reported that they located or "manufactured" solutions for the problems their children were facing. Often, in seeking an appropriate educational placement, parents of highly gifted children chose home schooling, for one or more years, much more frequently than did parents of less gifted children. This trend was especially true in rural areas, where in-school services tend to be limited in scope (Feldhusen, Van Tassel-Baska, and Seeley, 1989). Still, there is no magical elixir that meets the needs of all students at all times, as evidenced by the comments of two friends who both experienced home schooling:

CAM, AGE 13

I never thought I'd say this, but I'd like to return to regular school. I miss showing others what I've learned or created, wearing my new jacket to school, and sitting in class waiting for it to be over . . . and besides, how can you look forward to vacation when you're always on one?

RASHELL, AGE 16

It's not important to show others what I know, it's important that *I* know. Cam is much more outgoing than I am. . . . I have never missed being with students my own age because I don't like to stay in cliques like they do. . . . Home study gives me the chance to arrange my schedule. . . . I'd never go back to regular school. (Cornelius, 1988, p. 3)

Other, less drastic modifications than home schooling have been suggested by experts who have studied the field of highly gifted children. Among these modifications are the following:

1. *Appropriate, periodic assessments for placement purposes, involvement of the child in substantive decision making regarding placement, and assurance that at least one of the child's talents is stretched toward its current potential* (Lewis, 1984).
2. *Focused acceleration:* Grade placement, in areas of strength, four years above that typically expected. Social needs with children closer in age chronologically are met through common recess, art, lunch, and handwriting exercises (Kline and Meckstroth, 1985).
3. *Designing a "user friendly" home environment.* Even in highly gifted children, learning does not occur spontaneously or is it pervasive in all content and contexts (Feldman, 1979). Too, these children need behavioral limits and discipline as do all children. Using positive reinforcement, negotiation, and logic in setting limits takes advantage of these children's talents while imposing structure on their daily lives.
4. *Exposure to the arts, modern languages, and museums, combined with an exposure to adults who have succeeded in these areas* (White and Renzulli, 1987).
5. *Opportunities to explore areas of interest independently or with peers of similar abilities and support in pursuing projects with which even parents are not well-versed* (Sharkey, 1987).
6. *Adopting a "casual" approach to the highly gifted child's talents.* By not cajoling the child into "performing" for others, highly gifted children will come to accept their talents as natural *for them,* although they may be different from typical standards or expectations (Tolan, 1990).
7. *Make midcourse adjustments.* Even the best developed and most well thought out plans can go awry. The expected growth may not occur, or the highly gifted child may exhaust even advanced options quicker than anticipated. In other words, prepare for "plan B" before it is needed (Kearney, 1989).

Raising or teaching a highly gifted child requires a balance of temperament and expectations. Where does the point of encouragement become pushing? When does independence turn into chaos? When does appreciating a child's talents approach exploiting a child's talents? Whose gift is it, anyway?

These questions, among many others, confront adults who encounter highly gifted children. The broad smile and obvious pride on discovering a child's extraordinary gift soon give way to the realities of the daunting tasks that lie ahead. And, since no one "recipe" of genetics and environment goes into creating a highly gifted child, the path to success is not so well trod as to be obvious.

Mistakes will be made, decisions will be regretted, hindsight will rear its ugly head on a regular basis to expose us to our errors. Still, if it is kept in mind that the child, no matter the level of giftedness, remains a child, then we will be as ready to soothe the hurt feelings, and scrub the scraped knee, as we are to challenge the intellect.

David Huang, the 9-year-old college sophomore, is driven to "school" each day by his mom—who walks him across the street to his chemistry class, because "sometimes he forgets to look both ways."

Now *that's* good to know!

GIFTED GIRLS

Initially, I questioned long and hard as to whether this subtopic was legitimately placed in this book. Some gnawing male, knee-jerk reaction in me made me question the validity of this entire subject. After all, if gifted *girls* have special needs, does this imply that gifted *boys* do not? And if they *do,* who's writing about them? (Very few folks I could find.) Besides, at this time in our cultural history, haven't females progressed to the point where they have opportunities equal to those of males? I mean, really: My son, who is 12, has never been on a soccer or baseball team *without* girls, which was hardly the case with my own childhood teams. Certainly, "we've come a long way, baby."

But then I began to look around at who was writing about gifted girls. Most of them are respected colleagues, careful researchers, authors of note and integrity. Certainly, they wouldn't spend their valuable time and energies on a topic that was contrived. Thus began my reeducation about the importance of the topic of gifted girls.

It did not take long for me to find that this subtopic was not as "new" as I had assumed. Terman and Oden (1947) examined the adult lives of the 1500+ original "Termites" and found that women's adult achievement showed little relationship to their IQ scores. In fact, two-thirds of the highly gifted girls, now women (IQ = 170+), were employed as housewives or office workers. Men, on the other hand, showed high correlations between IQ and career prominence.

Watley (1969), in another longitudinal study, examined the career paths of National Merit Scholars from 1956 to 1957. The findings were parallel to those of Terman and Oden's study, as all areas of academic achievement beyond high school and career aspirations were lower for women than they were for men.

But do the results of these studies, now more than a generation old, still represent the world as it exists today? The answer is a conclusive yes and no. Kramer (1986) found that gifted boys and girls differ little in their career aspirations. However, Leroux (1985) found that twelfth-grade gifted girls had lower career and self-aspirations than did their male counterparts and that the girls perceived boys as more capable in math and science. Other research shows a similar lack of agreement.

Kerr (1985b) hypothesizes that young gifted children do not differ by gender in their life aspirations, but that differences begin to occur during adolescence. Whereas boys maintain their high-status profile of career aspirations throughout the teenage years, girls show a clear pattern of decline. This hypothesis is supported by Kaufmann (1981), who detected a similar trend among her subjects, Presidential Scholars.

Given this trend of declining female aspirations, it is logical to point to environmental conditions—home life, societal standards and expectations—as the culprits behind these diminished ambitions. Callahan (1979), though, cautions against such a blanket indictment:

> Underlying the problems of achievement and motivation of gifted and talented females lie hypotheses yet to be tested . . . until cultural or environmental factors are altered considerably to neutralize the potential effects, there will be no way of asserting how great that impact is. (p. 412)

Still, environmental conditions are responsible to at least some degree for the differential ambitions of gifted boys and girls. These barriers to achievement have been categorized as *external* or *internal* and are represented by some of the following (Hollinger and Fleming, 1984; Kerr, 1985b):

External Barriers	*Internal Barriers*
Sexism and discrimination	Fear of competition with men
Lack of role models	Fear of being "found out" as not really bright or competent
Societal expectations ("girls are pretty, boys are smart")	Self-defeating tendency to want to "fall back" onto expected societal roles
Lack of financial resources for professional development	Unwillingness to actively defy social norms
Family responsibilities that inhibit full participation in the workforce	Internalization of failure and externalization of success experiences

In order to circumvent these problems or to diminish their impact should they be present, Kerr (1985b) has suggested strategies and attitudes to guide gifted girls from preschool to professional school. Excerpted in the following list, it should be noted that the interventions begin from day 1 of a child's life and continue on through young adulthood. The undercurrents of emotional support, available role models, nonsexist caregivers, and the pursuit of academic excellence are all present in these suggestions. These attitudes, beliefs, and strategies can be implemented at home, in school, or in the community.

Guiding Gifted Girls: From Preschool to Professional School[2]

Preschool

If you don't want to treat your daughter like a fragile little flower, don't dress her as one.

Choose nonsexist, manipulative toys.

Choose day care that encourages play and reading activities.

Screen television shows that promote sexist or stereotypic roles for females.

Allow girls to see adults in various work roles that are not "typically" expected for that gender.

Primary/Elementary

Allow early and frequent reading.

Encourage mathematical interests and use of technology, for example, home or school computers.

Make available art materials, musical instruments, and manipulative toys and games (for example, Legos).

Try to find an older girl with similar interests to serve as a role model.

Acknowledge and respect her talents, let her know her areas of giftedness.

Junior High

Try to conceal your astonishment that she wants to now be like every other girl in her class.

Refuse to allow her to evaluate herself in terms of her attractiveness.

Continue to encourage her independence of thought and activities that promote her self-understanding.

Insist she continue to take math and science courses.

Encourage reading biographies to begin possible career options.

Senior High

Expect (and then encourage) a rekindled interest in academics.

Locate college and scholarship guides and information.

Seek competent, nonsexist career guidance, in or outside of school.

Require that she complete 4 years of math.

Locate a mentor, especially in an area of the girl's proficiency.

---

[2] Excerpted from: B. A. Kerr, *Smart Girls, Gifted Women*. Columbus, OH: Ohio Psychology, 1985.

Encourage "selective excellence" rather than "across the board perfection."

College

Locate an academically oriented college with a high proportion of female faculty.

Encourage social relationships with men and women who share common interests in campus organizations.

Initiate discussion related to her personal and professional ambitions and to how her current activities are providing for/leading to such fulfillment.

Maintain curiosity about her interests, even when they differ from your own.

Encourage her to speak up in class; to be assertive. She needs to be sure her professors notice and respect her.

Equal opportunity begins with the personal belief that you can be your personal best. No amount of dollars and no wealth of special programs can be accessed effectively if the recipient does not believe that she is worthy of them. First and foremost, the "I can" attitude underlies all approaches used in meeting the special needs of gifted girls.

CULTURALLY DIVERSE GIFTED STUDENTS

Cultural *diversity* for too long has been synonymous with cultural *disadvantage*. Our nation's melting-pot mentality, diminished somewhat since the 1920s, but not so far reduced as to be negligible, encourages assimilation into mainstream America. To hold onto one's heritage outside of the home or a few neighborhood festivals is to practice cultural anarchy; surely, a "good" citizen would want to adopt the language, standards, and customs of one's new home, not to hold on to the ways of some ancestral backwater farm, village, or ghetto.

In such a climate, cultural pluralism is discouraged. Reductions in federal funding of bilingual education programs and legislation in at least 12 states declaring English as the official language are but two examples of political movements that diminish the importance of cultural diversity. Even our newest federal holiday, Martin Luther King Day, is not recognized as a holiday in four US states and is seen by millions of people as nothing more than another Monday off with pay.

Against this backdrop exists the gifted child whose background, heritage, or lifestyle does not parallel those of most classmates. More often than not, gifted children from black or Hispanic families or from those where English is a second language (ESL) will not be selected for inclusion in programs for gifted students, as the gifts they possess, the talents they express, are not "picked up" by current identification methods (Cohen, 1990). Case in point: In Arizona, 16.17 percent of the school-age population consists of ESL students. However, a scant 0.14 percent of this population is enrolled in programs for gifted students—only 143 ESL students statewide (Maker, 1987). Other research, using populations of black, Hispanic, and native American students, shows a similar absence of identification among these culturally diverse groups. Kitano (1986) reports that the identification of giftedness among these groups is less than half of what is expected. In fact, the only culturally different population that has a proportional overabundance of children selected for inclusion in programs for gifted students is Asian Americans whose enrollment nationwide is twice what's expected (Kitano and Kirby, 1986; Machado, 1987).

Yet surely, giftedness exists in many forms within all cultures. As E. Paul Torrance wrote (1985) regarding John Torres, a 12-year-old sixth grader who was gifted in art, mechanics, leadership, and other language-free areas:

> Is John Torres gifted? Would it be better to treat John as gifted in the psychomotor and leadership areas or as a retarded non-reader and a behavior disorder case? Which is in John's best interest? Which is in society's best interest? (p. 2)

The identification of gifts and talents among culturally diverse groups, followed by appropriate educational planning and programming, is essential. Currently, 30 percent of all school-age students are from minority groups, and by the year 2000, minority enrollment in our nation's schools may surpass that of today's white majority ("Fifty-one percent of all teachers," 1987). If gifted education is to remain a vibrant and effective force in the next century, then educators will have to find *and implement* new strategies for identifying and educating culturally diverse students with exceptional promise.

Several researchers have suggested general methods and specific tests to identify talent in culturally diverse populations. Frasier (1980) recommended that objective test scores—IQ and achievement tests—be used with caution: "Students from culturally diverse backgrounds score, on the average, 15 points lower on intelligence tests than students from white, Anglo-Saxon Protestant groups" (p. 52). To partially compensate for this culturally based discrepancy, Frasier recommends that standardized tests scores be compared against other students from the same culture, rather than the norms based on the performance of white students. By using these "within-group norms," the possibility of *in*cluding a gifted child based on strengths rather than *ex*cluding that child based on perceived weaknesses will be enhanced.

In addition, Feldhusen, Van Tassel-Baska, and Seeley (1989) propose the use of subjective teacher checklists whose items correspond to traits and behaviors typically found among a specific culture. Torrance (1969) proposed the following roster that educators might consider in seeking talents among culturally diverse groups.

1. Ability to express feelings and emotion
2. Ability to improvise with commonplace materials and objects
3. Ability to articulate well in role playing, sociodrama, and storytelling
4. Enjoyment of and ability in visual arts such as drawing, painting, and sculpture
5. Enjoyment of and ability in creative movement, dance, dramatics, and so forth
6. Enjoyment of and ability in music, rhythm, and the like
7. Use of expressive speech
8. Fluency and flexibility in figural media
9. Enjoyment of and skills in group activities, problem solving, and so forth
10. Responsiveness to the concrete
11. Responsiveness to the kinesthetic
12. Expressiveness of gestures, body language, and so forth and the ability to interpret body language
13. Humor
14. Richness of imagery in informal language
15. Originality of ideas in problem solving
16. Problem centeredness or persistence in problem solving
17. Emotional responsiveness
18. Quickness of warm-up

The use of peer nomination, self-nomination, and product analysis are other techniques suggested for use. The "bottom line" in identification is to approach the task with the mindset that the object of our work is to find reasons to *in*clude rather than *ex*clude gifted or potentially gifted children into programs which will allow for the full expression of their talents.

> Identification is an individual matter and should never depend on a test score. If anything, it should depend more on the conclusions of teachers or specialists who are either trained to work with talented minority children, or sensitive to the less obvious 'signs' of talent. (Eby and Smutny, 1990, p. 121)

For individuals who do require the use of some objective test scores as a part of multicriteria assessment, several options are recommended. *The Kaufman Assessment Battery for Children—K-ABC* is an individually administered series of achievement and aptitude tests (Kaufman and Kaufman, 1983). The *K-ABC* is available in Spanish, and it has been found useful in assessing the mental processing abilities of children with both learning disabilities and cultural differences. Normed on children between the ages of 2.5 and 12.5, the

Kaufman is especially appropriate for use with gifted young children. *The Cattell Culture Fair Intelligence Series* is a brief screening tool that does not use language-based activities to assess general intelligence (Cattell and Cattell, 1970). Instead, subtests on classification and matrices are used to assess abstract reasoning. Similarly, the *Raven's Progressive Matrices Tests* has gained favor with educators of gifted children interested in assessing abstract mental ability through the use of problems using figures and designs (Raven, 1956; 1962). Totally nonverbal, the *Raven* may be used with specific cultural subgroups, as well as several other special populations (for example, deaf children). It is available for use with persons who are 8 to 65 years old and, like the Cattell, may be administered by teachers.

Other tools for identifying giftedness in culturally diverse populations are available, and Eby and Smutny (1990) provide a comprehensive list and analysis of these tests.

The ultimate purpose behind locating specific talents among culturally diverse groups is to follow through with educational services that match their talents. "Every time one of these students succeeds, his or her horizons are broadened, the vistas of his or her family are expanded, the reach of his or her community is extended, and the nation benefits" (McIntosh and Greenlaw, 1986, p. 107). The first step in *realizing* the fruition of these talents is identification *of* these talents, using instruments and strategies that allow these children to shine in the best of all possible lights.

Programming Concerns

In order for culturally diverse gifted students to develop their talents while preserving their cultural heritage, these students and their families must first understand that maintaining ethnic identity is compatible with achieving academically and artistically (Colangelo, 1985). However, culturally diverse gifted youngsters sometimes feel "caught" between maintaining their uniqueness and participating in a program for gifted students that is looked on with some suspicion by ethnic peers (Exum and Colangelo, 1981). Thus, Colangelo (1985) recommends that counselors acquaint themselves with the five stages of ethnic identity proposed by Banks (1979), so that they can help gifted students and their families accept and develop their special talents while holding on to their unique cultural heritage. The five stages are the following:

STAGE 1: *Ethnic Psychological Captivity:* Individuals who internalize negative stereotypes of their culture and strive vigorously to become a part of "mainstream" culture.

STAGE 2: *Ethnic Encapsulation:* Individuals at this level interact only with others of their same ethnicity, thinking themselves as superior to other groups.

STAGE 3: *Ethnic Identity Clarification:* Individuals who have "come to terms" with their own ethnicity and take pride in its uniqueness.

STAGE 4: *Biethnicity:* Individuals who have developed an appreciation for their own and other ethnicities and begin to interact with various ethnic groups, while maintaining primary affiliation with one's own ethnic heritage.

STAGE 5: *Multiethnicity:* Individuals who reach this stage have reached the ideal within a pluralistic culture. They function readily within several ethnic environments, appreciating the differences and uniqueness of each.

According to Colangelo (1985), "Counselors can make a significant contribution to gifted and talented programs by deliberately and systematically helping culturally diverse gifted (students) develop along this typology" (p. 35). Academic and social development will be enhanced, as culturally distinct groups share their uniqueness with students of other ethnic heritage, while members of the cultural "mainstream" (each of whom *also* has a cultural heritage to share) develop their own acceptance of multiethnicity.

Specific program designs for meeting the needs of gifted students from different cultural groups vary widely, yet they are not so unique as to be exclusive to this population. Thus, various authors suggest the use of resource rooms, enrichment classes, community outreach activities, and accelerated classes for culturally diverse gifted students (Barstow, 1987; Blanning, 1980; Cohen, 1990; Dannenberg, 1984; Frasier, 1980). However, there *are* some unique "reminders" to be aware of prior to program implementation.

Allow "trial participation" for students who may be questionable, for whatever reason, about program participation (Barstow, 1987).

Program directors should know the cultures they are inviting to participate, and they should provide home–school liaisons who are familiar with the cultural heritage of program participants (Eby and Smutny, 1990).

Manipulatives, especially in math, science, and problem-solving activities, should be provided throughout the school years (Lincoln, 1980).

Early career and college counseling should be provided (Dunbaum and Russo, 1983).

Integrate all gifted children into one program, to encourage multiethnicity, but provide individually determined goals, depending on a student's expressed need (Cohen, 1990).

This continuing challenge to provide optimal program services to gifted and talented children of all ethnicities is at the forefront of current issues in the field of gifted education. Our changing culture demands that this be so.

Our success *now* will be measured only in future generations, as the students who heretofore have been virtually bypassed by gifted program services begin to get identified for their strengths, not their differences, and their cultural differences are lauded, not tolerated.

CONCLUSION

The 1960s was an era where the unique aspects of many cultures became appreciated in ways that are only now beginning to reemerge (one step forward, two steps back). During that time, rock music—the voice and conscience of my youth—spoke directly to the thoughts expressed regarding the beauty and necessity of human diversity. Sly and his family told us that we're all "everyday people"; the Beatles reminded us that all we needed was love, and Janis Ian's "Society's Child" gave proof that growing up—for all of us—is not always pretty nor easy.

A smidgen of lyric here and there from bands said to have soul and singers said to have heart. Their collective messages were clear and are as timely now as in the era of bell bottoms and blue eye shadow: one world, one people, one common tune—acceptance and appreciation of differences.

Rereading what I have written in this chapter, I am appalled by the omissions. So many ideas presented; many, reviewed only in a cursory manner. Each topic, each subpopulation, worthy of their own book, rather than the brief mention that each gets here. Still, the resources are there now, and they continue to be published. Seek them out, please; or even better, write your own.

As we approach a new century that is sure to bring about changes that, today, cannot even be imagined, I look for the education of gifted children to grow toward those persons and topics that have not yet received the full attention they deserve. Gifted girls, gifted adults, adolescents at-risk, and young children with sensory impairments: gifted all, but still underserved and still misunderstood.

Hand in hand, adult and child; we are twenty-first-century pioneers.

CONTINUING QUESTS AND QUESTIONS

1. This chapter focused on "fringe" issues within education for gifted children. There were few references to curricular modifications and virtually no allusions to the importance of teaching higher level thinking skills or creative problem-solving strategies. Rather, the emphasis in Chapter 9 was on specific needs of gifted subgroups or specialized issues. Are these issues/topics/populations really as important as I make them out to be, or does this emphasis on the fringes detract from our main purpose in education for gifted students? What are your views on the impor-

tance of these topics, and how will you translate your views into visible actions for the gifted students with whom you are most familiar?

2. Teacher education programs in education for gifted children are still relatively scarce in our nation's colleges and universities, with only about 120 such programs available in our entire country. What are your views on the need for such programs? Is teaching in or coordinating such a program so unique that special certification should be required for those who do it? If so, what should that program entail? Given the focus of this chapter, it appears that skills in counseling, administration, and special education assessment would be helpful for professionals in education for gifted children—would you build these in to a certification program, or would you expect that these skills could be "picked up" through on-the-job experience? Who is the ideal "gifted" educator—what skills, knowledge, attitudes, and values should this person possess, and how does he or she get them?

3. Societal expectations for exceptional individuals seem to vary so much from the norm. Handicapped persons are often lauded for performing at levels that our own short-sighted expectations had simply placed too low. Conversely, gifted individuals are often shortchanged the credit they deserve for doing remarkable things, because we *expect* smart people to do great things. What role might these societal expectations—whether too low or too high—play in the onset of some of the problems reviewed in this chapter, especially depression, dissatisfaction with one's accomplishments, or denial of one's gifts in order to better "fit in"? What are your own attitudes regarding the role of the exceptional person in our society, and how can we guard against stereotypes in our own thinking and in that of our colleagues?

4. Is it possible to involve children in activities and projects related to global understanding and improvement without placing an undue pressure on them to "fix up" the world that their forebears have left them? In what ways can we help children to see that even small steps taken toward political, environmental, or social improvements are worthwhile? What can *we* do, as adults, that prove to our students that we, too, are taking an active part in our planet's improvement?

OUT OF THE WAY/OUT OF THIS WORLD RESOURCES

Digests on the Gifted, edited by Sandra Berger (Council for Exceptional Children, Reston, VA, 1990).

These 20+ "flyers" (one to four pages in length) present the current theory, research, and practice on such diverse topics as extreme giftedness, underachievement, identification of gifted minority students, and using computers with gifted children. The unique format (each flyer is self-contained, including its own reference list) makes these materials perfect for distribution at teacher inservice or parent-group meetings.

A Study of Successful Persons from Seriously Disadvantaged Backgrounds: Final Report, by E. M. Glaser and N. L. Ross (Office of Special Manpower Programs, Department of Labor, Washington, D.C., 1970).

This report details the many characteristics of successful students whose family or economic backgrounds place them seriously at risk. Among the common factors correlated with success are a strong sense of identity, pride, and self-worth; physical removal from the disadvantaged backgrounds at particular key times; the channeling of rage into appropriate actions; and an ability to take risks and endure anxiety and social norm humiliation. A must-read resource for anyone who works with economically deprived children and their families.

Mentor Relationships: How They Aid Creative Achievement, Endure, Change and Die, by E. Paul Torrance (Bearly Limited, Buffalo, NY, 1984).

Most successful adults credit significant others, at least partially, with their success. Whether this person was an academic advisor, a supervisor at work, or a familial or neighborhood colleague, the role of this mentor is often seen as a fundamental link in the chain of adult accomplishment. But mentor relationships often change over time, turn sour, or become deeper and more collegial. Torrance addresses the importance of mentor relationships and the complex twists and turns that often occur between the mentor and the protege.

Save Tomorrow for the Children, by E. Paul Torrance, Deborah Weiner, Jack H. Presbury, and Morgan Henderson (Bearly Limited, Buffalo, NY, 1987).

As members of a world community, gifted children have many concerns, dreams, and hopes for their future. This book addresses such themes as the world in 2010, the threat of cosmic radiation, programmed to care, and world discovery: peace causes war. Using writing samples selected from future world scenarios composed by over 5000 children, the authors present some startling and insightful views of today's world . . . and tomorrow's.

CHAPTER 10

From the Homefront: Parents as Helpers

The intent of this chapter is to

Review particular aspects of gifted education—labeling, sibling relationships, expectations—and explain how each impacts on the parenting of gifted children

Present case study research on gifted adolescents and adults who reflect on their own parents' childrearing methods

Introduce you to the distinctions between micro- and macroadvocacy and the purposes behind each as related to gifted education

Suggest some "do's and don't's" regarding childrearing techniques with gifted youngsters

KIDS AND KITES[1]

Kites
> *fly*
but they need an anchor.

Kids
> *roam*
but they need a home.

---

[1] From *Gifted Children Speak Out* by James R. Delisle. Copyright © 1984 by James R. Delisle. Reprinted by permission of Walker and Company.

If a kite loses its anchor
    it falls.
If a child loses his home
    he declines.

As a kite goes higher and higher
    you give it more string.

As a child grows older and older
    you give him more freedom.

But here
    the similarity ends;

for kites
    even with the most string imaginable
    crash sooner or later

but kids
    (if they are old enough)
    adjust safely
    and create new homes.

Robert Jellinghaus
Age 11

"Where did the years go?" parents ask. The fragile infant, totally dependent, soon begins to walk and talk, gaining assurance with each step, each word. Then, school becomes a daily routine: It is a new beginning, but it is also an end. Later years spin by in quick succession and, all-too-soon, our dependent children become independent adults, capable of visualizing and achieving their own dreams—which often include starting a family, making grandparents of those who feel too young to assume that role. The cycle of life continues. Our children, now parents themselves, have charted the course for a new generation. (Or, as Robert reminds us, they create new homes.)

What are the roles of parents in raising gifted children and are these responsibilities any different than those practiced by Dr. Spock and other gurus of childrearing? The answers to these questions lie somewhere in the recesses between common sense and clinical research. Certainly, it would be pompous to think of gifted children as so different from others as to make general parenting principles inappropriate; yet it is naive to believe that a characteristic as significant as giftedness would not have some unique impact on both the family and the child's role in the family, requiring some changes in parent–child interactions.

In this chapter, the important and dynamic roles of parents in fostering both giftedness and childhood will be addressed. Guidelines will be given, research will be cited, but the ultimate decision of "what to do when" will not be forthcoming; it's not that simple. Still, it is hoped that by listening to the experts—researchers, parents, children—some clear direction can be given.

PARENTING GIFTED CHILDREN:
WHAT THE RESEARCH SUGGESTS

Alexander Pope, in his "Essay on Criticism," wrote:

> *And still to-morrow's wiser than to-day.*
> *We think our fathers' fools,*
> *So wise we grow;*
> *Our wiser sons, no doubt, will think us so.*

Generation after generation, parents make the same mistakes and discoveries as did their forebears. Each sees its situation as different, made unique by world events and conditions that have never before existed. Still, how eerie is the sameness that pervades the concerns, century upon century, that parents encounter on the road of childrearing!

The same condition is true when we compare the early and later literature on parenting gifted children—the years may change, but the advice stays the same. Hollingworth (1942) wrote of the struggle between independence and dependence faced by parents whose children, though intelligent, still needed discipline. She suggested that parents respond quickly and consistently when undesirable behaviors appeared, and suggested "the silent treatment" as an especially effective technique to use with gifted children, who are often verbally facile enough to argue their way out of anything—except silence! Unwarranted or illogical punishments would go against the senses of fairness and reason so important to many gifted children, Hollingworth thought, and should thus be avoided at all costs. As she explained: "To find a golden mean between arbitrary abolition of all argument, on the one hand, and weak fostering of an intolerable habit of endless argumentation, on the other, is not always easy, but it is always worth while as a measure of retaining the respect of the child" (Hollingworth, 1942, p. 279). Ross (1964) believes that parents are unclear on what roles they should play in raising their gifted children; that, in fact, they react to their child's giftedness the same way that parents do when they are told that their child has a learning disability. Thus, they react more to the *differentness* of their children than to the physical and social *similarities* they share with other youngsters. Such a one-sided approach to childrearing—allowing the gift to assume a life of its own—often results in feelings of uncertainty and guilt. Parents often state, "I'm not doing enough for my child."

In 1956, Laycock wrote about the needs of gifted children within the family. "Gifted children need three things from parents: (1) acceptance, (2) understanding, and (3) guidance" (p. 109). How these needs differ from those of all other children is elaborated further in his article:

They need to be accepted as human beings and not because they bring prestige to parents because of their achievements.

In order to accept gifted children fully, parents must learn to note the specific behaviors that may indicate giftedness—superior insight, reasoning, abstract thinking skills, and so on.

Parents should not demean or lessen the presence of their gifted children's talents in an unhealthy attempt to "pull them down a peg."

Parents need to appreciate gifted children's need or preference for individuality. "Surely, democracy does not mean an attempt to secure a dead level of mediocre conformity" (Laycock, 1956, p. 109).

Parents should encourage gifted children's natural inclinations to pursue interests that may not be typical of their agemates, including reading, attendance at lectures, concerts, and exhibitions, and hobbies.

Parents should serve as "watchdogs" over their gifted children's education, ensuring that enrichment and acceleration options are offered and that vocational guidance is provided, when appropriate.

So many "shoulds"!

How about equal time for parents who followed through, who made an effort, consciously or unconsciously, to accept, encourage, and understand their gifted children? Several studies did just this, as gifted adults, adolescents, and their families were surveyed on the specific practices and attitudes that fostered the gifted child's talents.

David Henry Feldman wrote a book, *Nature's Gambit* (1986), in which he presents the results of his 10-year study of six remarkable children he classifies as prodigies. The children, all boys and all preadolescents at the study's onset, excelled in many areas: music, science, sports, math, chess, and writing. The lives of these children and their families were analyzed by Feldman with a precision seldom seen outside of a laboratory setting; Feldman learned much by looking and listening, and his readers benefit by the careful portraits he paints of the dynamics that exist between these prodigies and their parents. The following excerpts are from Feldman's findings, which are remarkable, I believe, because they can be generalized across all families that include a child with noticeably outstanding abilities.

The Author's Initial Expectation
I had expected the children and their parents to behave toward each other more like colleagues and peers than parents and children. After all, these children are as competent, if not more so, than their parents. . . . Instead I found . . . the prodigies tended to be treated even more as children than other youngsters their age. (pp. 151–152)

On Untying the Apron Strings
The boys' activities were carefully monitored and often included the presence of a parent . . . [yet] there seems to be an awareness that their children will have to begin making their own way . . . and they must be assisted in the process of growing up by assuming some level of independence and responsibility. (pp. 152–153)

On Parents' Role in Monitoring Development
They arrange and monitor educational experiences, advise and guide them in career decisions, and try at the same time to provide a stable emotional atmosphere and normal social life. (p. 153)

On Sibling Relationships
By and large (the parents are) sensitive to and appreciative of the individual strengths of each member of the family . . . [which] helps these unusually gifted children to put their talents in some perspective and to develop an appreciation for being one member of a larger enterprise—the functioning of a family unit—where sometimes prodigious talent is an asset and sometimes it is not. (p. 155)

On Enhancing a Child's Talents
No child was forced to study or to practice, nor was he denied other activities: no one was chained to a piano, or prevented from playing with his friends . . . possibly, this quality of responsiveness rather than control accounts for the easy, affectionate relationships between [these] children and parents. (p. 155)

Overall Finding on Parent–Child Relationships
I have observed dedicated and ambitious parents, but not parents who drive their children into activities that the children themselves do not seem inclined to attempt or pursue . . . it is the children who provide the primary source of energy and determination for developing their talents. The parents' role seems to be to respond, support and encourage these efforts (p. 156)[2]

The key elements in Feldman's findings—encouragement as opposed to pushing, responding to the child's interest instead of channeling the youngster down a path of the parents' choosing—are also present in a study by Cox, Daniel, and Boston (1985). These researchers surveyed creative adults who had received a MacArthur Foundation Fellowship—a "genius grant" of between $100,000 and $300,000—for the work they had accomplished to date.

---

[2] From *Nature's Gambit: Child Prodigies and the Development of Human Potential,* by David Henry Feldman with Lynn T. Goldsmith. Copyright © 1986 by Basic Books, Inc. Reprinted by permission of Basic Books, Inc., Publishers, New York.

The MacArthur Fellows submit no applications. They draw up no special plans or projects. They are not expected to submit reports or publish results.

They have qualified for the awards by uncommon abilities, demonstrated across a broad spectrum of creative pursuits. (Cox, Daniel, and Boston, 1985, p. 13)

In essence, the MacArthur Foundation serves as a sponsor for rewarding and encouraging the creative pursuits of gifted individuals whose work-to-date has already proven exceptional. Included among their ranks are Robert Coles, research psychiatrist at Harvard; Howard Gardner, developer of the theory of multiple intelligences; Francesca Rochberg-Halton, Assyriologist at the University of Chicago; and John Sayles, film maker and fiction writer. The insights, the remembrances of youth, and the vignettes of family interactions provided by these individuals give clear signals to parents who want to know what in the home environment stimulates creative behaviors. Some vital elements include the following (all from Cox, Daniel, and Boston, 1985):

Support: "They instilled in me a love of learning and knowledge as well as plenty of positive reinforcement for thinking, writing, and pursuing knowledge." (p. 21)

Communication: "Although my parents were not well educated, I believe that dinner-table conversation was . . . significant in instilling both social values and concern for knowledge." (p. 21)

Role Modeling: "I read a lot at home because I saw them reading all the time and I suppose that helped in school." (p. 21)

Quantity Time: "[My mother] drove us to the public library every Saturday morning of our lives. I used to think that everyone went to the library on Saturday and church on Sunday." (p. 22)

Trust: "My parents let me have a basement laboratory and darkroom, and they let me stay up into the early morning hours. The let me choose my hobbies, my friends, my activities." (pp. 22–23)

Exposure: "We were exposed to music long before we became active in it. And that is an important point, I think." (p. 23)

Some may argue against the somewhat simplistic suggestions offered here. Time, support, and interest may be necessary, but are they sufficient to ensure that giftedness will emerge? Also, these reflections are all contaminated by the selectivity of the respondents' own memories: They recall what they want to, or perhaps, what conveniently fits their current modes of thinking. Still, the magic formula that will guarantee that latent gifts come to bear fruit, or that expressed talents remain as such, seems to still be elusive. In my view, that will always be the case; for just as no two individuals are exactly alike, the same is true for families. Thus, I suggest, dear readers, that we be content with the general suggestions offered by the "experts" highlighted here rather than disappointed that a cookbook recipe doesn't appear at hand. From what we have learned from gifted children who have since grown up, they like the latitude of imprecision.

AT HOME: SPECIFIC DO'S AND DON'T'S

Here I go again, contradicting myself! For just after I've stepped down from my soapbox on which I extolled the praises of a recipe-free approach to childrearing, I get set to present a few more pages of specific strategies that usually work and those that usually fail. Bear with me, please, as I try to explain why I don't believe I'm speaking out of both sides of my mouth simultaneously.

Parents of gifted children, and parents of all children, desire some "how-to's" that are concrete; visible; doable. The admonition to "encourage your child" or to "support his or her efforts" seems trite and overplayed; you don't need a PhD in child psychology to appreciate the importance of caring or listening. We see the so-called big picture; it's the little details that often seem cloudy.

Here, then, are some of those specifics that help in the development of the gifted child within the family unit.

Avoid Comparisons

Whether the comparison is with a sibling, a classmate, a cousin, or a neighborhood child, gifted children detest being evaluated in relation to someone else. Oddly, it doesn't appear to matter whether the child gets compared favorably or unfavorably to another child; a comment such as "You are so much brighter than your brother was at this age" can be just as unwelcomed as is "If you tried harder you might do as well as your sister."

"But I don't *compare* my children," you may say. "I see each one as an individual." This, in fact, may be so between parent and child, yet it may *not* be the case when grandma visits or uncle calls. As the persons in charge of the household (presumably), parents are allowed to "call the shots" when it comes to who says what to whom. If well-meaning but errant elders pit children against each other in an intellectual sparring match, parents can serve as referees, calling off the bout due to a technical foul: that such verbal assaults are against the house rules.

When comparisons occur, no one wins; resentment reigns. A preferred mode is to cite positives that are individual to the child in question. For example, "I love to see you working so hard on your homework, Mary. You're so conscientious." Or, "Tony, that poem you wrote about the ocean really makes me feel as if I'm on the beach. You painted a word picture!" Go ahead, pick out who is "more gifted" than the other, Mary or Tony. You don't know, nor do I; for instead of reacting to a *label,* specific comments such as these allow parents (and others) to react to an *action*—a visible, concrete action. "This constant and public aknowledgement of *valuable individuality* reassures each child of her own worth and lessens the need to compete destructively with siblings" (Webb, Meckstroth, and Tolan, 1982, p. 166).

Avoid Bragging

"You'll just *love* the way Joey plays the piano—come on Joey, show us all."

"Annabel can recite the alphabet forward and backward—and she's only 4! Look, she'll show you."

"Go ahead, dear, tell Mrs. White your name, your age, and your IQ."

Bragging about a gifted child's talents isn't usually this blunt, but it might as well be. Putting the gifted child on display for others to ogle carries all sorts of unintended messages back to the child being bragged about, the most destructive of which is this: "If I'm to be accepted, I must be performing."

When self-worth is tied in with performance standards, the only time the child comes out a winner (in his own eyes) is during periods of *peak* performance. At other times—when a *B* is earned, when coming in third in an athletic competition, when messing up an etude at a piano recital—then a child's self-worth is diminished.

Certainly, there is nothing wrong with being proud of a child's accomplishments, nor is it a faux pas to encourage a young boy or girl who is trying something new, different, or difficult. When *we* are proud—as parents or teachers—we should share this pride with the source of our elation: the child.

. . . But do so in private; quietly. For example:

"Janie, this second draft of your short story on the westward movement contained all the right elements—plot, character, setting, dialogue. Do you mind if I share your work with the class?"

"Geraldo, I want you to know how much improvement I've noticed in your guitar playing. It's obvious you've been practicing."

The common features of these two comments are their *specificity of details, their acknowledgment of success or improvement,* and their *comparison to previous work done by the same individual, not others.* These are important components of verbal encouragement, as the child can begin to note not only the end results of his efforts, but the steps that pave the path toward eventual success. In essence, the child sees his work as noteworthy both along the way and at its conclusion.

Use Praise Appropriately

A common mistake made by adults in lauding gifted children's work is an error of focus: They praise the child instead of the act. Notice the distinction:

> CASE A: "What a smart girl! Look at that report card!"
>
> CASE B: "A report card with four *A*'s and three *B*'s shows real effort!"

In the first case, evaluation of the child's *work* is secondary to bestowing flattery. While the comment in *Case A* may seem an appropriate reinforcement for a job well done, frequent comments such as this one may cause the child to associate "smartness" with "goodness." Consequently, if the next report card (or test, or footrace) falls short of this present effort, the child might come to think, "I am a bad person." *Case B,* on the other hand, is a statement that lauds the act, not its performer, which is the appropriate focus for a well-deserved tribute.

Farson (1963), in his review of the effect of misplaced or too-frequent praise in adult interactions, believes that praise has become such an expected part of any performance or task that we have become a nation of "Praise Junkies," hooked so strongly on an external evaluation of our work that we go through withdrawal pains ("What did I do wrong? No one said anything about my work?") if praise is withheld. This addition to external evaluation of one's work demeans the importance of our personal interpretations and can, over time, make people unable to judge the quality of their own performance (Dinkmeyer and Losoncy, 1980). Other negative effects of praise are listed in Table 10.1 and are relevant both to parent–child interactions and employer–employee relations.

Is there ever a time for praise? Of course there is, but like every other potential vice we encounter in life, it must be used in moderation.

Other Suggestions: A Cornucopia

There are, of course, thousands of suggestions that could be given related to parenting gifted children. In fact, several books have been written on that very topic (Bloom, 1985; Moore, 1979; Perino and Perino, 1981; Saunders and Espeland, 1986; Webb, Meckstroth, and Tolan, 1982). Further, research studies have been conducted on such subjects as the impact of labeling when one child in a family is gifted and the other is not (Bottom line: The long-term impact is not significant on family members) (Colangelo and Brower, 1987);

Table 10.1. PRAISE . . . REAPPRAISED.

Praise	Which Implies
Is an evaluation	That its recipient may be found deficient or "wanting"
May be interpreted as a call to change or to improve beyond present levels	That praise may be noted as threatening, or even as negative, by its recipient
Assumes that the "praiser" knows what is good and what is not	That the "praisee" may feel he or she is being constantly evaluated, even when nothing is said
Is often used to "sandwich" bad news or negative comments	That praise benefits the speaker, not the person being praised
Pressures its recipient to continue to perform at a praiseworthy level	That anything noted by its recipient as less than perfect is totally inadequate

Source: Excerpted from Farson, R. E. 1963. Praise . . . reappraised. *Harvard Business Review, 41*(5), 61–66.

the relevance of birth order on intellectual precocity (Hint: Don't worry about this because there's nothing you can do about birth order anyway) (Boronson, 1973); the values that gifted children accept as they mature (Good news: Cross-generational values are adopted eventually) (Albert, 1978); and the success of gifted children from disadvantaged families (Big news: They are more successful in supportive families that provide encouragement and guidance) (Van Tassel-Baska, 1989). Still, research is most relevant to the persons who served as subjects, and all the statistically significant findings on earth may hold little weight when a specific parent wants to know how to get a gifted child to eat his or her cauliflower without compromising his or her individuality.

This being so, I believe that the best suggestions come from the heart more often than the mind, and from respected practices rather than high-faluttin' research. Such common sense is not so common, yet it does appear in the work of Jeanne Delp (1980) and William Purkey and John Schmidt (1982). The following list offers advice gleaned from these two sources and which may be applicable to many families, including those with gifted children.

Common Sense, Common Practice: Suggestions for the Home Front

Learn to live with the child's frequent change of interests—"passing fancies" that are intense but short-lived are common.

Point out occasions when you notice growth or achievement: "You know something about physics that you didn't know last summer—that's great!"

List and share your "nonnegotiables": instances or events where you *won't* give in even to a well-reasoned argument. Remember: "Because I'm the mommy, that's why" is sometimes acceptable.

Discipline in private and with dignity. Make the "punishment fit the crime" unless you desire a rebuttal of Perry Mason proportions.

Schedule weekly "alone time" with each sibling. Thirty minutes of total privacy between parent and child where the agenda is set by the child.

Gifted children hate arbitrariness, especially when it is disguised as authority. Prepare to compromise (except for the aforementioned nonnegotiables).

Gifted children often overcomplicate the simplest requests. Help them notice and implement step-by-step progress.

Allow "downtime" that is totally nonproductive. There's nothing wrong with *The Jetsons* on Saturday morning. (You might even watch it with them!)

Assign household responsibilities, and set a deadline by which the tasks must be completed: "You have to clean your room, change the car's oil and clean the cat litter before bedtime."

Touch your children—a hug, a pat, or a backscratch is appreciated even after your children grow taller than you.

Give expert advice sparingly, but always when asked. Gifted children have the potential to become more capable and self-supportive than we sometimes give them credit for. Ask, "How might you go about solving this problem?" before providing an adult-sized solution.

Allow some family feuds to put themselves out. If you get in the middle of every sibling squabble, you take away children's chances to make their own peace. Intervene only when one child is taking unfair intellectual advantage over the other or when physical or mental health is at stake.

Provide affection, discipline, an opportunity to make mistakes and a home environment where the adults share the household workload with their children. First and foremost, your gifted child is a child.

Finally, it is important to note the contributions that can be made by a gifted child's grandparents. Felice Kaufmann (1981a), in her review of the special roles that grandparents can play, cites four specific roles they can assume: role model, magician, mentor, and historian.

> The image of the grandparent is likely to represent to the child the end product of growing up. A focused role for the future, marked by the explicit modeling of family values and standards, is . . . one of the more significant contributions [grandparents] can make to a gifted child's development. (p. 3)

By sharing a grandchild's fantasy world ("Grandma, come meet my purple hippopotamus!"), imagination is encouraged. By acting as historian ("Gramps, what was it like fighting in World War II?"), family and world history take on a personal dimension. By serving as mentor ("Mimi, what was it like being the only woman in your medical school class?"), the attitudes, values, knowledge of, and excitement about career possibilities are imbued.

Parenting and grandparenting gifted children: an intergenerational link to the future.

POSITIVE PARENT ADVOCACY:
"BOTTOM UP" AND "TOP DOWN" CHANGE

Economists subdivide their area of study into two distinct camps: microeconomics and macroeconomics. The former deals with such issues as what to buy when on a family budget, or how many employees to hire during a factory expansion, while the latter covers more global principles behind the maintenance of economic equilibrium.

This important distinction should also be made by parents in dealing with schools. As advocates for gifted children and their appropriate education, parents need to be able to separate issues that relate only to their child and those that are more general to all gifted children. Both forms of advocacy—microadvocacy and macroadvocacy—are important, just as balancing one's home budget is as vital as reducing a state or federal fiscal deficit.

Here are some examples of the two types of advocacy:

Microadvocacy

Speaking to an individual teacher about your child's performance

Attending a PTA meeting

"Buttonholing" a school board member, informally, to express your views on a certain issue

Voting for a school budget increase

Volunteering in your child's school

Writing a letter to your child's school principal asking for more attention to gifted programming

Macroadvocacy

Forming a parent support group to inform the school board about your collective views toward education for gifted children

Lobbying the state or federal legislatures for laws or funds to support education for gifted children

Serving on the planning council for your state association for gifted children

Sponsoring letter writing campaigns to elected officials regarding education for gifted children

Involving local media in promoting the needs of gifted children

Often, parents of gifted children participate in all forms of microadvocacy. Adhering to the belief that "the squeaky wheel gets the grease," these parents see to it that *their* child's talents are challenged by appropriate educational options. But their advocacy stops as soon as graduation from high school occurs; their personal stake in improving the schools is withdrawn when their last child is awarded a twelfth-grade diploma.

Microadvocacy is effective as far as it goes—which, as I said, is usually not much further than a family's youngest child. Yet long-term changes in school districts seldom occur when parents advocate only as individuals, not as coalitions. School boards know this. School administrators know this. Anyone who serves at the whim of the voting public knows this, too. Thus, if education for gifted children (or any other "movement") is to progress beyond its current state, the strategies of macroadvocacy must be employed.

"But why?" you may ask. "If *I* had to fight for the rights of my child, why shouldn't others do the same?" For an answer to this bordering-on-selfish question, parents need look no further than to their colleagues in special education for handicapped children. Prior to 1975 and the passage of Public Law 94-142: The Education for All Handicapped Children Act, parents of handicapped children were at the mercy of sympathetic state legislators and school boards as regards education services for their special needs children (United States Congress, 1975). The passage of P.L. 94-142 mandated educational services for those youngsters for whom a typical classroom curriculum was too hard, while residential treatment in a special school was too limiting. Today, such specialized services within public schools for students with developmental delays, learning disabilities, or sensory/motor problems are common—and expected. That's the good news. The bad news is that gifted and talented children were excluded from this law's provisions, leaving mandated services for gifted students as a decision to be made by individual state legislatures [thus far, less than half the states have mandated gifted education (Dodd, 1987)].

Without question, the major impetus behind P.L. 94–142's enaction was parent macroadvocacy. It took parents who could look beyond their own backyard to coalesce into a force to be reckoned with in Washington before special education services became a right for all rather than a privilege for few. If similar inroads are to be made toward the full education of gifted and talented children, then this same path of macroadvocacy, well trodden by our predecessors, will have to be followed (Fichter, 1987).

Strategies and materials for use by persons interested in such efforts have become available. The Gifted Child Society of Glen Rock, New Jersey developed an "Advocacy Packet" that contains 36 reproducible loose-leaf enclosures with information about giftedness in general, school–home communication, public relations efforts, and macroadvocacy skills (Riggs, 1984). Tannenbaum (1980) produced a short book that guides readers through the organizational processes of macroadvocacy and includes sample materials and resource lists used by local and state parent advocacy groups. Further, an entire issue of the *Journal for the Education of the Gifted* focused on effective advocacy techniques that can be applied on a small scale (in schools) as well as on a grand scale that is national in scope (Mitchell, 1987).

In addition to print resources, human resources are also available—and are probably more helpful. Mitchell (1988) reports that 48 states have at least one individual in the State Department of Education who has primary responsibility for programs for gifted and talented children within that jurisdiction. And every state has at least one statewide organization that was formed to advocate for special services for gifted and talented children (Alvino, 1988). And at the national level, the federal government has approved legislation under the Jacob K. Javits Gifted and Talented Student Education Act of 1989 that will help fund research projects, especially those aimed at identifying and educating historically underrepresented groups of gifted students. This act also reestablishes a federal office to oversee these projects, as well as a national center for disseminating information about effective practices for use with gifted students. So, indeed, many advocacy links have already been established.

In an editorial acknowledging the long road ahead for advocates of gifted and talented children, Greer (1990) wrote: "It sometimes feels much like we are now arriving at the place to where we ought to have begun" (p. 289). Micro- and macroadvocacy strategies will certainly promote growth and continuity of programs for gifted children, and the grassroots efforts that are within reach of parents of gifted children will be effective only to the degree that they are successfully implemented.

In other words, stop complaining . . . and start advocating!

ERRONEOUS ASSUMPTIONS

The adjective *just* should be eliminated from our vocabularies, as in *just* a housewife, *just* a teacher, *just* a secretary. This misplaced modifier downplays the very real contributions that can be made by individuals who have become their own worst enemies.

Parents often fall victim to this un*just* self-appraisal. "Oh, I'm *just* a parent—I don't claim to have all the answers about educating gifted children" is a common justification for not becoming fully involved in a child's schooling. But it is based on two faulty assumptions: namely, that parents are not reliable identifiers of giftedness in their children and that education should be provided primarily by people with college degrees and teaching credentials.

This section of Chapter 10 serves to erase erroneous assumptions that have, *in fact,* no basis *in fact.*

Erroneous Assumption 1: Parents Are Not Reliable Identifiers of Giftedness in Their Own Children

Ask most school administrators why parents are not used as sources in a school district's plan for identifying gifted students and here's what you'll hear: "*All* parents think their kids are gifted, now don't they?"

Wrong.

If this comment has any basis in fact whatsoever, it is due, more than likely, to the district's mistakes rather than the parents' misperceptions. Case in point: A school district for which I worked once sent home a letter to parents stating that a program for gifted children would begin in the next school year. "If you think your child would qualify for this program," the note stated, "please sign this letter and return it to your child's teacher." As could have been predicted by farsighted people, the floodgates opened. Parents, given no guidance whatsoever in defining or identifying giftedness, answered yes by the hundreds, causing the letter-senders to moan, "See, we *told* you all parents think their kids are gifted."

The solution, and one that benefits educators and parents, is *specificity*. Parents need to answer specific questions regarding the traits and behaviors of their children, rather than record a yes/no tally mark regarding whether or not a particular child is gifted. One such form, "Things My Child Likes To Do" (Figure 10.1), is offered as an example of a checklist on which parents detail specific incidents in a child's life that may indicate precocity or creative performance. By requiring an example in the far-right column, parents are *less* likely to overstate their child's talents and *more* likely to provide data that will help in both the identification of and programming for gifted students.

Parent identification of giftedness is especially important in the early years, when test data are not readily available and test scores that *are* available are considered suspect by many school personnel (Roedell, Jackson, and Robinson, 1980). Research studies have shown that the judgments made of young children's talents by their parents is reliable and valid. For example, a survey of 1039 parents of gifted children from 43 states showed that 72 percent of the respondents first suspected giftedness in their children between birth and 3 years of age; only 13 percent of parents were unsure until their children were older than 5 years (Gogel, McCumsey, and Hewett, 1985). Also, in a study by Jacobs (1971), it was found that parents identified 76 percent of children in a kindergarten class, while teachers identified these same children with only 4 percent accuracy. Further, Hanson (1984) reported that parents who enrolled their children (ages 4 to 6) in a gifted classroom based only on their perceptions of the child's verbal giftedness were accurate 90 percent of the time in their informal evaluation. A battery of achievement tests were administered to the children on enrollment in school, and these data substantiated the parents' beliefs.

Figure 10.1. "Things My Child Likes To Do"

COVER LETTER

TO: Parents of Students in the ————— Program

FROM:

SUBJECT: Things My Child Likes To Do

One of the major goals of our overall school program is to provide each child with an opportunity to develop his or her individual strengths and creative thinking abilities. We also would like to provide your child with an opportunity to do some work in an area of study that is of personal interest to him or her. In other words, we would like to supplement our basic curriculum with experiences that are interesting, challenging, and enjoyable to individual children.

Although the work that your child does in school gives us many opportunities to observe his or her strengths and areas of interest, the activities that your child pursues at home can also help us to find ways for enriching his or her overall school program. For this reason, we are asking you to complete the attached questionnaire and return it to us at your earliest convenience.

The attached questionnaire contains 14 items. Each of the items deals with a general type of interest or activity that you may or may not have seen in your child. The interests or activities might be the result of school assignments, extra-curricular, club activities such as—Girl Scouts or 4-H Club projects or other activities in which your child has developed an interest. To help clarify each of the 14 items, we have also provided an example. Please keep in mind that each example is included only to help clarify the meaning of the item. In other words, you should remember that you are rating your child on each of the fourteen general items rather than the specific example. It will, of course, be very helpful if you can jot down specific examples of your child's interests or activities in the righthand column of the questionnaire.

If you should have any questions about this questionnaire, please contact the person whose name and telephone number are listed below. We very much appreciate your assistance in helping us to provide the very best possible educational program for your child.

204

"THINGS MY CHILD LIKES TO DO"

Your Name _____ Child's School _____ Your Child's Name _____ Today's Date _____

Child's Age _____

	Seldom or Never	Some-times	Quite Often*	Almost Always	Example From Your Own Child's Life
1. My child will spend more time and energy than his/her agemates on a topic of his or her interest. (For example: Joan is learning to sew and spends every free minute designing new dress patterns and trying to sew them herself.)					
2. My child is a "self-starter" who works well alone, needing few directions and little supervision. (For example: After watching a film about musical instruments, Gary began to make his own guitar from materials he found around the garage.)					
3. My child sets high personal goals and expects to see results from his or her work. (For example: Marj insisted on building a robot from spare machine parts even though she knew nothing about engines or construction.)					
4. My child gets so involved with a project that he or she gives up other pleasures in order to work on it. (For example: Don is writing a book about his town's history and spends each night examining historical records and documents—even when he knows he's missing his favorite TV show.)					

5. My child continues to work on a project even when faced with temporary defeats and slow results. (For example: After building a model rocket, Sally continued to try to launch it, despite several failures and "crash landings.")			
6. While working on a project (and when it is finished) my child knows which parts are good and which parts need improvement. (For example: After building a scale model of a lunar city, Kenny realized that there weren't enough solar collectors to heat all the homes he had built.)			
7. My child is a "doer" who begins a project and shows finished products of his or her work. (For example: Mary began working on a puppet show four months ago and has since built a stage and puppets and has written a script. Tomorrow she's presenting her play to the PTA!)			

	Seldom or Never	Some-times	Quite Often*	Almost Always*	Example From Your Own Child's Life
8. My child suggests imaginative ways of doing things, even if the suggestions are sometimes impractical. (For example: "If you really want to clean the refrigerator, why don't we move it out-side and I'll hose it down—that will defrost it, too.")					
9. When my child tells about something that is very unusual, he or she expresses himself or herself by elaborate gestures, pictures, or words. (For example: "The only way I can show you how the ballet dancer spun around is if I stand on my tiptoes on the record player and put the speed up to 78.")					
10. My child uses common materials in ways not typically expected. (For example: "I'll bring a deck of cards when we go camping. If it rains, we can use them to start a fire, and if it's dry, we can play 'fish' around the campfire.")					
11. My child avoids typical ways of doing things, choosing instead to find new ways to approach a problem or topic. (For example: "I had trouble moving this box to the other side of the garage so I used these four broom handles as rollers and just pushed it along.")					

12. My child likes to "play with ideas," often making up situations which probably will not occur. (For example: "I wonder what would happen if a scientist found a way to kill all insects and then went ahead and did it.")

13. My child often finds humor in situations or events that are not obviously funny to most children his or her age. (For example: "It was really funny that after our coach showed us a movie on playground safety, he sprained his ankle while lining us up to go back to class.")

14. My child prefers working or playing alone rather than doing something "just to go along with the gang." (For example: "I always misspell the first word in a spelling bee; then I get to sit down and do something I like.")

*If your child scores in either of these two columns, it would be helpful if you would write a specific example in the last column, using the reverse side of this page if necessary.

It is clear, then, that parents can be helpful in the identification of giftedness in their own children, but the all-important phrasing of the questions determines the accuracy of the information obtained.

Erroneous Assumption 2: Educators Know Exactly How to Work with Gifted Children

If there is an undergraduate teacher-training program in any of our nation's colleges and universities that requires a course in teaching gifted children, I am unaware of its existence. Even persons trained in special education seldom hear mention of giftedness as a part of their course content. At most, there might be a chapter on education for gifted children in an "Introduction to Special Education" text, but as often as not, this chapter is skipped over by the professor teaching the course.

This is not to imply that all teachers without specialized training in education for gifted children are unable to meet the needs of highly able children. On the contrary, there are some educators whose teaching styles and flexibility mesh perfectly with the intellectual challenges presented by gifted students. Still, the majority of teachers do need some assistance in designing curriculum and exploring educational options that tap both the talents and interests of gifted children. And parents, as one source among many, can help teachers explore these options.

Here's why, and how: Parents are their children's first teachers, acting in the role of educators long before "Sesame Street" and preschool come on the scene. From this dual vantage as participant and observer, parents learn of their children's talents, specialities, quirks, and mannerisms. They become, in fact, "expert witnesses" as regards their children's strengths and weaknesses and can testify eloquently to the range and limits of their children's abilities. It is a wise teacher who knows this and who seeks out information from parents that may have an impact on a child's social performance or attitude. Such first-hand data are unavailable through test scores, report card grades, or anecdotal notes made by the previous year's teacher. Together this information—parent input and school records—provides a most complete picture of a developing child, unique among others, yet similar in so many ways to agemates.

Several programs for young gifted children have gained national recognition for their emphasis on establishing and maintaining an effective home–school link. The Astor Program in New York City is a public school program for 4- and 5-year-old gifted children (Ehrlich, 1980). Among the screening tools used prior to placement are a telephone interview with parents and an observation of the child, in either the home or preschool, to observe attention span, social maturity, and good skills in following directions. The Seattle Child Development Preschool, incorporated in 1982 under parent direction, uses a comprehensive parent questionnaire prior to entrance (Robinson and Roedell, 1980). The New Mexico State University Preschool for the Gifted uses a battery of standardized tests of intelligence and creativity for entrance and includes a parent on the school's selection committee to determine whether a specific child would benefit from the program offerings (Kitano and Kirby, 1986).

But parental involvement in their children's education does not end once school entrance begins; in fact, it is at this time that parents can become most helpful. Takacs (1986) stresses that "cooperation rather than confrontation should be the thrust of parental interaction with the schools" (p. 125), and she provides the following specific guidelines for ensuring this cooperative relationship.

> Assume that teachers want *all* their students to prosper to the best of their abilities.
>
> When requesting special provisions (e.g., early entrance, dual enrollment, independent work) parents should provide specific evidence from their child's life that justifies the need for these provisions.
>
> Avoid use of the term "boring" when describing a child's attitude toward school. The term is vague and, often, misleading. Instead, focus on the types of activities the child plays and/or learns from. If a particular activity or teacher is "boring," give specific examples of the child's dissatisfaction.
>
> Parents should stress to teachers that *learning* is more important than *grades,* and that they do not expect their child to be a straight-A student.
>
> When problems arise in a child's attitude or performance, do not look for a scapegoat to blame. Instead, listen to the child's and the teacher's perceptions of the problem, and work together to arrive at an equitable solution. (Takacs, 1986, pp. 125–135)

No one ever said parenting would be easy—in fact, it is probably the most difficult and vital of life's endeavors that does not require a special license to perform. But as Marvin Fine (1977) concludes, "There is a need for parents to be very self aware regarding their personal investments in the child and also to maintain an accurate and balanced perception of the child as a total and growing person" (p. 488). Such a balancing act is not easy—good things seldom are—yet if parents become partners with schools, the child will become the ultimate beneficiary.

COMMON PITFALLS

Overscheduling

The phone rang. It was a business call (I *hate* those at home!). The long-distance caller had a concern about her 12-year-old daughter. It went something like this:

ME: "Hello?"

CALLER: "Yes, Dr. Delisle, this is Mrs. Tardif. You don't know me, but . . ."

ME: "Yes?"

M.T.: "I have a question about my daughter. Beth is 12, and she's in her school's gifted program. She gets good grades, plays violin, loves swimming and computers, and is in the Girl Scouts."

ME: (Pause) . . . "So what's the problem?"

M.T.: "I'm concerned that she has too much spare time—can you give me some advice?"

Which I did, but only after I had picked my jaw up off the floor. What I suggested was free time, downtime, time to lay around on the couch pondering life's little mysteries, such as, "if butter melts yellow, why doesn't snow melt white?"

Mom huffed and puffed, telling me this is what Beth already does, and what-business-did-I-have-calling-myself-a-counselor anyway when it was obvious that I didn't see a problem when it hit me in the face.

"Hey," I thought, "*you* called *me.*"

This example, exaggerated only slightly for the sake of a good story, is not common among parents of gifted children; neither is it rare. *Overscheduling,* the attitude that able youngsters must be constantly on the go, seeking new challenges, exploring new options, is the "stuff" from which young workaholics are made. Advise parents to advise their children to live by the Roman playwright Terence's advice: "Everything in moderation." For while too hectic a schedule can leave even able children bewildered and anxious, too much free time can turn those same children into video junkies— kids whose daily workout is highlighted by pushing the remote control channel selector.

So, Mrs. Tardif, calm down. There are benefits to a balance between busy time and quiet time.

Overorganizing

A gifted student shows an early interest in reading the classics—so parents purchase a complete collection of the greatest books of the western world.

Another youngster picks up a baseball bat and starts hitting pebbles into the nearby vacant lot—so her parents enroll her in Little League.

A curious child picks up a paintbrush and dabbles with mixing yellow and green—so parents register him for Saturday morning art classes.

The presence of interest in something new and different on the part of the child does not necessarily imply that this child wants to become an expert in that subject. Art, music, sports, reading: Each can be a *leisure* activity, explored for fun, not for fame. By *overorganizing* free-time activities, parents can unwittingly *decrease* their children's interests in new undertakings. Such comments as "What fun is music now if I have to take lessons?" or "Soccer was great before I got on a team" aren't necessarily indicators of a lack of initiative, but may, in fact, relay to parents the child's interest in just having fun. *So what* if she doesn't grow up to be a great performer; there is joy in knowing that you can like something for no other reason than because it suits your style. Overorganizing, a close relative to overscheduling, sends a message that only things done *well* are worth doing *at all,* which is a precursor to that terrible beast called perfectionism.

Albert Einstein, in response to the question, "If you had your life to do over, what one thing would be the most important to you to change?" stated his wish thusly: "Simply to be average in everything I did." Certainly, it is beyond the scope of any researcher, in retrospect, to determine the source of this desire. Still, the simplistic idea to be more typical than deviant, more like others than unlike them, *may* tie in with the topics of overscheduling and overorganizing. Sometimes, there are benefits derived from "just being."

Overinvestment

Mark Fritz, a freelance writer, penned a modern parable about parents who live their own lives through those of their children (Fritz, 1985). He wrote especially about parents who want their children to become something they, themselves, may not have been—the ace, the star, the performer:

> He thought for a moment about some of those parents on the sidelines and their disappointment in some facet of their children, when, in fact, they should fault their own absurd expectations. Being grown men and women they should know that, after all, their insecurities eventually become their children's. (p. 11-A)

It is a far, far different thing for parents to hope for and guide their children to do well than it is to *expect* them to because of the parents' own unfulfilled ambitions. Comments such as "You have the brains to become a doctor, and you will; I never did, and I've regretted it all my life" speak more to the adults' desires and dreams than those of their children. To measure the effectiveness of one's skills as a parent by using the yardstick of a child's eventual achievements dismisses the importance of the child's vantage point, the child's goals, and the child's individuality.

Should parents have hopes for their offspring and wishes for their success in life? Of course. Should these values and ideas be imposed on young people against their will? Of course not, but parents should be on the alert to safeguard from this possibility.

Overreliance

Almost directly opposite the previous three pitfalls, this dilemma occurs when parents of gifted children relinquish their responsibilities to what *others* think is best. Often, those "others" are school personnel:

> "No, Martha shouldn't skip a grade; it'll hamper her social development and she'll be very unhappy down the line."
>
> "Enrico really doesn't need a program for gifted children. In our school we use cooperative learning, so everyone's needs are met whatever their intellectual level."
>
> "Sandy should really be retained in kindergarten. I *know* he's very bright, but he can't even color within the lines yet."

Since education began, and most likely until it ends, parents, teachers, and administrators will seek a panacea that doesn't exist. Whether it takes shape in a back-to-basics movement, individually guided education (IGE), cooperative learning, or any of a number of as yet unnamed provisions, it should be obvious that any instructional treatment, no matter how effective overall, will not work for some students. However, this obvious conclusion is drawn too seldom, so the zealots of a particular trend or "package" dominate for a year, or two, or more. In the meantime, children who do not benefit from the newest trend (often, gifted children) continue to lose out on an appropriate education. This is true not only in general education, but in education for gifted children as well. For example, if a program for gifted children is based entirely on a particular program model that demands that children complete a visible product or project (for example, Renzulli's enrichment triad/revolving door models), then children who are gifted but nonproductive will most likely be excluded from receiving program services. Or, if a school district has established a policy against early entrance to kindergarten, early graduation from high school, or any form of grade skipping whatsoever, then students for whom these provisions are in their best interests will be shortchanged by policies that may work for the masses, but do not work for the few.

Parents should demand that their children be considered as *the exceptions* until such time that it is shown that they more resemble *the rule*. If an existing program for gifted children doesn't meet the needs of a particular child, is the child to blame? If a child is one year ahead of agemates developmentally, does this imply that the current school placement will suffice until the other children catch up? The resounding answer to these questions is no! but parents of gifted children will have to speak up if their voices are to be heard at all.

CONCLUSION

It is the rare educator who cannot learn from students; it is the rare parent who cannot learn from offspring. So often, the adult assumes the task as tutor, guide, and mentor—all appropriate roles. Still, there are times and circumstances when children teach the grownups with whom they live or work.

The teacher or parent who can distinguish what to do when—when to listen instead of talk; when to be led instead of when to guide; when to learn instead of when to instruct—will find the greatest degree of success in working (and living) with children of high potential.

Happy journeys to us all, as we explore life's many roads alongside the children with whom we work and live.

CONTINUING QUESTS AND QUESTIONS

1. Our society prizes *excellence,* yet too often this high regard for high performance gets translated into a quest for *perfection.* How can educators help parents to note the distinction between these two qualities? Also, when gifted children look around them and see the societal push to get into the "right" college and enter the "right" career, how can we convince them that there is more to life than right answers and perfect solutions?

2. An essay appearing several years ago in the *New York Times* and written by the principal of an elementary school began: "Oh oh, here comes another parent of a bright kid . . ." It went on to present views that many would find derogatory (I did!) regarding the "pushiness" of parents who ask school personnel about special provisions made for gifted students. Does this view exist in your community, and if so, is there is a basis for this animosity? Why is it that when parents of handicapped children approach the schools they are seen as "advocates" for their children, but when parents of gifted students do the same thing, they are considered "pushy"? What can be done to eliminate this negative bias if, indeed, it does exist?

3. No one discounts the role of parents in encouraging self-concept and achievement, and few would argue that parents have no role in the identification of talents in their children. Yet what happens when life circumstances or conditions—economic, emotional, cultural—prevent parents from full participation in fostering their children's development? What steps can and should school personnel take to ensure that *all* parents have an equal opportunity to note the special gifts possessed by their children?

4. Twenty years hence, will the same questions being asked today by parents of gifted children still be voiced? Will a concern still exist for mandating educational services for highly able youngsters, or will program offerings be so vast and varied that all individual learning needs within our schools will be met? Will parenting concerns change as our culture evolves via technological and other advances? Will this latter piece of the twentieth century be seen as the "golden age of education for gifted children" or the dark ages? Why do you believe this to be so?

OUT OF THE WAY/OUT OF THIS WORLD RESOURCES

Perfectionism: What's Bad about Being Too Good, by Meriam Adderholdt-Elliott (Free Spirit Publishing, Minneapolis, MN, 1987).

This book, written primarily for use by students in grades 5 and above, is equally appropriate for parents and educators. If you live with or work with a child for whom nothing but number 1 will do, then this book is for you. Don't be surprised if you see yourself in various sections of this book—either as a perfectionist or someone who may be promoting such behaviors unintentionally—but don't be dismayed either; for Adderholdt-Elliott provides solutions and alternatives to the perfectionist who resides inside many of us.

A Parents' Guide to Raising a Gifted Child, by James Alvino (Little, Brown and Company, Boston, MA, 1985).

The subtitle of this book, "Recognizing and Developing Your Child's Potential," says it all. Every aspect of a gifted child's development—intellectual, social, emotional, physical—is addressed in this volume. The advice given in this book is very practical and positive and will be appreciated by parents of all gifted children.

The Encouragement Book, by Donald Dinkmeyer and L. Losoncy (American Guidance Services, Circle Pines, MN, 1980).

Using the work of Abraham Maslow and Carl Rogers as their humanistic base, the authors provide specific suggestions on how parents (and others) can become more encouraging. The use of humor as a powerful antidote to self-defeating behavior is explained, and suggestions are also offered for how to sharpen your perceptive powers, turn stubbornness into determination, and "read" unwritten and unspoken messages. A fine, usable resource well steeped in theory.

Smart Kids with School Problems: Things to Know and Ways to Help, by Patricia L. Vail (E. P. Dutton, New York, 1987).

Vail calls them "conundrum kids": the math whiz who can't read, the budding artist who can't solve a simple equation, the coordinated athlete who has undecipherable handwriting. She's talking about gifted students with learning disabilities, and, in her highly readable book, Vail suggests practical programs for helping these children. Also, a variety of case studies, informally presented, highlights conundrum kids who have succeeded.

Epilogue

Long before I ever put pen to paper, this book existed. Each concept, each chapter, each child—all were part of a collection of ideas and images that were linked in my mind by a common focus. So, I wrote this book for you (the reader) but I also wrote it for me (the writer). By doing so, I hope to have enriched the base of professional literature about the social and emotional needs of gifted children as much as I have benefited personally by addressing issues that have been the focus of my career for over a decade.

The formal writing of this book began in an informal milieu—at a beach in the summer overlooking wave after wave after wave. Daily, equipped with my writing pad and pen, SPF 15 sunscreen, and an idea or two on which I could elaborate, I wrote. As the tide shifted, so did I.

Time passed quickly, each day and each week, until all-too-soon the world of teaching and paychecks resumed, 800 miles to the north. Classes began, obligations piled up, but my writing continued at 500 words per day. (Sometimes, I stopped writing midsentence, so that the next day I would be "on a roll," with a set idea of how to begin.) By the time November's first snow fell and memories of the South Carolina shore, while still warm, were quite distant, 60,000 words had been written—half a book.

"Is this leading anywhere?" you might be asking.

The answer, of course, is yes—if nothing else, the stories told in this book are meant to serve as guides, as natural analogies showing the connections between seemingly disparate parts of our lives. So, indeed, the analogy is there, and the analogy is this: Just as this book was written one word, one day, one wave at a time, so does self-worth, self-confidence, and self-knowledge accrue gradually in children:

You say you don't have a program for gifted children in your school, therefore able students' needs are not being met? [Don't discount the worth of your own importance; as an individual educator you can (and you have) made a difference.]

You say that there *is* a program for gifted children in your school, therefore "all is well," educationally speaking? (Assume nothing. Programs for gifted children supplement, but do not replace, a school's other offerings.)

You say there are so many needs, so many kids, and so many times when you question whether your work has merit? (So do I, with every word I write; so does anyone, who wants to make a positive difference.)

Bottom line—just one last time: Do what you can today—the next minute, next hour, next child is too precious to lose; and your time to make a difference is cut short each moment that you believe that what you do doesn't add up to anything.

It does, though; kind words, caresses, unexpected smiles, and genuine encouragement add up to social and emotional growth as surely as my individual words here eventually grew into a book. Who would've believed it?

It's snowing—still—as I compose these closing thoughts. But spring will soon follow, with its longer days, warmer temperatures, and flowers. Before long, it's back to the beach for a summer full of fun with family, Matt and Deb. We'll have grown between last July and this, and we'll change again as surely as do the tides and the dunes.

Looking ahead, looking back: There is a lot to remember, and even more to anticipate.

References

Adderholdt-Elliott, M. 1987. *Perfectionism: What's bad about being too good?* Minneapolis: Free Spirit.

Agency for Instructional Technology. 1988. *Empty Chairs.* Bloomington, IN: Agency for Instructional Technology.

Albert, R. S. 1978. Observations and suggestions regarding giftedness, familial influence and the achievement of eminence. *Gifted Child Quarterly, 28*(3), 201–211.

Alexander, M. 1989. *We are one. Reaching their highest potential, VI* (II). Phoenix: Zephyr Press.

Allen, J. 1989. Here's what missing boy had to say in letter to Journal. *Milwaukee Journal,* January 12, 8A.

Alvino, J. 1988. Support in your state. *Gifted Children Monthly, 9*(8), 9.

Alvino, J. 1989. From the editor. *Gifted Children Monthly, 10*(2), 23.

American Association for Gifted Children. 1978. *On being gifted.* New York: Walker.

Antia, S. 1985. Chapter reaction: Hearing impaired gifted persons. In J. R. Whitmore & C. J. Maker (Eds.), *Intellectual giftedness in disabled persons.* Austin: Pro-Ed, pp. 60–62.

Arrick, F. 1980. *Tunnel vision.* New York: Bradbury Press.

Asbury, C. 1974. Selected factors influencing over and underachievement in young school-age children. *Review of Educational Research, 44,* 409–428.

Austin, A. B., & Draper, D. C. 1981. Peer relationships of the academically gifted: A review. *Gifted Child Quarterly, 25,* 129–133.

Bandura, A. 1977. *Social learning theory.* Englewood Cliffs, NJ: Prentice-Hall.

Banks, J. A. 1979. *Teaching strategies for ethnic studies (2nd ed.).* Boston: Allyn and Bacon.

Barrett, T. C. 1987. *Youth in crisis: Seeking solutions to self-destructive behavior.* Longmont, CO: Sopris West.

Barstow, D. 1987. Serve disadvantaged and serve all gifted. *Gifted Children Monthly, 8*(10), 1–3.

Barton, J. M., & Starnes, W. T. 1989. Identifying distinguishing characteristics of gifted and talented/learning disabled students. *Roeper Review, 12*(1), 23–29.

Baum, S., Emerick, L. J., Herman, G. N., & Dixon, J. 1989. Identification, programs, and enrichment strategies for gifted learning disabled youth. *Roeper Review, 12*(1), 48–53.

Berger, S. L. 1989. *College planning for gifted students.* Reston, VA: Council for Exceptional Children.

Berman, S. 1986. *The courage of conviction.* New York: Dodd, Mead.

Betts, G. T., & Knapp, J. 1985. *Autonomous learner model for the gifted and talented.* Greeley, CO: ALPS.

Betts, G. T., & Neihart, M. F. 1985. Eight effective activities to enhance the emotional and social development of the gifted and talented. *Roeper Review, 8*91), 18–23.

Binet, A., & Simon, T. 1905. Methodes nouvelles pour le diagnostic du niveau intellectuel des anormaux. *L'Année Psychologique, 11,* 191–244.

Bingham, M., Edmondson, J., & Stryker, S. 1983. *Choices: A teen woman's journal for self-awareness and personal planning.* El Toro, CA: Advocacy Press.

Blanning, J. M. 1980. *A multi-dimensional inservice handbook for professional personnel in gifted and talented.* Hartford, CT: Connecticut State Department of Education.

Bloom, B. S. 1977. Affective outcomes of school learning. *Phi Delta Kappan, 59*(3), 193–198.

Bloom, B. 1985. *Developing talent in young people.* New York: Ballantine Books.

Blos, P. 1979. *The adolescent passage.* New York: International Universities Press.

Boronson, W. 1973. First-born: Fortune's favorite? *Annual Editions: Readings in Human Development, 1973–74.* Guilford, CT: Dushkin, pp. 193–196.

Brandwein, P. 1987. On avenues to kindling wide interests in the elementary school: Knowledges and values. *Roeper Review, 10*(1), 32–40.

Brophy, J. E. 1979. Teacher behavior and its effects. *Journal of Educational Psychology, 71*(6), 733–750.

Buescher, T. (1984). Gifted and talented adolescents: Challenging perspectives. *Journal for the Education of the Gifted, 8*(1), 1–8.

Buescher, T. M. 1986. Understanding the impact of adolescence on the social and emotional growth of highly talented students. In T. M. Buescher (Ed.), *Understanding gifted and talented adolescents,* 5–10. Evanston, IL: Northwestern University.

Callahan, C. M. 1979. The gifted and talented woman. In A. H. Passow (Ed.), *The gifted and the talented.* Chicago: University of Chicago Press.

Callahan, C. M. 1980. The gifted girl: An anomoly? *Roeper Review, 2*(3), 16–20.

Carlson, D. 1977. *Triple boy.* New York: Atheneum.

Cattell, R., & Cattell, A. K. 1970. *Cattell Culture Fair Intelligence Series.* Indianapolis: Bobbs-Merrill.

Chamberlin, J. G. 1981. *The educating act: A phenomenological view.* Washington, DC: University Press of America.

Clark, B. 1988. *Growing up gifted* (3rd ed.). Columbus: Charles Merrill.

Cohen, L. M. 1988. National secondary options for the gifted. *Illinois Council for the Gifted Journal, 8,* 42.

Cohen, L. M. 1990. Meeting the needs of gifted and talented minority language students: Issues and practices. In S. M. Berger (Ed.), *ERIC Flyer File.* Reston, VA: Council for Exceptional Children.

Colangelo, N. 1985. Counseling needs of culturally diverse gifted students. *Roeper Review, 8*(1), 33–35.

Colangelo, N. 1989. Moral dilemmas as formulated by gifted students. *Understanding our gifted, 1*(6), 1; 10–12.

Colangelo, N., & Brower, P. 1987. Labeling gifted youngsters: Long-term impact on families. *Gifted Child Quarterly, 31,* 75–78.

Coleman, J. M., & Fults, E. A. 1982. Self-concept and gifted classroom: The role of social comparisons. *Gifted Child Quarterly, 26*(4), 116–120.

Coleman, J. S. 1961. *The adolescent society.* New York: Free Press.

Coleman, Z. 1983. Loss of hearing: Coping with a new reality. In R. L. Jones (Ed.), *Reflections on growing up disabled.* Reston, VA: Council for Exceptional Children, pp. 42–49.

Combs, A. W., Avila, D., & Purkey, W. W. 1978. *Helping relationships: Basic concepts for the helping professions* (2nd Ed.). Boston: Allyn and Bacon.

Coopersmith, S. 1967. *The antecedents of self-esteem.* San Francisco: W. H. Freeman.

Cornelius, H. M. 1988. Home sweet school: For some, not all. *Gifted Children Monthly, 9*(4), 1–3.

Cox, J., Daniel, N., & Boston, B. 1985. *Educating able learners: Programs and promising practices.* Austin: University of Texas Press.

Csikszentmihalyi, M., & Larson, R. 1984. *Being adolescent.* New York: Basic Books.

Daniels, P. R. 1983. *Teaching the gifted/learning disabled child.* Rockville, MD: Aspen Systems.

Dannenberg, A. C. 1984. *Meeting the needs of gifted and talented bilingual students: An introduction to issues and practices.* Quincy, MA: Massachusetts Department of Education, Office of Gifted and Talented.

Davis, C. J. 1980. *Perkins–Binet test of intelligence for the blind.* Watertown, MA: Perkins School for the Blind.

Davis, G. A. 1986. *Creativity is forever* (2nd Ed.). Dubuque, IA: Kendall-Hunt.

Davis, G. A., & Rimm, S. B. 1989. *Education of the gifted and talented* (2nd Ed.). Englewood Cliffs, NJ: Prentice-Hall.

DeBruin, J. 1988. *Scientists around the world.* Carthage, IL: Good Apple.

Delisle, J. R. 1982. Learning to underachieve. *Roeper Review, 4*(4), 16–18.

Delisle, J. R. 1984. *Gifted children speak out.* New York: Walker.

Delisle, J. R. 1986. Death with honors: Suicide and the gifted adolescent. *Journal of Counseling and Development, 64,* 558–560.

Delisle, J. R., & Galbraith, J. 1987. *The gifted kids survival guide II.* Minneapolis: Free Spirit.

Delisle, J., & Squires, S. 1989. Career development for gifted and talented youth: Position statement, Division on Career Development (DCD) and The Association for the Gifted (TAG). *Journal for the Education of the Gifted, 13*(1), 97–104.

Delp, J. 1980. *How to live successfully with the gifted child.* Ventura, CA: National/State Leadership Training Institute.

DeSalvo, M. 1988. Personal communication, Kent, OH.

Dinkmeyer, D., & Losoncy, L. 1980. *The encouragement book.* Circle Pines, MN: American Guidance Services.

Crabbe, A. B. 1979. *The 1979 future problem solving bowl. G/C/T,* September/ October, 15–16.

Dodd, D. 1987. Special without special education. *Journal for the Education of the Gifted, 10*(2), 65–77.

Dowdall, C., & Colangelo, N. 1982. Underachieving gifted students: Review and implications. *Gifted Child Quarterly, 26,* 179–184.

Dreyer, S. S. 1985. *The bookfinder: When kids need books.* Circle Pines, MN: American Guidance Service.

Driscoll, M. 1988. Transforming the "underachieving" math curriculum. *ASCD Curriculum Update,* January, 1–8.

Dunbaum, G., & Russo, T. 1983. Career education for the disadvantaged gifted: Some thoughts for educators. *Roeper Review, 5*(3), 26–28.

Dunn, R., & Dunn, K. 1975. *Educator's self-teaching guide to individualizing instructional programs.* West Nyack, NY: Parker.

Eby, J. W., & Smutny, J. F. 1990. *A thoughtful overview of gifted education.* White Plains, NY: Longman.

Education Consolidation and Improvement Act. 1981. Public Law 97-35. Washington DC: U.S. Government Printing Office.

Ehrlich, V. Z. 1980. The Astor Program for Gifted Children. In *Educating the preschool/primary gifted and talented.* Ventura, CA: Office of the Ventura County Superintendent of Schools, pp. 248–250.

Ellis, A. 1961. *A guide to rational living.* Englewood Cliffs, NJ: Prentice-Hall.

Ellis, A. 1971. *Growth through reason.* Palo Alto: Science and Behavior Books.

Ellis, A. 1977. Rational-emotive therapy: Research data that support the clinical and personality hypotheses of RET and other modes of cognitive therapy. *Counseling Psychologist, 7*(1), 2–42.

Exum, H. A., & Colangelo, N. 1981. Culturally diverse gifted: The need for ethnic identity development. *Roeper Review, 3,* 15–17.

Farson, R. E. 1963. Praise . . . reappraised. *Harvard Business Review, 41*(5), 61–66.

Feldhusen, J., Van Tassel-Baska, J., & Seeley, K. 1989. *Excellence in educating the gifted.* Denver: Love.

Feldman, D. H. 1979. The mysterious case of extreme giftedness. In A. H. Passow (Ed.), *The gifted and the talented: Their education and development.* National Society for the Study of Education. Chicago: University of Chicago Press.

Feldman, D. H. 1986. Nature's gambit: *Child prodigies and the development of human potential.* New York: Basic Books.

Feldman, D. H. 1987. Extreme giftedness: A bit less mysterious—an editorial. *Roeper Review, 10*(2), 72–74.

Fichter, G. 1987. Special education for gifted children is a good idea. *Journal for the Education of the Gifted, 10*(2), 79–86.

Fifty-one percent of all teachers possess an advanced degree, Union survey finds. 1987. *Education Week, Extra Edition: Editorial Projects in Education,* August, 20.

Fine, M. 1977. Facilitating parent–child relationships for creativity. *Gifted Child Quarterly, 21*(4), 487–500.

Fox, L. H., Brody, L., & Tobin, D. 1983. *Learning disabled gifted children: Identification and programming.* Baltimore: University Park Press.

Frasier, M. M. 1980. Programming for the culturally diverse. In J. B. Jordan & J. A.

Grossi (Eds.), *An administrator's handbook on designing programs for the gifted and talented*. Reston, VA: Council for Exceptional Children, pp. 56–65.

French, J. N. 1982. The gifted learning disabled child: A challenge and some suggestions. *Roeper Review, 4*(3), 19–21.

Fritz, M. 1985. Comparing kids is a guilty pastime. *Cleveland Plain Dealer,* November 26, 1985, p. 11-A.

Frymier, J. 1988. Understanding and preventing teen suicide: An interview with Barry Garfinkel. *Phi Delta Kappan, 70*(4), 290–293.

Galbraith, J., & Espeland, P. 1988. Ten tips for talking to teachers. *Free Spirit: News and Views on Growing Up, 2*(1), 7.

Gallagher, J. J. 1985. *Teaching the gifted child* (3rd ed.). Boston: Allyn and Bacon.

Gardner, H. 1983. *Frames of mind.* New York: Basic Books.

Gaunt, R. I. 1989. A comparison of the unpublished perceptions of parents of highly and moderately gifted children. (Doctoral dissertation, Kent State University)

Gibson, R. L., & Mitchell, M. H. 1981. *Introduction to guidance.* New York: Macmillan.

Glasser, W. 1976. *Positive addiction.* New York: Harper and Row.

Goertzel, V., & Goertzel, M. 1962. *Cradles of eminence.* Boston: Little, Brown.

Goertzel, M. G., Goertzel, V., & Goertzel, T. G. 1978. *Three hundred eminent personalities.* San Francisco: Jossey-Bass.

Gogel, E. M., McCumsey, J., & Hewett, G. 1985. What parents are saying. *G/C/T,* November–December, 7–9.

Good, T. L. 1981. Teacher expectations and student perceptions: A decade of research. *Educational Leadership, 38*(5), 415–422.

Gowan, J. C. 1972. Improving the mental health and performance of children. In Westmoreland Intermediate School District (Ed.), *Emotional disturbance and the gifted child: Implications for school people.* Harrisburg: Pennsylvania Department of Education, pp. 12–15.

Grahame, K. 1981. *The wind in the willows.* New York: Dell.

Greer, J. V. 1990. Shattering the monolith. *Exceptional Children, 56*(4), 286–289.

Gudeman, J. 1986. *Creative encounters with creative people.* Carthage, IL: Good Apple.

Gudeman, J. 1988. *Learning from the lives of amazing people.* Carthage, IL: Good Apple.

Gysbers, N. C., & Moore, E. J. 1987. *Career counseling.* Englewood Cliffs, NJ: Prentice-Hall.

Hafen, B. Q., & Frandsen, K. J. 1986. *Youth suicide: Depression and loneliness.* Evergreen, CO: Cordillera Press.

Hansen, J. C., Stevic, R. R., & Warner, R. W. 1977. *Counseling: Theory and process* (2nd ed.). Boston: Allyn and Bacon.

Hanson, I. 1984. A comparison between parent identification of young bright children and subsequent testing. *Roeper Review, 7*(1), 44–45.

Haugland, P. 1986. The use of puppetry to modify nonhandicapped students' attitudes toward the handicapped. (Doctoral dissertation, California State University, Los Angeles)

Hawkins-Grider, S. G. 1985. A study of an effort to modify nonhandicapped students' attitudes toward the handicapped. (Doctoral dissertation, College of William and Mary)

Hawton, K. 1986. *Suicide and attempted suicide among children and adolescents*. Beverly Hills: Sage.

Hayes, M. L., & Sloat, R. S. 1990. Suicide and the gifted adolescent. *Journal for the Education of the Gifted, 13*(3), 229–244.

Hesse, H. 1974. *Steppenwolf.* New York: Bantam Books.

Hipp, E. 1985. *Fighting invisible tigers*. Minneapolis: Free Spirit.

Hollander, L. 1987. Music, the creative process and the path of enlightenment. *Roeper Review, 10*(1), 28–32.

Hollinger, C. L., & Fleming, E. S. 1984. Internal barriers to the realization of potential: Correlates and interrelationships among gifted and talented female adolescents. *Gifted Child Quarterly, 28*(3), 135–139.

Hollingworth, L. S. 1942. *Children above 180 I.Q. Stanford Binet: Origin and development*. Yonkers-on-Hudson, NY: World Book.

Horner, M. S. 1972. Toward an understanding of achievement related conflicts in women. *Journal of Social Issues, 28*, 129–156.

Hoyt, K., & Hebeler, J. (Eds.). 1974. *Career education for gifted and talented students*. Salt Lake City: Olympus.

Husain, S. A., & Vandiver, T. 1984. *Suicide in children and adolescents*. New York: Spectrum.

Itard, J. M. G. 1962. The wild boy of Aveyron. George and Muriel Humphrey, trans. Englewood Cliffs, NJ: Prentice-Hall.

Jacobs, J. 1971. Effectiveness of teacher and parent identification of gifted children as a function of school level. *Psychology in the Schools, 8*, 140–142.

Janos, P. J., Fung, H. C., & Robinson N. M. 1985. Self-concept, self-esteem, and peer relations among gifted children who feel "different." *Gifted Child Quarterly, 29*(2), 78–82.

Johnsen, S. K. 1988. The validity and reliability of instruments used in identifying gifted and talented students. Paper presented at the Annual Conference of the National Association for Gifted Children, Orlando, Florida.

Johnson, L. 1987. Teaching the visually impaired gifted youngster. *Journal of Visual Impairment and Blindness, 81*(2), 51–52.

Jones, J. A. 1987. *Teen suicide: A guide to understanding adolescents who take their own life*. Waterford, MI: Minerva Press.

Karnes, F. A., & Koch, S. F. 1985. State definitions of the gifted and talented: An update and analysis. *Journal for the Education of the Gifted, 8*(4), 285–306.

Karnes, M. B. 1979. Young handicapped children can be gifted and talented. *Journal for the Education of the Gifted, 1*(3), 157–171.

Kaufmann, F. 1981a. *Guideposts for grandparents of gifted and talented children*. New York: American Association for Gifted Children.

Kaufmann, F. 1981b. The 1964–68 Presidential Scholars: A follow-up study. *Exceptional Children, 48*(2), 164–169.

Kaufman, A., & Kaufman, N. 1983. *Kaufman Assessment Battery for Children: (K-ABC)*. Circle Pines, MN: American Guidance Services.

Kearney, K. 1988. The highly gifted. *Understanding our gifted, 1*(1), 13.

Kearney, K. 1989. The highly gifted: School placement (Part II). *Understanding our gifted, 1*(3), 14.

Kerr, B. A. (1983, Fall). Raising aspirations of gifted girls. *Vocational Guidance Quarterly, 27–34.*

Kerr, B. A. 1985a. *Smart girls, gifted women.* Columbus, OH: Ohio Psychology.

Kerr, B. A. 1985b. Smart girls, gifted women: Special guidance concerns. *Roeper Review, 8*(1), 30–33.

Khatena, J. 1982. *Educational psychology of the gifted.* New York: Wiley.

Kitano, M. K. 1986. Gifted and talented Asian children. In M. K. Kitano & D. C. Chinn (Eds.), *Exceptional Asian Children and Youth.* Reston, VA: Council for Exceptional Children.

Kitano, M. K., & Kirby, D. F. 1986. *Gifted education: A comprehensive view.* Boston: Little, Brown.

Kline, B. E., & Meckstroth, E. A. 1985. Understanding and encouraging the exceptionally gifted. *Roeper Review, 8*(1), 24–30.

Kramer, L. R. 1986. Career awareness and personal development: A naturalistic study of gifted adolescent girls' concerns. *Adolescence, 21,* 123–131.

Laffoon, K. S., Jenkins-Friedman, R., & Tollefson, N. 1989. Causal attributions of underachieving gifted, achieving gifted, and non-gifted students. *Journal for the Education of the Gifted, 13*(1), 4–21.

Lajoie, S. P., & Shore, B. M. 1981. Three myths? The overrepresentation of the gifted among dropouts, delinquents, and suicides. *Gifted Child Quarterly, 25*(3), 138–143.

Lanker, B. 1989. I dream a world. *National Geographic, 176*(2), 209–225.

Laycock, S. R. 1956. Counseling parents of gifted children. *Exceptional Children, 23*(3), 108–110.

Laycock, F. 1979. *Gifted children.* Glencoe, IL: Scott Foresman.

Leder, J. M. 1987. *Dead serious: A book for teenagers about teenage suicide.* New York: Atheneum.

Leroux, J. A. 1985. Gender differences influencing gifted adolescents: An ethnographic study of cultural expectations. (Doctoral dissertation, University of Connecticut)

Levine, A. 1987. Getting smart about IQ. *U.S. News and World Report, 106,* November 23, 1987, 53–55.

Lewis, G. 1984. Alternatives to acceleration for the highly gifted child. *Roeper Review, 6*(3), 133–136.

Lincoln, E. 1980. Tools for teaching math and science students in the inner city. *School Science and Math, 80,* 3–7.

Lockwood, A. T. 1989. Peer influences: High school seniors speak. *National Center on Effective Secondary Schools Newsletter, 4*(2), 5–8.

MacCurdy, E. 1939. *The notebooks of Leonardo da Vinci.* New York: Reynal and Hitchcock.

McGuffog, C., Feiring, C., & Lewis, M. 1987. The diverse profile of the extremely gifted child. *Roeper Review, 10*(2), 82–89.

Machado, M. 1987. Gifted Hispanics under-identified in classrooms. *Hispanic Link Weekly Report,* February, 1.

MacKinnon, D. W. 1978. *In search of human effectiveness.* Buffalo: Creative Education Foundation.

McIntosh, M. E., & Greenlaw, M. J. 1986. Fostering the post-secondary aspirations of gifted urban minority students. *Roeper Review, 9*(2), 104–107.

McKean, K. 1985. The assault on IQ. *Discover, 6*(10), 25–41.

MacLeish, R. 1984. Gifted by nature, prodigies are still mysteries to man. *Smithsonian, 14*(12), 71–79.

Maker, C. J. 1977. *Providing programs for the gifted handicapped.* Reston, VA: Council for Exceptional Children.

Maker, C. J. 1987. *Project DISCOVER: Discovering intellectual skills and capabilities while providing opportunities for varied ethnic responses.* Tucson, AZ: University of Arizona, Special Education and Rehabilitation.

Maker, C. J., Redden, M. R., Tonelson, S., & Howell, R. M. 1978. *The self-perceptions of successful handicapped scientists.* Albuquerque, NM: University of New Mexico, Department of Special Education.

Marland, S. P. 1972. Education of the gifted and talented: Report to the Subcommittee on Education, Committee on Labor and Public Welfare. Washington, DC: U.S. Government Printing Office.

Marshall, B. 1981. Career decision-making patterns of gifted and talented adolescents: Implications for career education. *Journal of Career Education,* June, 305–310.

Maslow, A. 1970. *Motivation and personality* (2nd ed.). New York: Harper and Row.

Mehorter, J. T. 1964. Self and society: An independent study course for gifted high school students. (Doctoral dissertation, University of Virginia). *Dissertation Abstracts International, 25,* 3879-A (University Microfilms #64-10909).

Melichar, J. F. 1978. ISARE, a description. *AAESPH Review, 3,* 259–268.

Mitchell, B. M. 1988. The latest assessment of gifted education. *Roeper Review, 10*(4), 239–240.

Mitchell, P. B. 1987. Special topical issue: Advocating for the gifted and talented. *Journal for the Education of the Gifted, 7*(4), 225–299.

Montemayor, R. 1984. Changes in parent and peer relations between childhood and adolescence: A research agenda for gifted adolescents. *Journal for the Education of the Gifted, 8*(1), 9–23.

Moore, L. P. 1979. *Does this mean my kid's a genius?* New York: McGraw-Hill.

National Commission on Excellence in Education. 1983. *A nation at risk.* Washington, DC: U.S. Government Printing Office.

Newland, T. E. 1976. *The gifted in socio-educational perspective.* Englewood Cliffs, NJ: Prentice-Hall.

Nielsen, M. E., & Mortorff-Albert, S. 1989. The effects of special education service on the self-concept and school attitude of learning disabled/gifted students. *Roeper Review, 12*(1), 29–36.

Obringer, S. J. 1984. Survey of physician expertise with developmentally disabled children and attitudes toward mainstreaming. *Educational and Psychological Research, 4*(2), 91–95.

O'Shea, H. E. 1960. Friendship and the intellectually gifted child. *Exceptional Children, 26*(6), 327–335.

Passow, A. H. 1986. *Issues and trends in curriculum for the gifted.* Paper presented at the 32nd Annual Convention of the National Association for Gifted Children, Las Vegas.

Passow, A. H. 1988. Educating gifted persons who are caring and concerned. *Roeper Review, 11*(1), 13–15.

Peck, M. 1968. Suicide motivation in adolescents. *Adolescence, 3,* 109–118.

Peck, R. F., & Havighorst, R. J. 1960. *The psychology of character development.* New York: Wiley.

Perino, S. C., & Perino, J. 1981. *Parenting the gifted.* New York: Bowker Books.

Perrone, P. A., Karshner, W. W., & Male, R. A. 1979. Identification of talented students. In N. Colangelo & R. T. Zaffran (Eds.), *New voices in counseling the gifted.* Dubuque, IA: Kendall-Hunt.

Phi Delta Kappa Task Force on Adolescent Suicide. 1988. *Responding to adolescent suicide.* Bloomington, IN: Phi Delta Kappa Educational Foundation.

Piechowski, M. M. 1986. The concept of developmental potential. *Roeper Review, 8,* 190–197.

Piechowski, M. M. 1989. Developmental potential and the growth of the self. In J. L. Van Tassel-Baska & P. Olszewski-Kubilius (Eds.), *Patterns of influence on gifted learners.* New York: Teachers College Press, pp. 87–101.

Porter, R. M. 1982. The gifted/handicapped: A status report. *Roeper Review, 4*(3), 24–25.

Powell, K. 1985. Disability awareness and attitudes of nonhandicapped children toward the severely disabled. (Doctoral dissertation, Arizona State University)

Purkey, W. W., & Novak, J. J. 1984. *Inviting school success* (2nd ed.). Belmont, CA: Wadsworth.

Purkey, W. W., & Schmidt, J. J. 1982. Ways to be an inviting parent: Suggestions for the counselor–consultant. *Elementary School Guidance and Counseling, 17*(2), 94–99.

Raph, J. B., Goldberg, M. L., & Passow, A. H. 1966. *Bright underachievers.* New York: Teachers College Press.

Raph, J. B., & Tannenbaum, A. J. 1961. *Underachievement: Review of literature.* New York: Teachers College, Columbia University.

Raven, J. 1956. *Standard progressive matrices.* New York: Psychological Corporation.

Raven, J. 1962. *Advanced progressive matrices.* New York: Psychological Corporation.

Renzulli, J. 1978. What makes giftedness? Reexamining a definition. *Phi Delta Kappan, 60,* 180–184; 261.

Renzulli, J. S., Reis, S. M., & Smith, L. 1981. *The Revolving Door Identification Model.* Mansfield Center, CT: Creative Learning Press.

Riggs, G. G. 1984. *Advocacy packet.* Glen Rock, NJ: The Gifted Child Society.

Rimm, S. B. 1986. *Underachievement syndrome: Causes and cures.* Watertown, WI: Apple.

Roberts, D. 1988. Cloisonne and steel. *Vis a Vis.* May, 70–71.

Robertson, J. 1985. Gifted adults incurring severe disabilities. In J. R. Whitmore & C. J. Maker (Eds.), *Intellectual giftedness in disabled persons.* Austin: Pro Ed, pp. 135–169.

Robertson, J., & Robertson, C. (Eds.) 1976. *The brown paper school book series.* Boston: Little, Brown.

Robinson, H. B., & Roedell, W. C. 1980. Child development preschool. In *Educating the preschool/primary gifted and talented.* Ventura, CA: Ventura County Superintendent of Schools, pp. 237–241.

Roedell, W. C., Jackson, N. E., & Robinson, H. B. 1980. *Gifted young children.* New York: Teachers College Press.

Roeper, A. 1989. Empathy, ethics and global education. *Understanding our gifted, 1*(6), 1; 7–10.

Roeper Review. September, 1989. *Special Issue: Gifted students with disabilities,* vol. 12. Bloomfield Hills, MI: Roeper School for the Gifted.

Ross, A. O. 1964. *The exceptional child in the family.* New York: Grune and Stratton.

Sah, A., & Borland, J. H. 1989. The effects of a structured home plan on the home and school behaviors of gifted learning-disabled students with deficits in organizational skills. *Roeper Review, 12*(1), 54–57.

Sanborn, M. P. 1979. Differential counseling needs of the gifted and talented. In N. Colangelo & R. Zaffran (Eds.), *New voices in counseling the gifted.* Dubuque, IA: Kendall-Hunt, pp. 154–165.

Sanborn, M. P., Pulvino, C. J., & Wunderlin, R. F. 1971. *Research reports on superior students in Wisconsin high schools.* Madison: Univ. of Wisconsin, Research and Guidance Laboratory for Superior Students.

Saunders, J., & Espeland, P. 1986. *Bringing out the best: A resource guide for parents of young gifted children.* Minneapolis: Free Spirit.

Sears, P. S. 1963. *The effect of classroom conditions on the strength of achievement motive and work output of elementary school children.* U. S. Department of HEW, Office of Education, Cooperative Research Project No. 873. Stanford, CA: Stanford University.

Seeley, K. 1984. Perspectives on adolescent giftedness and delinquency. *Journal for the Education of the Gifted, 8*(1), 59–72.

Seibel, M., & Murray, J. N. 1988. Early prevention of adolescent suicide. *Educational Leadership, 45,* 48–51.

Seligman, M. E. 1975. *Helplessness: On depression, development and death.* San Francisco: W. H. Freeman.

Shannon, C. K. 1989. In the service of children: An open letter to global educators. *Roeper Review, 11*(4), 184–185.

Sharkey, O. C. 1987. Tony Lai, Age 14, B. Sc., Prodigy. *Roeper Review, 10*(2), 94–96.

Sherburn, G. 1929. *The best of Pope.* New York: Ronald Press.

Shneidman, E. S. 1972. *Death and the college student.* New York: Behavioral Publications.

Silverman, L. S. 1986. Parenting young gifted children. In J. R. Whitmore (Ed.), *Intellectual giftedness in young children.* New York: Haworth Press.

Silverman, L. S., & Kearney, K. 1989. Parents of the extraordinarily gifted. *Advanced Development, 1,* 41–56.

Simpkins, K., & Stephens, B. 1974. *Cognitive development of blind subjects.* Proceedings of the 52nd Biennial Conference of the Association for the Education of the Visually Handicapped, pp. 26–28.

Smith, D. C. 1962. Personal and social adjustment of gifted adolescents. National Education Association, Council for Exceptional Children. *Research Monograph No. 4.* Washington, DC: The Association.

Smith, J. D. 1985. *Minds made feeble: The myth and legacy of the Kallikaks.* Rockville, MD: Aspen.

Smith, R. M., & Mauceri, P. K. 1982. Suicide—The ultimate middle school trauma. *Middle School Journal, 14*(1), 21–24.

Spredemann-Dreyer, S. 1989. *The bookfinder.* Circle Pines, MN: American Guidance Services.

Starko, A. J., & Schack, G. D. 1989. Perceived need, teacher of efficacy, and teaching strategies for the gifted and talented. *Gifted Child Quarterly, 33*(3), 118–122.

Sternberg, R. J. 1982. Lies we live by: Misapplication of tests in identifying the gifted. *Gifted Child Quarterly, 26*(4), 157–161.

Sternberg, R. J., & Davidson, J. (Eds.). 1986. *Conceptions of giftedness.* New York: Cambridge University Press.

Stewart, E. 1981. Learning styles among gifted/talented students: Instructional technique preferences. *Exceptional Children, 48*(2), 134–138.

Strang, R. 1951. Mental hygiene of gifted children. In P. Witty (Ed.), *The gifted child.* Lexington, MA: D. C. Health and Company, pp. 131–162.

Strang, R. 1960. Helping your gifted child. New York: E. P. Dutton.

Takacs, C. A. 1986. *Enjoy your gifted child.* Syracuse, NY: Syracuse University Press.

Tannenbaum, A. J. 1962. *Adolescent attitudes toward academic brilliance. Talented Youth Project Monograph.* New York: Bureau of Publications, Teachers College, Columbia University.

Tannenbaum, A. 1980. *Reaching out: Advocacy for the gifted and talented.* New York: Teachers College Press.

Tannenbaum, A. J. 1983. *Gifted children: Psychological and educational perspectives.* New York: Macmillan.

Terman, L. M. 1954. The discovery and encouragement of exceptional talent. *American Psychologist, 9,* 221–230.

Terman, L. M., & Merrill, M. A. 1973. *Stanford-Binet Intelligence Scale—Third Revision Form L–M.* Boston: Houghton-Mifflin.

Terman, L. M., & Oden, M. H. 1947. *The gifted child grows up: Genetic studies of genius, 4.* Stanford, CA: Stanford University Press.

Tolan, S. 1989. Special problems of young highly gifted children. *Understanding our gifted, 1*(5), 1; 7–10.

Tolan, S. 1990. Helping your highly gifted child. *ERIC Flyer File.* Reston, VA: Council for Exceptional Children.

Torrance, E. P. 1962. *Guiding creative talent.* Englewood Cliffs, NJ: Prentice-Hall.

Torrance, E. P. 1966. *Torrance tests of creative thinking.* Bensenville, IL: Scholastic Testing Service.

Torrance, E. P. 1969. Creative positives of disadvantaged children and youth. *Gifted Child Quarterly, 13,* 71–81.

Torrance, E. P. 1985. Who is gifted? *Illinois Council for the Gifted Journal, 4,* 2–3.

Treffinger, D. 1975. Teaching for self-directed learning: A priority for the gifted and talented. *Gifted Child Quarterly, 19*(1), 46–59.

United States Congress. 1975. Public Law 94-142: The Education for All Handicapped Children Act. Washington, DC: U.S. Government Printing Office.

Van Tassel-Baska, J. 1989. The role of the family in the success of disadvantaged gifted learners. In J. Van Tassel-Baska & P. Olszewski-Kubilius (Eds.), *Patterns of influence on gifted learners,* pp. 60–80.

Vars, G. F. 1987. *Interdisciplinary teaching in the middle grades.* Columbus, OH: National Middle School Association.

Vonnegut, K. 1950. Harrison Bergeron, In *Welcome to the Monkey House.* New York: Delacorte, pp. 7–14.

Wallas, G. 1926. *The act of thought.* New York: Harcourt, Brace and World.

Ward, V. S. 1961. *Educating the gifted: An axiomatic approach.* Columbus: Charles Merrill.

Ward, V. S. 1980. *Differential education for the gifted.* Ventura, CA: Ventura County Superintendent of Schools.

Watley, D. J. 1969. Career progress: A longitudinal study of gifted students. *Journal of Counseling Psychology, 16*(2), 100–108.

Webb, J. T., Meckstroth, E. A., & Tolan, S. 1982. *Guiding the gifted child.* Columbus, OH: Psychology Publishing.

Whaley, C. E. 1980. The study of global futures and the gifted. *Roeper Review, 2*(4), 28–29.

White, W. L. 1990. Interviews with Child I, J, and L. *Roeper Review, 12*(3).

White, W. L., & Renzulli, J. S. 1987. A forty year follow-up of students who attended Leta Hollingworth's school for gifted students. *Roeper Review, 10*(2), 89–94.

Whitmore, J. R. 1980. *Giftedness, conflict and underachievement.* Boston: Allyn and Bacon.

Whitmore, J. R. 1981. Personal communication, October 10.

Whitmore, J. R., & Maker, C. J. 1985. *Intellectual giftedness in disabled persons.* Austin: Pro-Ed.

Whitrock, M. C. 1979. The cognitive movement in instruction. *Educational Researcher, 8,* 5–11.

Williams, K. 1988. Profiles and perspectives: Annemarie and George Roeper. *Roeper Review, 11*(1), 53–54.

Willings, D. 1983. The gifted at work. In B. M. Shore (Ed.), *Face to face with giftedness.* New York: Trillium.

Willings, D. 1985. The specific needs of adults who are gifted. *Roeper Review, 8*(1), 35–38.

Witty, P. A. 1940. Some considerations in the education of gifted children. *Educational Administration and Supervision, 26,* 512–521.

Worden, W. 1983. *Grief counseling and grief therapy.* London: Tavistock.

Yewchuk, C. R., & Bibby, M. A. 1989. Identification of giftedness in severely and profoundly hearing impaired students. *Roeper Review, 12*(1), 42–48.

Ziv, A. 1977. *Counseling the intellectually gifted child.* Toronto: The Governing Council of the University of Toronto.

Index